Rough Road to Justice

The Journey of Women Lawyers in Texas

by Betty Trapp Chapman

Two-Minute Histories of Houston
Historic Houston
Houston Women: Invisible Threads in the Tapestry
100 Years—100 Stories: The Houston Public Library 1904–2004
Historic Photos of Houston

ROUGH ROAD to JUSTICE

The Journey of Women Lawyers in Texas

BETTY TRAPP CHAPMAN

Austin 2008

The State Bar of Texas, through its TexasBarBooks Department, publishes practice books prepared and edited by knowledgeable authors to give practicing lawyers as much assistance as possible. The competence of the authors ensures outstanding professional products, but, of course, neither the State Bar of Texas, the editors, nor the authors make either express or implied warranties in regard to their use. Each lawyer must depend on his or her own knowledge of the law and expertise in the use or modification of these materials.

International Standard Book Number: 978-1-892542-46-5
Library of Congress Control Number: 2007937154

Austin, TX 78711

The State Bar of Texas gratefully acknowledges the permission of the rightsholders to reproduce the photographs in this book.

Printed in the United States of America

Women in the Profession Committee
2003–2008

Debra Baker
Patrice Barron
Melinda Kyle Becker
Karmen Binka
Kathy Boutchee
Melissa Caro
Michelle Hoogendam Cash
Theresa Chang
Karin Crump
Ellen Elkins Grimes
Yvonne R. Guaderrama
Amy Karff Halevy
Lauren Harrison
B.J. Hemmeline
Pauline Edwards Higgins
Paula Weems Hinton
Leila Safi Hobson
Hillary Hunt Holmes
Karen Hurwitz
Sherylynn Kime-Goodwin
Rita Lucido
Mandi Lee Matlock
John H. Miller
Judy Ney
Deborah Penner
Carmen Perez
Velva Price
Nancy Rapoport
Serina Ayn Rivela
Veronica Rivera
Marvina Robinson
Iris Hefter Robinson
Elizabeth Rogers
Laura Frances Sharp
Jan Soifer
Cynthia Spanhel
Rosemarie Williams Swan
Catherine Tram Than
Karen Tillman
Charlene Hsi-Lin Tsang-Kao
Barbara Van Duyne
Tracy Willi
Kathleen J. Wu
Moha PradhanYepuri

Staff Liaisons

Caren Blackwell
Kristie Brasfield
Zeenia Challa
Cristina De La Garza

CONTENTS

STATE BAR OF TEXAS

The State Bar of Texas proudly presents *Rough Road to Justice: The Journey of Women Lawyers in Texas*. This book by historian Betty Trapp Chapman documents the hardships and victories in the lives and careers of women who paved the way for later generations of women lawyers in Texas.

Our sincere thanks go to the Women in the Profession Committee, whose dedication to this project has resulted in a valuable contribution to legal history. We are also grateful to the Texas Bar Foundation and the many sponsors who contributed to the funding for this project. Without the help of all of these people, publication of this book would have been impossible.

The State Bar of Texas is committed to educating the public about the roles of judges and lawyers in the American system of justice. We hope this publication helps to illuminate the role of women in advancing the cause of justice for all Texans.

Gib Walton
President 2007–2008
State Bar of Texas

Harper Estes
President 2008–2009
State Bar of Texas

P.O. Box 12487, Capitol Station, Austin, Texas 78711-2487, (512) 463-1463

ACKNOWLEDGMENT

The idea for a book regarding the history of women lawyers in Texas began in 2004 when I was asked to give a speech about the women who paved the way for women lawyers practicing today. In researching, I discovered fascinating stories about the pioneers from other parts of the country but realized there was very little research regarding the female lawyers in Texas. Thus, the idea for a book was born.

The Women in the Profession Committee of the State Bar of Texas has the mission to report on the status of the women lawyers of Texas so this history project seemed a perfect fit. The committee decided to have a book written without any idea of how to do it.

First, we applied to the Texas Bar Foundation for a grant to fund the project and received $7500 as seed money. We funded the remainder of the project through donations from the following firms, corporations, bar associations, and individuals: Andrews Kurth, Baker Botts, Locke Liddell & Sapp, Vinson & Elkins, Houston Bar Association, Gregg County Bar Association, Jefferson County Bar Association, ExxonMobil, Shell Oil, B.J. Hemmeline, Nancy Rapoport, Deborah Penner, Leila Hobson, and Ellen Grimes.

The enthusiastic response we received from everyone allowed the book to be researched and written.

Fortunately, we found and persuaded Betty Trapp Chapman, a noted historian, to write the book. She has devoted herself to the research and writing beyond the call of duty. As she researched, she became more and more excited about our history. She has completed the book as a labor of love and produced a product beyond our expectations.

The committee was fortunate in having TexasBarBooks agree to publish this book which is unique to the type of book it normally publishes. We would also like to thank Caren Blackwell and the Minority Affairs Department at the State Bar of Texas for their advice, patience, and encouragement.

We are so proud of our history which continues to unfold today and pleased that this story will be available to the public.

Ellen Elkins Grimes
Chair, History of Texas
Women Lawyers Project
Women in the Profession Committee
State Bar of Texas

Prologue

THE HISTORY OF WOMEN LAWYERS IN TEXAS is a powerful story of women's search for equality and autonomy in American society. Filled with hardship and rejection, it also is marked by achievement and success. Our story begins in 1902 when a woman petitioned the courts in west Texas to grant her a license to practice law. It follows women lawyers over a century as they learned the law, established professional careers, integrated state bars, and tried to balance traditional responsibilities of private lives with demands of new careers.

More than any other profession women sought to enter, law was the most closed to them. Women were more readily accepted in other professions because of their womanly natures. Female physicians could treat other women, thus preserving female modesty. Teachers merely extended the role of mothers as moral instructors of children. Even as ministers, women could build on beliefs about women's spiritual nature. But there was no way to feminize the meaning of being a lawyer.

The legal profession was especially difficult to integrate because sexual discrimination was rooted in the legal system. Our nation's laws were patriarchal in intent and form, favoring the masculine gender while discriminating against women. Under the common law adopted in the United States, once a woman married she lost the right to inherit property on her own, to enter into contracts in her name, and to independently obtain goods and service. Decisions about her property and her style of living belonged exclusively to her husband. While single women did not face these particular constraints, they, too, faced gender discrimination when a woman's proper role in society was addressed. Moreover, since the legal profession was dominated by men, women had to access it through male-controlled institutions: courts, bar associations, law schools, and law firms.

It is ironic that the figure representing the law is a woman. Lady Justice—Justitia, the Roman Goddess of Justice—is a symbol of the American system of justice and the ideals it embodies. Typically depicted blindfolded, wearing flowing robes and holding a sword and the scales of justice, the image has since antiquity symbolized the fair and equal administration of justice without prejudice or favor.[1] But what of women in our judicial system throughout the country?

Margaret Brent was the first woman known to have acted as an attorney in America. The daughter of a wealthy landowner who had emigrated from England to St. Mary's Parish, Maryland, she was a cousin of Lord Baltimore. He appointed her as counsel to the governor, even though she did not have a license from either the crown or the colony to act as an attorney. Brent shattered all the restrictions facing seventeenth century women by appearing in public trials. Because the colonists did not quite know what to call such a unique woman, they frequently addressed her, in person and in court, as Gentleman Margaret Brent. Court records show that her name figured in 124 cases in eight years.[2]

Despite Brent's legal prowess, it would be more than two centuries before a woman was licensed to practice law in America. Arabella Mansfield, valedictorian of her class at Iowa Wesleyan College and a skilled debater, read law in her brother's office and applied to the Iowa Bar in 1869. Mansfield was allowed to take the bar examination even though the procedure was supposedly limited to "any white male person" who had adequately studied law.[3] Mansfield scored so high on the examination that the court was urged to admit her "because in her examination she has given the very best rebuke possible to the imputation that ladies cannot qualify for the practice of law."[4] Arabella Mansfield thus became the first woman recognized as a lawyer by a state bar association. Not every state, however, was as progressive as Iowa.

In the same year that Mansfield was admitted in Iowa, Myra Bradwell applied to the State Bar of Illinois. Bradwell had worked in her husband's law office before the Civil War. She founded and edited the *Chicago Legal News*, the most important legal newspaper of the West and Midwest. After her application was received, Bradwell received a polite letter from the clerk of the Illinois Supreme Court informing her that as a married woman she had no legal right to contract in her own name. Thus, she could not be admitted to the practice of law. Bradwell then petitioned the Illinois court for reconsideration as she publicly protested its decision in her newspaper. The Illinois Supreme Court again denied Bradwell admission. The court rejected her due to "the disability imposed by your married condition." Bradwell then filed a writ of error to the United States Supreme Court. The decision, which was not rendered for nearly two years, once again ruled against Bradwell because of her gender. Finally in 1890 the Illinois Supreme Court granted the aspiring lawyer her license to practice law.[5] Bradwell, by this time more concerned with the rejection of women in the legal profession than practicing law herself, placed her energies into campaigning for expanded rights for women using the *Chicago Legal News* as her pulpit.[6]

The state of Wisconsin, like Illinois, had a closed mind about accepting women as lawyers. In 1875 Lavinia Goodell, who had been licensed as a lawyer at the local level and had a successful practice in Janesville, appealed to the Wisconsin Supreme Court when the ruling on one of her cases was reversed. Since only members of the state bar were allowed to address the supreme court and since only men were members of the bar, Goodell was not allowed to appear before Wisconsin's highest court. She prepared all of the briefs and had a male lawyer represent her. Goodell argued in her brief that references to "he" and "him" were obviously meant to refer to women as well as men.

Goodell did not prevail in her argument.[7] The justices' opinion, disguised as protection for women, read: "The peculiar qualities of womanhood, its genteel graces, its quick sensibility, its tender susceptibility, its purity, its delicacy, its emotional impulses, its subordination of hard reason to sympathetic feeling, are surely not qualifications for forensic strife. Nature has tempered woman as little for the juridical conflicts of the court room as for the public conflicts of the battle-field . . . [Our profession] has essentially and habitually to do with all that is selfish and malicious, knavish and criminal, coarse and brutal, repulsive and obscene, in human life. It would be revolting to all female sense of the innocence and sanctity of their sex, shocking to man's reverence for womanhood and faith in woman, on which hinge all the better affections and humanities of life, that woman should be permitted to mix professionally in all the nastiness of the world which finds its way into courts of justice. . . . "[8] These sentiments were widespread in America, but the following year the Wisconsin state legislature revised its statutes and admitted Goodell to the bar.[9] The view that women had no place in a courtroom, however, would prevail.

Contrary to some popular opinion, many of these early women lawyers had men who supported them in their efforts. The sympathetic judge who admitted Arabella Mansfield, Myra Bradwell's husband who encouraged her not to give up, the lawyer who represented Lavinia Goodell in court when she could not make her own appeal—

these and other men allied themselves with women in their struggles. These allies were frequently family members who enabled women to study and practice law. Husband and wife teams provided an acceptable environment for women to remain in the background while contributing to the office practice. Progressive male lawyers often became mentors to aspiring female lawyers.

White women had a difficult time obtaining the right to practice law, but their struggles were mild compared to those of black women. Charlotte E. Ray, a graduate of Howard University School of Law in 1872, was the first black woman lawyer in the United States. Ray impressed everyone with her intelligence and legal skill, but the prejudice of the time discouraged clients from using her. Reluctantly, she returned to her teaching career.[10] The number of black female attorneys rose ever so slowly. By 1910, U.S. census data listed only two female black attorneys in the entire country while there were 556 white female attorneys.[11] Minority females had to overcome the double barriers of gender discrimination and racial prejudice.

In spite of some successes, experiences similar to those of Arabella Mansfield, Myra Bradwell, Lavinia Goodell, and Charlotte Ray were rare and progress was slow for women entering the legal profession over the next forty years. Some states, including Texas, allowed women to practice law while others resisted. Not until 1923 did every state admit women to the bar.[12] This was nearly three centuries after Margaret Brent had proved that a woman could, in fact, be at least as effective in public life as the men to whom the prerogative was reserved.

Women were hampered not only by legal precedent but also by social convention, which defined women as belonging to a separate sphere of society from men.[13] This feminine sphere kept women out of the public eye which included, of course, the practice of law. Even when new laws were enacted state by state to admit women to the bar, societal disapproval remained intact. This disapproval erupted into rank discrimination which would become ingrained in the struggle of female lawyers to achieve equality with male members of the bar. As might be expected, the number of women lawyers in the country continued to be quite low—between 1 and 3 percent—until the renewed women's movement of the 1970s.[14] The civil rights movement helped raise concerns not only for racial equality but also for the rights of women.

The last quarter of the twentieth century saw an extraordinary increase in both licensed women lawyers and their acceptance in the profession. As more women became "friends of the court," substantive law has become friendlier to women. The number of women students in law school rose from 4 to 20 percent in less than a decade.[15] Women students streamed into institutions that did not know how to make them feel welcome or how to integrate them into the classroom setting. Many law schools had never hired a woman professor. Women, whether student or faculty, still felt like outsiders in the heavily male environment. Gradually, however, new gender-related courses were introduced into the curriculum and women formed their own organizations for bonding and networking.

Yet one aspect of being a woman lawyer is still problematic. The practice of law, in most instances, is not accommodating to women's lives. Many of the early female lawyers were single and childless.[16] Today women who are the primary caregivers in their families find themselves caught between the demands of family and those of career. Trying to balance these two aspects of their lives is causing many women to leave the profession.

Another problem that lingers for some women is that of sexual discrimination, including subtle bias, unequal treatment, and harassment. Admittedly, it is less overt than in the past, but its very existence indicates that women are not yet viewed as equal participants in all areas of the legal profession. Surveys have shown that women especially feel discrimination in advancement opportunities.[17] The glass ceiling has occasionally been penetrated, but for many women it is still there.

Though firms are hiring women with greater frequency, the road to a partnership is not assured. Few women are managing partners in major Texas firms. Female deans are a minority among the country's law schools. While the judiciary now has scores of women on the bench, they are not always well represented on the highest courts. Considering that none of these possibilities even existed fifty years ago, we recognize the progress women have made in the legal arena.

Although women lawyers still represent a minority of the profession in Texas, they have achieved success in all areas: litigation, corporate law, large firm practice, small firm and solo practice, government, politics, academia, the judiciary, and bar leadership. Their success has been built on the foundation created by those who came before them. The pioneers in the field proved that women lawyers were as intelligent, hardworking, and capable as their male counterparts. Here are their stories.

Notes

1. "Lady Justice," http://en.wikipedia.org/wiki/Lady_Justice (accessed June 22, 2007).

2. Karen Berger Morello, *The Invisible Bar: The Woman Lawyer in America, 1638 to the Present* (New York: Random House, 1986), 3, 6–7; Mary Jane Mossman, *The First Women Lawyers: A Comparative Study of Gender, Law and the Legal Professions* (Portland, Ore.: Hart Publishing, 2006), 26–27.

3. Morello, 12.

4. Annie Nathan Meyer, ed., *Woman's Work in America* (New York: Henry Holt and Company, 1891), 222.

5. Mossman, 42–48.

6. Meyer, 222–24.

7. Mossman, 48–49.

8. Meyer, 227.

9. Ibid., 222. Meyer expressed confidence that women would "push on and upward, keeping pace with her brother . . . until, like him, she shall have finally reached the highest pinnacle of legal fame." (244)

10. Morello, 145–47.

11. Lorraine Dusky, *Still Unequal: The Shameful Truth About Women and Justice in America* (New York: Crown Publishers, Inc., 1996), 142.

12. Virginia G. Drachman, *Sisters in Law: Women Lawyers in Modern American History* (Cambridge, Mass.: Harvard University Press, 1998), 251–53. Texas was the 35th state to admit women if the licensing date (1902) of Edith Locke is used.

13. See Nancy F. Cott, ed., *No Small Courage: A History of Women in the United States* (New York: Oxford University Press, 2000). Karen Manners Smith, *New Paths to Power: American Women, 1890–1920* (New York: Oxford University Press, 1994), Chapter 7, 353–412, is especially relevant to a discussion of women's separate sphere.

14. Cynthia Fuchs Epstein, *Women in Law* (Urbana, Ill.: University of Illinois Press, 1993), Table 1.1, 4.

15. Ibid., Table 3.1, 53.

16. Drachman, 79.

17. Dusky, 165–68.

Chapter One

Pushing the Gate Open

A MOST UNUSUAL HEADLINE APPEARED IN THE *El Paso Herald* on May 20, 1902. In bold letters it announced, "A Woman Lawyer Qualifies for Practice in This City." Mrs. Edith W. Locke had applied to the courts in El Paso County for admission to the bar. A panel of three judges had given her, according to the article, "a most searching examination ransacking all of the law from the foundations of the Roman Empire through the English common law and down to the latest Texas statutes." On completion of the examination, the jurists praised Mrs. Locke's answers on every principle of law and granted her a license,[1] presumably making her the first female lawyer in Texas.[2] Edith Locke had previously taught school in Nebraska and Iowa, where she became interested in the study of law. After marrying, she lived in Chicago and worked in the advertising department of Marshall Field & Co. When her health failed, she moved to the warmer climate of El Paso where she had family members. In her interview for the *El Paso Herald*, she indicated that she took up the study of law as a "pastime."[3] There is no record of Edith Locke having eventually practiced law in Texas,[4] but she did prove—like Iowa's

Mansfield before her—that a woman was capable of learning the law. This fact was still in dispute in much of the country.

In the early twentieth century, the status of women continued to be defined principally by their roles in the family. They had little or no access to higher education or professional employment and were completely excluded from the political process. Under the common law, women lost their economic independence when they married and were considered subject to the control of their husbands. Thus, many women were isolated within the confines of marriage. Most professions were closed to them by virtue of their gender and lack of education, and the demands of raising large families precluded regular work outside the home.[5] While single women were not constrained by the legal hardships of marriage, they too were deemed unfit for the "tough and aggressive" endeavor of practicing law. Women were seen as being nurturing and gentle and therefore not good candidates for such a combative profession. When single women worked outside the home, they were expected to engage in employment "suitable to the female temperament," such as teaching or nursing.[6]

Practicing medicine was considered closely related to nursing as a nurturing profession. Female physicians explained that their medical careers simply extended their womanly responsibility to care for family health. In addition, they argued that it was only because they were women that they could understand the pain and suffering other women endured from gynecological ailments. Moreover, they insisted, only a woman physician could protect the modesty and virtue of a sick woman. In an age that placed a high value on feminine modesty, women doctors argued that women often chose to endure their pain rather than seek the care of a male doctor.[7] Women lawyers, however, did not find it so easy to argue that the practice of law was a natural extension of woman's proper place. It is no surprise, then, that at the turn of the century reports show Texas had one hundred women physicians, but no female lawyers.[8]

Higher education for women was also controversial. Some advocates claimed that education made women better wives and mothers and gave single women the tools they needed to be self-supporting. In contrast, critics voiced concern that educating women posed a serious assault on marriage and the family, pulling women from the home into the workplace.[9] More deceptive criticism insisted that women were biologically inferior to men and could not withstand the physical and mental demands of a rigorous educational curriculum. A Harvard University physician went so far as to claim that excessive study diverted energy from the female reproductive organs to the brain, causing a breakdown in women's health and threatening the existence of future generations.[10] Critics pointed out that fortunately little education was required for most work performed by women. Teaching did not require a college degree at that time, and professions like law were not considered suitable for women whose separate sphere demanded piety, purity, domesticity, and submissiveness.[11]

Attending law school was not the only avenue of learning for pioneer women attorneys. Before law schools began to open and for years afterward, working in an established law office as a stenographer or office manager was the most readily accessible path to passing the bar exam for women, just as clerking was the path to a law career for men. "Reading" the law, or studying the law under the supervision of a licensed attorney, was the most available means of legal education for women, particularly if they did not live near a school offering law classes.[12] Correspondence courses were also available from places such as Blackstone and LaSalle universities.[13]

In spite of the public's widespread disapproval of higher education for women, colleges and universities began to admit them in larger numbers. All-female institutions such as Incarnate Word College[14] and Our Lady of the Lake University[15] in San Antonio and the College of Industrial Arts[16] in Denton were established by proponents of higher education for women to provide them with additional access to education. From its inception, the University of Texas admitted women into the undergraduate program and had no restrictions against women enrolling in its law department.[17] Nevertheless, no female enrolled in law classes at the University of Texas until 1906 when Ella Crim Lynch entered. Apparently Mrs. Lynch attended for only one year, and no records have been found of her further involvement in the legal field.[18]

In 1914, the law department of the University of Texas graduated its first two women, Irene Gertrude Brown of San Antonio and Rose Zeloski of Fort Worth. Two years later Anna Sandbo of Austin was the first woman to receive a master of laws degree.[19] These pioneers chose divergent paths on graduating. Brown returned to her hometown and opened a solo practice that she maintained after her marriage,[20] while Zeloski ventured to New York to become the first woman on the legal staff of American Telephone and Telegraph Company.[21] Brown and Zeloski completed their legal education four years before women were allowed to vote in Texas. That, within itself, was an ironic accomplishment. Sandbo became interested in a law career when she married an attorney. Having already received a B.A. degree, she worked as a stenographer in her husband's office. After completing work for her master of laws, she joined his firm, which she continued to operate after his death in 1925. Sandbo began conducting study courses for young law graduates as they prepared for the bar examination. She continued her coaching for more than thirty years until she retired at the age of eighty.[22]

In 1915 female law students at the University of Texas formed the Texas Women's Law Association. These pioneering women chose for their motto, "Not what we give but what we share." The officers in 1918 were Bertha Wallace Lewis, Mildred Marshall, Nellie Gray Robertson, Annie Maxwell, Mary Wallace Savage, and Anna Sandbo.[23] They wanted to have an organization that could help create a context for bonding among the scant number of women in the school.

By 1918 the law department at the University of Texas boasted five women in a graduating class of thirty-four.[24] They were Alice Jane Drysdale of Houston, Annie Maxwell and Mildred Marshall of Austin, Helen Lord Leary of San Antonio, and Nellie Gray Robertson of Granbury. The comments under the women's photographs in the *Cactus*, the university yearbook, were tongue-in-cheek, always alluding to their gender and their determination. One read, "[i]s too modest to be a lawyer. We are surprised she was able to weather the course in Domestic Relations. She is a good student, though and intends to 'sure nuff' practice law." Another declared, "[g]oes after law work like she did after the goats on her father's ranch in her childhood and will make the men hustle whenever she decides to practice."[25] Despite the yearbook's ribbing, each of these women was admitted to the bar.[26]

In the years ahead, as additional law schools opened, more women received a university-related education. When Texas Christian University moved from Waco to Fort Worth in 1911, the school approved a department of law whereby a student could receive both the B.A. and LL.B. degrees in six years. By 1917 the law program was extended to three years. That same year Texas Christian University enrolled its first female law student, Geneva Bradley, the daughter of a judge. The student newspaper headline read, "Texas Has a Lady Law Student." The story related that the male students seemed pleased to have a "lady student." The reporter, however, noted, "It is needless to say that it adds a certain amount of stimulus to the work for the young men when they feel that there is a young lady in the class who is likely to show them up in their chosen work at any time." There is no further word on Bradley's study of law, and the law department at Texas Christian University closed in 1920 because the board of trustees was not prepared to make the substantial financial investment required to maintain the law department.[27]

The University of Texas and Texas Christian University were not the only accessible institutions of higher education for women attorneys in the early twentieth century. Baylor University School of Law, organized in 1857 as the second university west of the Mississippi to teach law, had closed in 1883 but reopened in 1920,[28] while Southern Methodist University established its law school in Dallas in 1925.[29]

In addition to these universities, a number of proprietary law schools were being operated across the state. Dallas offered four such schools: Jefferson and Madison, both founded in 1919, Somerville (later renamed Dixie University), and Dallas Law School, operated by the Young Men's Christian Association.[30] Jefferson and Madison merged in 1929 and placed a branch in Fort Worth that same year.[31] South Texas School of Law, founded in 1923, operated under the auspices of the education committee of the Houston YMCA.[32] The Galveston Institute of Law opened in 1926[33] while San Antonio had three privately operated schools. The San Antonio Bar Association opened the San Antonio Law School in 1927. Another school, the San Antonio Public School of Law, met in a high school building and was presided over by the superintendent of the San Antonio School District. The third such school in San Antonio was Colonel John K. Weber's School of Law.[34] The oldest of the proprietary schools, Houston Law School, opened in 1912.[35]

Those privately operated schools conducted classes in the evening using a faculty of local practitioners and emphasized mastery of subject matter necessary to pass the bar examination. These schools were chosen by many women because they were inexpensive—as little as $6 a month—and they allowed students to work at full-time jobs or handle family responsibilities while pursuing their legal studies.[36] In spite of the numerous law schools in Texas at this time, the overall ratio of women students to male ones remained low through the 1920s.[37] Women were not encouraged to study law. In fact, they were discouraged by those who portrayed the study of law as an environment that women would find distasteful. Women were constantly reminded that their place was in private confines, and they were not to venture into public ones.

In reality, the requirements for being licensed to practice law in Texas at the turn of the century were not rigorous. Basic requirements included possessing a "good reputation for moral character and honest and honorable deportment," being twenty-one years of age, being an American citizen, being a Texas resident for at least six months, and having a knowledge of legal rules and court proceedings. This knowledge could be obtained by working as a legal secretary, studying in a lawyer's office, or attending classes in a law school.[38] Applicants were required to take an examination unless they held a diploma from the University of Texas law department, in which case they were exempt from being examined.[39]

In 1903 the primary responsibility for granting admission to the bar moved from the district courts to the nine courts of civil appeals. Each of these courts appointed a three-member board of examiners, whose duty it was to conduct examinations in conformity with standards set by the Supreme Court of Texas. Although this action resulted in more uniformity, there were still substantial variations in admission procedures in the different jurisdictions.[40]

A radical change in 1919 established the Supreme Court of Texas as the sole licensing agent for Texas attorneys at law.[41] At the same time, written examinations under a single board of law examiners brought greater consistency to the application process. Educational requirements for enrolling in law school were gradually raised from a high school diploma to two years of college,[42] and then to three years of college study.[43] Eventually, a college degree was necessary to enroll in a Texas law school.[44] Nowhere was gender mentioned as a reason for exclusion.

Why did women choose to pursue a field of work in which the doors were tightly closed against them? Women who worked as stenographers in law offices became interested in the formal study of law due to this exposure. Still others saw themselves as mediators and problem solvers by nature and believed this was a necessary attribute for lawyers. Additionally, many recognized that being an insider in the legal arena was an opportunity to expand women's rights and to establish reform measures within society. Few of them realized that the journey to realize these goals would be an incredibly difficult one just because they were women.

Many had family connections to the law. While it was less likely that a daughter rather than a son would be expected to join her father in a law office, there were some women who saw this as carrying on a family tradition. Those who were married to attorneys felt it was an opportunity to work closely with their husbands and to benefit their families financially. It was natural for the wife of an attorney to join her husband in his office. There was actually a precedent in our state for a wife assisting her husband in his law practice. Frances Cox Henderson, whose husband, James Pinckney Henderson, was the first governor of the state of Texas in 1846, learned enough law from her husband to carry on his practice when he was away from their home in San Augustine. Frances had been educated in Europe, where she reputedly learned to speak eighteen languages. Although she was never licensed to practice law, her neighbors in San Augustine continued coming to Frances for counsel.[45]

Since no formal courses of study or degrees were required—indeed, many male lawyers did not possess these credentials—a wife would study under her husband's tutelage before taking the bar examination. Her husband not only provided a secure and welcoming place to work but also shielded his wife from public disapproval. The wife usually remained in the office where she prepared legal documents and managed the office business while her husband conducted public transactions.[46] Although the tasks of a notary public were considered public ones, and thus not fitting for women to assume, they nevertheless fell to the woman in the office, along with the secretarial duties.[47] For this reason, an aspiring female attorney was frequently cautioned against becoming a "typewriter"—as they were called—lest she be hired as a legal secretary rather than as a practicing attorney.[48]

Hortense Ward and Alice Tiernan were two of the earliest women to become associated with their attorney husbands. Ward, a divorced mother of three daughters, was a court stenographer who married attorney W. H. Ward in 1908.[49] After studying law in her husband's office and taking a correspondence course, Ward was admitted to the bar in 1910 after making a score of 95 on the bar examination. When notified of her success on the examination, Ward explained that she would "assist her husband" and "counsel and advise."[50] Ward did just that for almost thirty years as a partner in the firm, Ward and Ward. She seldom appeared in court, remaining in the background writing briefs and conducting research. This is an interesting revelation when one understands the active role Hortense Ward played in the women's suffrage movement and in expanding women's legal rights.[51] She was admitted to the United States Supreme Court Bar on February 24, 1915, making her the first woman in Texas, and perhaps in the entire South, to claim this distinction.[52]

Alice Tiernan was listed in the Galveston City Directory as working with her husband in his office some six years before her admission to the bar in 1909.[53] It is likely that she received her legal training from her husband, as did Ward in Houston. Tiernan and her husband relocated their practice to Houston about 1910.[54] In October of 1912, Richard and Alice Tiernan found themselves the object of a lawsuit. The Harris County Bar Association, claiming that the Tiernans were guilty of barratry and extortion, filed malpractice charges against the couple. In an unusual turn of events, Richard was dropped from the barratry charge, leaving Alice to face it alone. It is not known whether Alice was brought to trial, but she apparently was not disbarred, because she continued to practice law. The Tiernans subsequently filed a suit against the *Houston Chronicle*, claiming that the newspaper had defamed them in an article. A trial was held and the jury returned a verdict and judgment in favor of the Tiernans for $15,000. The judgment, however, was reversed on appeal.[55] Alice received a great deal of unfavorable publicity, which did not seem to concern her. Richard died shortly thereafter, but Alice continued as a lawyer, practicing from her home until 1918 when she left the city.[56] Alice Tiernan, unlike Hortense Ward, was not reluctant to appear in a public role as a female lawyer.

The University of Texas law school continued to graduate a few women every year from 1917 until 1925.[57] Women, as expected, remained an overwhelming minority in classes. One solution to this problem was the founding of law school sororities, which offered women a common social and intellectual community. The first legal sorority in the country, Kappa Beta Pi, was founded in 1908 by ten women students at Chicago-Kent College of Law. Just three years later, five women in the law school at the University of California at Los Angeles organized another legal fraternity, Phi Delta Delta. Both sororities grew quickly beyond their local settings.[58] The Eta chapter of Kappa Beta Pi was organized on the University of Texas campus in 1916 with fourteen charter members. Anna Sandbo was installed as dean, the lead officer. In an effort to support women's professional goals, the Eta chapter held monthly meetings to help its members stay up to date on changing state laws.[59] The legal sororities also functioned in important ways on the national level through their publications, the *Kappa Beta Pi Quarterly* and the *Phi Delta Delta*. They reported events that impacted women's professional lives, including announcements regarding office openings, address changes, and professional appointments and accomplishments. There was, however, a negative aspect to the sorority. They could be restrictive in their membership, and for that reason, many women chose not to join.[60] Nevertheless, these groups were a means of forming a community among women in law—an ideal that would be pursued in the years ahead by the formation of other professional organizations for women lawyers. Lucy Moore, a 1920 University of Texas law graduate, served as the grand dean—the equivalent of national president—of Kappa Beta Pi in 1921–22. After her graduation, Moore remained on the Austin campus as librarian at the law school and as an instructor on the faculty, as well as advisor to the Kappa Beta Pi chapter.[61]

A small number of women continued to brave the halls of the University of Texas law school where they were a rare sight. Frances McQueen graduated in 1917 and Doris Connerly in 1919, each as the only woman in her class.[62] There is no indication whether McQueen pursued a legal career after graduation. Connerly, however, was hired by a prominent Houston firm, Baker Botts Parker & Garwood, and placed in the job of librarian. She remained there for four years after which she returned to her hometown of Austin to become the librarian of the University of Texas School of Law. In 1928 she was appointed librarian for the state legislature, a post she held for thirty-four years.[63] In those days when a woman was hired by a firm, the library was her usual assignment. Connerly found this to her liking, but her successor at Baker Botts, Dorothy Most, thought otherwise. Most, the only female in her class in 1925, apparently had no trouble finding a job when she graduated. Letters in her scrapbook, which she kept during her university years, reveal strong support from her professors, other students, and friends. She was first offered a legal position with the Gainesville Girls' Reform School. Through the intervention of the law school dean, however, she acquired a position with Baker Botts.[64] After two years with the firm, where she did little more than library duties, Most resigned and took a position as Dean of Women at St. John's College of Law in New York. After a few years, Most abruptly left the legal field and entered Juilliard School of Music in New York City to pursue study of the violin—an instrument on which she was already quite accomplished.[65] Her scrapbook revealed Most's thoughts about becoming a lawyer. She wrote, "[n]ot every woman can make a lawyer. But if a girl has brains, perseverance and the will to do, she will get ahead. It is a hard road to hoe."[66]

Not all of the women licensed during these early years had attended law school. Lilian Aveilhe passed the bar examination in 1914 after studying in the Dallas firm of Spellman & Murray. The *Daily Times Herald* announced shortly after she was admitted to the bar, "Dallas Woman in Court as Lawyer; Starts New Era." Aveilhe's appearance in court apparently caused quite a stir, attracting a large number of spectators. The reporter noted with some astonishment that the young lawyer seemed quite familiar with the statutes. For some undetermined reason, Aveilhe disappeared from Dallas legal circles one year later.[67]

Frances Hexamer was also admitted to the bar in 1918. She had begun working as a secretary for a Dallas firm at the age of 18. Based on what she learned from working in the firm's office, she passed the bar examination and opened her own practice. A comment in the 1922 *Men of Texas Encyclopedia* had this to say about the young attorney: "Frances is a refutation of man's old contention that a woman would lose her feminine charm by mingling in the affairs of men." Hexamer was quite serious about her chosen profession. She became the legislative chairman of the Texas State Federation of Business and Professional Women, and, in this capacity, she lobbied for equal treatment of women in hiring and promotion. Despite encouraging women to enter professions such as law, Hexamer, like Aveilhe, disappeared from the legal scene within a year.[68]

Florence Rabe Ramer was another promising young lawyer who ultimately changed her mind about her chosen profession. Ramer earned a degree in math from the University of Texas, after which she taught school and engaged in social work for three years. Following a divorce, she was encouraged by a San Antonio judge to use his private library to study law. She studied for six months and then passed the bar examination. After her admission to the bar in 1914, Ramer practiced in San Antonio for four years before deciding to try another profession. Moving to California, she became a successful Hollywood character actress at the age of fifty under the name of Florence Bates.[69]

With the advent of World War I, women lawyers expected that new opportunities would open for them, as occurred in so many other professions in which women found jobs vacated by men who went to fight the war. But even in the war years, women were not welcome in established legal fields. The work they performed consisted mainly of serving on draft boards, advising committees supporting the war effort, and filing naturalization petitions, as Irene Brown O'Connor did in San Antonio.[70] After the war and the passage of women's suffrage, women attorneys were hopeful that their time for advancement had come.

Considering that these women were breaking out of the mold of traditional female work, it is surprising that more of them were not ardent suffragists. An examination of their biographical information, however, seldom mentions this involvement. In reality, it appears that only a few of these women lawyers evidenced their support of women's rights by being active in the movement. The women's suffrage movement began in 1848 with a conference at Seneca Falls, New York, which was organized by a small group agitating for women to be given legal rights equal to those enjoyed by men. The movement was initiated in Texas in 1868, but it plodded along for forty years before it caught fire. Among the most avid suffragists were professional women who advocated for change, not only in voting rights but also in other areas that would benefit women in the workplace.[71] Houston lawyer Hortense Ward was an enthusiastic and relentless suffragist. She believed that if women could vote they would be in a position to choose public officials who supported women's rights.[72] Little thought was given to electing women themselves to public office, but Edith Wilmans, a Dallas attorney and active suffragist, would soon throw herself into the fray and run for the state legislature.[73] Bertha Wallace Lewis, who was admitted to the bar in 1918, was a member of the National Woman's Party, a more militant arm of the suffrage movement. Lewis served as Texas legislature chairman for the organization. This position would indicate that Lewis was active in lobbying the legislature to support the suffrage bill.[74] Much to the dismay of these women, not much changed after the Nineteenth Amendment was passed in 1920. Many white women were apathetic, and black women still could not vote because of state laws prohibiting blacks from voting in the Democratic primary election, which was tantamount to being the only election that mattered in a predominantly one-party state. A poll tax requirement also increased the likelihood that women of lesser means would not be on the list of eligible voters.[75] Furthermore, the sense of being part of a movement all but disappeared. There was no agreement on an agenda to be achieved by securing the vote. Professional women, especially lawyers, placed no faith in what suffrage could mean to them. Recognizing that having the vote would not be sufficient to advance their causes, women quickly turned to the model of male lawyers and sought to attain their success.

Even if only a few women lawyers were active suffragists, nearly all of them were interested in reform. They were concerned about education, temperance, child labor practices, married women's property rights, and world peace.[76] One venue they used for this activity was membership in the Business and Professional Women organization. Its federation was founded in 1919 in St. Louis as the first national organization for working and professional women. There were units of the B&PW in many parts of Texas, in towns both small and large.[77] This involvement provided them with a network, national and local, to address inequities that women faced. It would prove to be a strong instrument for reform in the years ahead.

A 1925 article in the *Daily Times Herald* featured "Eight Portias in Dallas' Legal Profession." The writer touted the ability of these women, even admitting that many in his opinion had made better attorneys than some men. Helen Viglini was described as "a self-made woman" who was strongly attracted to criminal law. Hattie Henenberg practiced civil law but also administered the Free Legal Aid Bureau established by the Dallas Bar Association. Grace Fitzgerald handled bankruptcy cases in both federal and state courts from her own law office. Isabelle Abright worked in the legal department of the Cotton Belt Railroad. Sarah Menezes had been appointed assistant U.S. attorney for the Northern District of Texas. Hollie Martin worked in the credit department of a large mercantile firm. Edith Wilmans had just completed a term in the state legislature as the first woman elected to that body. Only Sarah Hughes practiced in a firm—previously all-male—and she revealed that her first job with the firm was as the receptionist.[78] This glowing article probably led readers to think that Dallas' first female lawyers were having an easy time in this new field. In actuality, they had encountered strong discrimination in landing jobs of any kind that related to their legal studies. Two decades after Edith Locke passed the bar examination, women were still viewed as being interlopers.

What motivated these particular women to become lawyers? Viglini, a widow with five children, was candid in saying she hoped a law practice would provide a good income for her family.[79] Henenberg wanted to have a role in child welfare issues, just as Wilmans and Martin expressed interest in expanding the rights of women. Fitzgerald believed that women would prefer to have a woman represent them, while Menezes was influenced by her attorney father to study law. Abright unabashedly said she was waiting for "that carved chair in the White House" to be available for a woman.[80] Hughes decided to study law after two years of teaching in a girls' school in North Carolina where she was not adequately challenged. She became convinced to become a lawyer when she worked for the Washington, D.C., Police Department while she was in law school.[81] Ten years after the article appeared, five of the eight women—Helen Viglini, Sarah Hughes, Hattie Henenberg, Grace Fitzgerald, and Sarah Menezes—were still pursuing a career in law in Dallas. Several had also assumed positions within the Dallas Bar Association.[82]

While Dallas may have had the largest concentration of women attorneys in 1925, there were others who had been admitted to the bar in various places across the state. Each was one of the earliest female attorneys in her locale. They were Mae Ament in Alpine;[83] Bertie Puntney in Amarillo;[84] Pauline Franks in Austin;[85] Leola Chauvin in Beaumont;[86] Myrtle Hancock in Bonham;[87] Elizabeth Bellah[88] and Susette Meyer[89] in Bowie; Pearl Patterson Gibson in Brownwood;[90] Emma Stullken Webb in Elgin;[91] Ruth Brazzil in Galveston;[92] Lillie May Bradley in Groesbeck;[93] Marjorie Rogers Church in Marlin;[94] Willie Zac Drummond in Mission;[95] Amanda Dunlay,[96] Kate Weidekind,[97] and Inez Elizabeth Lohman[98] in Houston; Elizabeth Threadgill in Laredo;[99] Margaret Hill in Longview;[100] Emma Boone Bledsoe in Lubbock;[101] Esther Mary Schneider[102] and Pauline Feller[103] in San Antonio; and Bezie Dee in Wichita Falls.[104]

Available information describing the women who were admitted to the bar between 1909 and 1925 paints an interesting profile. Regarding marital status, 48 percent were single, 46 percent were married, and 6 percent were widowed. Of the married women, 66 percent of them had children, but only 40 percent had more than two children. In reviewing their education, 50 percent had received an LL.B. degree, 15 percent had some formal legal education without receiving a degree, 32 percent had studied in a law office, and 3 percent had taken correspondence courses. As to the nature of their law practice, 42 percent practiced with a male family member, 26 percent were in a solo practice, and the remainder were scattered among positions in government, businesses, title companies, and law libraries. Among married female lawyers, small families were the norm and a few women reported that they chose not to have children so that they could focus on their careers. Single women gravitated toward a solo practice, but also found employment in other places.[105]

These findings likely indicate the difficulty encountered in securing legal positions. The most surprising result was the number of women who had received a degree in law or had some formal legal education. This appears to indicate a growing awareness by 1925 of the value of not just the additional training available through law school but also the law degree itself as a credential that might help them access a broader range of law practice opportunities.

Although the number of women practicing law slowly increased, they still faced problems posed by the conflicts present in the two worlds in which they found themselves. As a woman she was to be modest, sentimental, and caring. As a lawyer she was to be assertive, rational, and objective. As a woman, her place was at home and her role was the caretaker of domestic concerns. As a lawyer, her place was in the office and the courtroom and her task was to protect freedom and justice. These conflicts influenced every aspect of those women's professional lives: the type of practice they chose, their relationship to social reform, whether they remained in the office or ventured into the courtroom, and even how they dressed.[106]

Since they faced limited opportunities in law practice, they chose their areas of expertise carefully in order to secure a niche in the world of the small practitioner. A survey in 1920 revealed that the practice areas most often selected by women were probate, real estate, domestic relations, and general office practice. These fields relied on qualities traditionally associated with femininity.[107] Women lawyers saw themselves as problem solvers who could assist individuals and families. Most women did not see themselves as combatants in the male-dominated courtroom. The idea that women could compete equally with men resonated through Beatrice Doerschuk's *Women in the Law*, a guide to legal training and opportunities in law for women in New York City published in 1920. Doerschuk insisted that women were avoiding trial practice, to the detriment of their careers. In spite of Doerschuk's admonition, few women pursued trial work because they had been told over and over again that a woman's nature was not suitable for the courtroom environment.[108] At the same time, women argued that the legal profession would benefit from their feminine virtues. They claimed that their womanly sympathies, morality, and domestic nature would ameliorate the competitive and aggressive qualities that men brought to the law.[109]

Women had a number of practical concerns as well. One of the most visible issues centered on hats. The custom of the day in the early twentieth century was that women wore hats whenever they were in public. Judges, however, required that male attorneys remove their hats when entering a courtroom. Women attorneys faced the dilemma of maintaining their femininity or lining up with the men. It appears that decisions were frequently made on an individual basis by the ruling judge, but women's legal publications firmly stated that women lawyers, like men, should appear before the bench with uncovered heads. Interestingly, it was during these years that the *Ladies' Home Journal* began to advise business and professional women on appropriate dress.[110] Attire would continue to be a debated topic in the years ahead.

Women admitted to the bar in these early years were intent on proving that they could successfully practice law, maintain their womanhood, and break through legal restrictions. They continued to face cultural mandates telling them to stay home, labeling those who ventured into the public realm as unladylike, and excluding them from the power structure within the profession. Women of color faced even greater prejudice, and their journey would be a delayed one. The history of the first generation of women lawyers in Texas is full of triumphs and defeats, but it was their perseverance and their day-to-day dedication to the fight that opened the profession to women. They had pushed the gate open. Those that followed would push it open a bit more.

Notes

1. "A Woman Lawyer Qualifies for Practice in This City," *El Paso Herald*, May

20, 1902.

2. The United States Census for 1900 reports seventeen women lawyers in Texas for that year. Exhaustive research has failed to uncover those women. Some errors were found in recording the census information (i.e., entering *lawyer* by the wife's name instead of by the husband's, as was correct). This could account for the reported seventeen women. The El Paso news article referred to Mrs. Locke as the first woman lawyer in Texas, as did the *Chicago Legal News*, May 24, 1902, 317, col. 4.

3. *El Paso Herald*, May 20, 1902.

4. Justice Ann Crawford McClure in correspondence to author, April 18, 2005, indicated there were no records in the El Paso courts of Edith Locke having appeared in them. Since Mrs. Locke had two-year-old twins and her husband worked in Chicago, it is possible that she returned there.

5. Elizabeth York Enstam, "Women and the Law," *The New Handbook of Texas* (Austin: The Texas State Historical Association, 1996), 6:1046–1047; Cott, 369. As late as 1920, more than 75% of all adult women in the country reported that they functioned exclusively as wives, mothers, and housekeepers in their homes. At the same time, the divorce rate was rising. By 1915 one in nine couples sought a divorce, perhaps indicating that more women were unwilling to remain in unsatisfactory marriages and were willing to become independent. As single women they were able to control their own interests.

6. Nancy Woloch, *Women and the American Experience: A Concise History* (New York: Alfred A. Knopf, 1984), 247–49. Teaching was the only profession that women, both white and black, could enter in any numbers. It was, however, directed toward single women. Most school systems required female teachers to resign when they married. Although women comprised the majority of teachers, administrative posts were usually assigned to men.

7. Ibid., 284–85. See also Elizabeth Silverthorne and Geneva Fulgham, *Women Pioneers in Texas Medicine* (College Station: Texas A&M University Press, 1997).

8. *Census Occupation Report of the Twelfth Census of the United States, 1900* (Washington, D.C.: U.S. Census Office, 1902), II: 541. In comparison, there were 715 female stenographers in Texas. In 1900 there were 9,000 female physicians in the U.S. while there were only 1500 female lawyers. Medical schools for women were established more frequently than law schools for women, giving women more access

to professional training and less competition with men.

9. Women in the nineteenth century were bombarded on all sides with reminders of what true womanhood required of them. Popular magazines of the time, sermons in church, household manuals and, of course, public sentiment hold fast to the idea that women were only suited for the domestic role. Naturally, all women could not model their lives in this way even if they chose to do so. Many women had to work to provide an income either for themselves if they were single or for their families if they were married.

10. Drachman, 114. Dr. Edward H. Clarke published *Sex in Education; or, A Fair Chance for Girls,* which explained the supposed weakness of female physiology. In reality, it was an assault on the new phenomenon of coeducation. *Sex in Education* was widely read, going through seventeen editions in thirteen years. When Lavinia Goodell, the early Wisconsin lawyer, died at the age of forty-one, the question arose again as to whether women could endure the severe mental strain of a legal career. The retort of those who supported women lawyers was that an outstanding male lawyer had died at thirty-two and no one questioned whether his death was due to mental exertion. Cited in Lelia Robinson, "Women Lawyers in the United States," *The Green Bag*, 1890, vol. 2, 24.

11. See Barbara Welter, *Dimity Convictions: The American Woman in the Nineteenth Century* (Athens, Ohio: Ohio University Press, 1976), 21–41.

12. Nancy Jo Newton and W. Frank Newton, "Legal Education in Texas," *Centennial History of the Texas Bar 1882–1982* (Burnet: Eakin Press, 1981), 160.

13. Blackstone Career Institute, "History of Blackstone Career Institute," http://www.blackstone.edu/about/history (accessed June 3, 2007). Founded in 1890 in Chicago, Blackstone Institute was a pioneer in "distance education." In 1912 the institute developed a commentary on law education that simplified the technical style in which most textbooks were written. Drawing on the knowledge of the best legal talent in the country, the books became highly successful and were used by many aspiring lawyers. In the late 1970s, Blackstone Institute changed from a school of law to a training school for paralegals and legal assistants. "LaSalle Extension University," http://en.wikipedia.org/wiki/La_Salle_Extension_University (accessed June 3, 2007). Another Chicago-based school, LaSalle Extension University, included an accredited program in law from 1908 until 1980.

14. June Rayfield Welch, *The Colleges of Texas: A Survey of the Lone Star State's Institutions of Higher Learning, Past and Present* (Waco: Texian Press, 1981), 98–

100. Incarnate Word College was founded in 1900 by the Sisters of Charity of the Incarnate Word of San Antonio as a secondary academy. By 1910 four years of college instruction had been added.

15. Ibid., 118. Our Lady of the Lake Academy and Normal School opened in 1896 with female boarders and day students. Operated by the Sisters of Divine Providence, it began offering junior college courses in 1911 and was accredited as a senior college in 1919. Graduate courses were added in 1942. All programs became coeducational in 1969.

16. Ibid., 26–28. The Girls' Industrial College opened in 1900 and changed its name to College of Industrial Arts in 1905. The school had a strong vocational program with a domestic emphasis. The first four-year degree was conferred in 1915. A name change resulted in Texas State College for Women, and in 1957 the school became Texas Woman's University. During the early years of the twentieth century, higher education for women was dedicated to training them as wives, mothers, or teachers. Colleges for women with more exacting academic credentials had opened in the East, but few women from Texas attended them at this early date because of the distance and the cost. See Barbara Miller Solomon, *In the Company of Educated Women: A History of Women and Higher Education in America* (New Haven: Yale University Press, 1985), for a comprehensive discussion of women accessing higher education in spite of those who opposed it.

17. Allegra Jordan Young, "Celebrating 100 Years of Women at UT Law," *UT Law* (Spring 2006), 20. Note that the law department was one of several academic departments until 1920 when it became the University of Texas School of Law.

18. Hans Baade, "Law at Texas: The Roberts-Gould Era (1883–1893)," *Southwestern Historical Quarterly*, Vol. 86, October 1982, 183. Although there is no record of women having enrolled in the university's law department before Mrs. Crim, there is evidence that women had expressed interest in registering as law students and that one woman, Jennie Scott Wilson, was permitted to attend law classes along with her brother in 1891. My thanks to Mark W. Lambert, former special collections librarian, Fred Parks Law Library, South Texas College of Law, for bringing this to my attention.

19. Young, *UT Law*, 20.

20. *Texas Bar Journal*, Vol. 8, No. 5, p. 245 (hereafter cited as 8, 5:245).

21. "Mrs. Fisher, UT Law Grad, to be buried," *Dallas Morning News*, January 11,

1971, Section A, 12.

22. *Texas Bar Journal*, 28, 6:555–556.

23. *1918 Cactus*, 222, Special Collections, Tarlton Law Library, University of Texas at Austin.

24. *1918 Cactus.* While men outnumbered women in the law department, the reverse was true in undergraduate classes. The 1918 senior class at UT had 102 females and thirty-seven males. This followed a national trend in which more women were seeking a higher education than were men, except in professional areas. The ratio of women to men in the 1918 law class would be the highest in the law school until the 1970s.

25. Ibid., 86.

26. The records of the Texas Supreme Court reveal these dates of admission: Drysdale (1918), Leary (1920), Marshall (1918), Maxwell (1919), and Robertson (1918). Drysdale returned to Houston and accepted a job with Gulf Oil Corporation. Alice Drysdale Sheffield's career as associate general counsel at Gulf Oil allowed her to amass considerable wealth, and on her death in 1983 the UT law school received a bequest of $3.5 million, making her the school's most generous benefactor to that time.

27. Ann Arnold, *History of Fort Worth Legal Community* (Austin: Eakin Press, 2000), 39–41.

28. Newton and Newton, 164.

29. Ibid., 170–71.

30. Ibid., 162.

31. Arnold, 44.

32. Newton and Newton, 168.

33. Ibid., 162.

34. Jay Brandon, *Law and Liberty: A History of the Legal Profession in San Antonio* (Dallas: Taylor Publishing Company, 1996), 11.

35. Newton and Newton, 162. The proprietary law schools discussed here were not the only such schools in Texas, but they appeared most often in women lawyers' biographies. For a comprehensive review of proprietary law schools in the United

States, see Robert Stevens, *Law School: Legal Education in America from 1850 to the 1980s* (Chapel Hill: The University of North Carolina Press, 1983), 73–91.

36. Arnold, 44.

37. The University of Texas graduated twenty-six women in law during the 1920s while other schools graduated a scattered few. No records have been found for most of the proprietary schools, but their numbers are also apparently low when compared to the number of male graduates.

38. Stephen K. Huber and James E. Myers, "Admission to the Practice of Law in Texas: An Analytical History," *Houston Law Review* 15:3, 490–92.

39. Ibid., 499. Schools, both in Texas and out of state, were periodically added to the exemption list. By the 1920s these Texas schools were included: UT, Baylor, SMU, South Texas, Dallas School of Law, Jefferson University School of Law, San Antonio School of Law, and San Antonio Public School of Law. This rule remained in place until 1935 when the bar examination became mandatory for all law graduates.

40. Ralph Yarbrough, "A History of Law Licensing in Texas," *Centennial History of the Texas Bar*, 186.

41. Huber and Myers, 542.

42. Ibid., 513.

43. Ibid., 517.

44. Ibid. The rule requiring a college degree to enter law school was adopted in 1976.

45. Mary D. Farrell, "Frances Cox Henderson," *Handbook of Texas*, 3:554.

46. Epstein, 168.

47. Drachman, 26. Some states prohibited women from serving as notaries because public offices were not open to women. Still others held the view that women could not serve as notaries since they could not vote. Texas, apparently, was more open in its views since there were women notaries in Texas in the nineteenth century.

48. Morello, 84.

49. Janelle D. Scott, "Hortense Sparks Ward," *Handbook of Texas*, 6:818.

50. *Houston Post*, August 18, 1910, 9.

51. Michelle Skinner, "Hortense Sparks Ward," Stanford University Law School, Spring 2005, http://womenslegalhistory.stanford.edu/papers05/WardH-Skinner05.pdf (accessed September 10, 2007). Ward admitted to having a "colossal ego," which led to her listing in the 1920 Houston City Directory being much more prominent than that of her husband. She, nevertheless, stayed in the background in their law practice because of negativity toward women lawyers. Ward not only championed women's property rights, but she lobbied for a shorter work week for women, a domestic relations court, a women's division in the state department of labor, and the right for married women to serve as officers in corporations. In 1912 Ward authored a commentary, "The Kernel of the Thing," in *Delineator* (80, 5: 317) as part of a larger article titled "Will Texas Do Better By Its Married Women?" The preface to Ward's words were "Every last mention in this short statement carries with it the chance of injustice, oppression, and tragedy in any home in which the husband chooses to experience his legal rights."

52. Patricia McCade, Clerk's Office, United States Supreme Court, telephone conversation with author, May 11, 2007.

53. *Morrison and Fourmy Directory of the City of Galveston 1905, 1908–09, 1909–10* (Galveston: Morrison and Fourmy). Alice Tiernan is listed in the Texas Supreme Court records as having been admitted to the bar in 1909. Since she participated in numerous court cases with her attorney husband as early as 1902 and was listed in the Galveston City Directory as an attorney at that early date, it is possible that this 1909 admission was to practice before the Texas Supreme Court. She, no doubt, was admitted to practice by a state district court prior to 1903.

54. *Morrison and Fourmy Directory of the City of Houston 1911–12* (Houston: Morrison and Fourmy, 1912).

55. Court of Civil Appeals of Texas at Galveston, *Houston Chronicle Publishing Co. v. Tiernan,* December 1, 1914. The Tiernans were charged by the Houston Bar Association with soliciting clients at the jail. The other charge which led to the malpractice suit was extortion of clients for payments they received for legal service never rendered. When Alice remained a party to the suit and Richard was dropped, one scholar suggested that this could have been gender discrimination since women were still not welcome in the courtroom as litigants.

56. *Morrison and Fourmy Directory of the City of Houston 1920* (Houston: Morrison and Fourmy, 1920).

57. Baade Collection, Special Collections, Tarlton Law Library, University of Texas at Austin. There were twenty-eight female graduates over this period of time. No class had more than four women graduates. Women currently comprise 48.2 percent of the UT law school enrollment.

58. Drachman, *Sisters in Law*, 146–61.

59. Kappa Beta Pi Legal Sorority Records, Tarlton Law Library, University of Texas at Austin.

60. Drachman, *Sisters in Law*, 147.

61. Fiona Hale Cook, ed., *Who's Who Among Women Lawyers 1939* (Boston: Fiona Hale Cook, 1939), 66–67.

62. Baade Collection, Tarlton Law Library, University of Texas at Austin.

63. *Handbook of Texas Online* s.v. "Connerly, Doris Hayne," http://www.tsha.utexas.edu/handbook/online/articles/CC/fcocq.html (accessed November 8, 2004).

64. Dorothy Most Scrapbook, Special Collections, Tarlton Law Library, University of Texas at Austin. See also Allegra Young, "A Most Remarkable Woman," *UT Law*, 2 (Winter 2004) 3:64.

65. "Sees Many Fields for Woman Lawyer," undated article, Houston Women Biography Scrapbooks, Vol. 17c, Houston Metropolitan Research Center, Houston Public Library.

66. Most Scrapbook, n.p. Most's scrapbook includes moot court competition papers, law school assignments, chamber concert flyers, dance cards, photos of campus buildings (including a photograph of the cafeteria burning), and a letter from Baker Botts Parker and Garwood offering her a position. This piece of history was almost lost. It was found in a trash bin, having been thrown away by Most's heir after her death. It was retrieved by a young girl who took it home and asked her parents if it should be saved. The family took the scrapbook to the UT law school where it resides today.

67. Darwin Payne, *As Old as Dallas Itself: A History of the Lawyers of Dallas, the Dallas Bar Association, and the City They Helped Build* (Dallas: Three Forks Press, 1999), 125–26.

68. Vivian Anderson Castleberry, *Daughters of Dallas: A History of Greater Dallas Through the Voices and Deeds of Its Women* (Dallas: Odenwald Press, 1994),

256.

69. Ruthe Winegarten and Cathy Schecter, *Deep in the Heart: The Lives and Legends of Texas Jews* (Austin: Eakin Press, 1990), 106; *Handbook of Texas Online* s.v. "Jacoby, Florence Rabe," http://www.tsha.utexas.edu/handbook/online/articles/JJ/fjact.html (accessed March 24, 2007). She played comic and dramatic supporting roles with some of Hollywood's biggest names. She made her acting debut in *Rebecca*, directed by Alfred Hitchcock, who was credited with discovering her.

70. Payne, *Dallas*, 126; *Who's Who*, 71.

71. Ruthe Winegarten and Judith N. McArthur, ed., *Citizens at Last: The Woman Suffrage Movement in Texas* (Austin: Ellen Temple Publishers, 1987), 13–48.

72. Nancy Baker Jones and Ruthe Winegarten, *Capitol Women: Texas Female Legislators, 1923–1999* (Austin: University of Texas Press, 2000), 37.

73. Ibid., 77.

74. Laura Miller Derry, ed., *Digest of Women Lawyers and Judges* (Louisville, Ky.: Dunne Press, 1949), 210.

75. Enstam, *Handbook of Texas*, 1048–49.

76. Morello, 108.

77. "Business and Professional Women," http://en.wikipedia.org/wiki/Business_and_Professional_Women (accessed March 17, 2007). Clubs were established in some places before the National Federation was formed. Both Dallas and Houston had local organizations by 1917.

78. *Daily Times Herald*, February 1, 1925, http://freepages.history.rootsweb.com/~jwheat/miscellany.html (accessed March 20, 2005).

79. In 1920 women lawyers made $1,000–$3,000 yearly. The median income for all lawyers was $4,000 so males, obviously, earned more than females. The income of women lawyers, however, compared well with other professional positions that women held.

80. *Daily Times Herald*, February 1, 1925.

81. Darwin Payne, *Indomitable Sarah: The Life of Judge Sarah T. Hughes* (Dallas: Southern Methodist University Press, 2004), 17–19.

82. Payne, *Dallas*, 126, 128–30.

83. *Texas Bar Journal,* 34, 10:1123–24. Ament considered her role in the acquisition of the Big Bend National Park the highlight of her fifty-year career in law.

84. *Martindale American Law Directory 1920* (New York: G.B. Martindale Publisher, 1920), 785.

85. *1925 Martindale,* 794.

86. *1920 Martindale*, 725.

87. Derry, 153.

88. *Texas Bar Journal,* 8, 7:336.

89. Ruthe Winegarten, *Finders' Guide to the Women's Exhibit*, Texas and Local History Collections, Houston Metropolitan Research Center, Houston Public Library.

90. *Derry*, 135.

91. *Texas Bar Journal,* 45, 1:129.

92. *Handbook of Texas,* 5:673.

93. *Texas Bar Journal,* 24, 5:472.

94. *1930 Martindale,* 900.

95. *1925 Martindale*, 828.

96. *1925 Martindale*, 820.

97. *Morrison and Fourmy Directory of the City of Houston 1925.*

98. Records of the Texas Supreme Court, June 14, 1921.

99. *1922 Martindale*, 752.

100. *1920 Martindale*, 726.

101. *Texas Bar Journal,* 46, 9:1449; Dr. Monte Monroe, Southwestern Collection Archivist, Texas Tech University, correspondence to author, April 11, 2005. Dr. Monroe confirmed that Emma Bledsoe in 1918 was the first Lubbock County woman admitted to the Texas Bar. Although Bledsoe did not actively practice law, she assisted her attorney husband, who as a state legislator authorized the bill that brought Texas Tech College (as it was then named) to Lubbock.

102. Records of the Texas Supreme Court, June 24, 1921.

103. Records of the Texas Supreme Court, June 9, 1924.

104. Dr. Jeff Campbell, correspondence to author, May 24, 2005.

105. Information was compiled by author using the Supreme Court Records, Martindale and Hubbell directories, Texas Bar Journals, archival collections in libraries, and personal accounts.

106. Drachman, *Sisters in Law*, 64–65.

107. Ibid., 181.

108. Ibid., 168–72. Doreschuk, contrary to popular opinion within the legal profession, believed that women were more naturally suited to a court practice than to an office practice. She complained that the low educational standards of many law schools were not preparing women to compete with males. Doreschuk had such faith in the capabilities of women that she seemed to discount the discrimination they faced as they tried to enter the profession.

109. Ibid., 71–72. See also Virginia Drachman, "Women Lawyers and the Quest for Professional Identity in Late Nineteenth-Century America," *Michigan Law Review*, 88:2414. Not all women agreed with this rationale. In 1887 a female lawyer, Lelia Robinson, argued in a letter to her fellow lawyers, "Do not take sex into the practice. Don't be a 'lady lawyer.' Simply be lawyers and recognize no distinction —no existence of any distinction between yourselves and the other members of the bar."

110. Drachman, *Sisters in Law*, 209.

CHAPTER TWO

Traveling the Narrow Road

WHICH CAREER IS THE BEST ROAD TO A HAPPY and successful life? As Joyce Burg pondered this question, she was advised, "Don't practice law. It is not a woman's game."[1] So, like many of her peers, she chose teaching, which was considered an acceptable job for a woman. After two years in the classroom, however, Burg still felt the pull of the law. She entered the University of Texas School of Law and graduated in 1926 as one of two women in her class. She recalled that the women were not treated badly but were just merely tolerated and made to feel out of place by their sixty-five male peers. She sought a job in Houston but was faced with repeated rejections. Burg then moved to New York City where she found a job in the legal department of the largest title company in the city. In 1933 she returned to Houston and discovered that nothing had changed. Established firms were still not receptive to hiring women, so she opened an office across the street from the courthouse, paid a monthly rent of $30, and formed one of the first female partnerships in the state with a recent law graduate from the University of Texas, Helene Daily.[2] Burg, who retained her maiden name during her seventy-year career, and Daily, who became Helene Susman after marriage, became outstanding attorneys in spite of any obstacles placed before them. Even during the depression years, their practice survived due to the number of foreclosures they handled.[3]

The other woman in Burg's class followed a different path. Helen Hargrave became assistant librarian at the University of Texas School of Law, a position she held until 1939. The following year she enrolled at Columbia University to specialize in law librarianship. She then returned to Austin and became head librarian at the University of Texas School of Law. For the next thirty-one years, she was instrumental in developing one of the largest academic law libraries in the Southwest. Hargrave also received a faculty appointment and regularly taught a course in legal bibliography. When asked about her career, Hargrave responded, "I just kept after it." Her contributions were recognized in 1979 when she became the first woman to receive the University of Texas School of Law Distinguished Graduate Award.[4]

Legal education became more available for both men and women as additional law schools opened. Baylor Law School graduated its first woman, Emeline Katherine Jackson, in 1926.[5] Jackson first practiced with a male partner in Corpus Christi and then opened a solo practice in 1934.[6] Mabel Grey Howell, a member of the class of 1933, had a varied career in law. After practicing in Waco for five years, she became an assistant city attorney there. Relocating to Houston in the early 1940s, she practiced both alone and with a major firm, served as a substitute corporation judge, and lectured part-time at the University of Houston Law Center.[7] It is likely that her single status allowed her more flexibility in her career pursuits. Female enrollment at Baylor remained low during these early years. Records reveal that only eight female law students had graduated by 1940.[8]

Margaret Harris Amsler grew up on the Baylor University campus where her father taught at the law school. She always knew that she would eventually become a lawyer herself. She once told a reporter, "I was supposed to have been Chief Justice of the Supreme Court."[9] She entered law school in 1932 but withdrew for two years to marry and begin a family. When she returned to law school, she carried a full load of classes, taught French, cared for an infant daughter, and graduated first in her class in 1937. That same year she divorced her husband, often telling the story of how she was her own first client in handling her divorce. When she remarried in 1942, she and her new husband formed a law practice which continued for forty-eight years.[10] Unlike most women lawyers at the time, Amsler never felt she suffered from discrimination. "If I was ever discriminated against, I was never conscious of it," she recalled in her later years.[11]

Josephine Myrick Jameson, like Margaret Harris Amsler, was influenced by family members to study law. In this instance, however, both Jameson's mother and father were lawyers. She graduated from Baylor Law School in 1939 and received her LL.M. degree from the University of Texas in 1940, becoming only the second woman to earn a master of laws in the state at the time. She then became a partner in her father's law firm in Harlingen. During World War II and after her marriage, Jameson worked as a War Department investigator and in the land department of an oil company.

Houston's second law school, South Texas School of Law, opened in 1923 and was established as one of the schools across the country associated with the YMCA. Its curriculum was patterned after that of the University of Texas, but classes met in the evening to accommodate students who worked full-time during the day.[12] Its first class included five women, but South Texas did not graduate a woman until 1928 when Ann Marie Hollenberg received her LL.B. degree. The college yearbook noted under Hollenberg's photograph that "a Teutonic maid proves that beauty and brains do mix."[13] At twenty-two years of age, she was the youngest lawyer that South Texas School of Law had produced. Hollenberg had worked as a legal stenographer for Gulf Oil while attending school. She remained in that position after graduation and continued as a stenographer even after relocating, first to Shreveport, Louisiana, and then to California.[14] Like many women who worked as stenographers in law firms, Hollenberg was drawn into studying law. Although additional education should have moved them beyond the secretarial ranks, that did not always happen. Why Hollenberg remained a legal stenographer rather than become a fully practicing attorney is not known. Over the next ten years South Texas granted LL.B. degrees to twelve women.[15]

Founded in 1915, Southern Methodist University had considered establishing a law school as early as 1919, but nothing was done until the local legal community convinced the administration that no university could achieve first-rank status without the presence of a law school. Classes began in the fall of 1925 with twenty first-year students, all men.[16] The first graduating class three years later included a woman, Erin Bain Jones, who had entered the program late yet graduated early.[17] Jones, who was admitted to the bar in 1929, went on to earn a master's degree in law, as well as a master's in comparative literature. Jones used her legal background in oceanography and the environment, writing two books on these subjects. She traveled to study energy and pollution-related issues at both the North and South Poles.[18] Jones' career clearly indicated that a legal education could have widespread use.

Frances Spears Cloyd, class of 1931, was another early graduate of Southern Methodist University School of Law and later received an LL.M. degree. Cloyd never actually practiced law, but she remained involved with legal organizations in Dallas.[19] In recognition of her pioneering studies, a scholarship endowment for female law students was established in her name at SMU's law school.[20] Although a small number of women studied law at SMU during this time, the majority of female students in the north Texas area attended proprietary schools.[21]

As the clouds of the Depression gathered, jobs were still scarce. Some fortunate women were able to join family businesses. Wilminor

Morris was encouraged by her family to study law. Her attorney uncle even gave her a summer semester at the University of Wisconsin Law School as a gift when she graduated from Rice Institute. Morris' mother, whose father was a judge, agreed it would be permissible for her to study law but cautioned her against ever going to the courthouse, a place she considered dangerous for women to be seen. Morris, nevertheless, entered the University of Texas law school and graduated in 1929. She later told the story of closing a real estate transaction after she began working at Stewart Title Co. Morris remembered that the buyer asked for a lawyer to look at the papers. When the very young Morris replied that she was a lawyer, she said that he stood up, bowed from the waist, and said, "Well, now I have seen everything!" Seventy years later, at the age of ninety, Wilminor Morris Carl was planning to attend the annual meeting of the National Association of Women Lawyers in London.[22]

Title companies proved to be a welcoming work environment for women. The increased number of female lawyers seeking employment coincided with the expansion of Stewart Title Guaranty Company. Incorporated in Galveston in 1908, the company added offices in Dallas, San Antonio, and Houston, and by the 1920s had spread to El Paso and Fort Worth. Its subsidiary, Stewart Title Company, employed lawyers in these locations to issue abstracts and title insurance.[23] Herminie McDonald, a Galveston native, began in Stewart Title's home office in 1928 as a stenographer, but by 1930 she was listed as an attorney.[24] After fourteen years with Stewart Title in Beaumont, Nellie Gray Robertson became the office manager,[25] while Murray Brownlee Cameron spent forty-five years with Stewart Title, becoming vice-president and manager of the Houston office.[26] An Austin lawyer, Sarah Jane Sumner, was employed for many years by the Gracy Abstract Co.,[27] and Ruth Brazzil managed an abstract company in Wharton.[28] A Grimes County attorney, Artie Fultz Davis, even operated her own title company in Anderson while practicing law with her husband in nearby Navasota.[29]

Proprietary schools continued to be a source of legal education for women. A branch of Jefferson School of Law (sometimes called Jefferson University School of Law) opened in Fort Worth in 1929, and it was placed on the list of approved law schools by the Texas Supreme Court a year later.[30] In 1932 its first graduating class had thirteen members, including four women.[31] One of those graduates, Eva Bloore Barnes, later recalled that in 1928 her choices for employment had been Woolworth, Montgomery Ward, or the telephone company. She approached a lawyer whom she had met and succeeded in landing a clerical job in his office, for which she was paid $17.50 a week. This position drew her to the legal profession. When she learned that Jefferson School of Law was opening a branch in Fort Worth, she persuaded the school's president to let her work there doing odd jobs in exchange for tuition. For three nights each week over a period of three years, she went from her job in the law firm to the school where she opened the building, kept the books, and performed other odd jobs before and after class. She passed the bar in 1932 at the age of twenty-two, but jobs were scarce. She worked first as a clerk for a male attorney. Then she went to New York and worked in a large firm for a year. Her mother's illness brought her back to Fort Worth where she clerked in a law firm. Barnes received her first job as a full-fledged lawyer in 1945—thirteen years after graduation—when she became an assistant district attorney, the first woman to hold that position in Tarrant County.[32] Barnes reflected on how difficult it was to work in a "male world" but added, "I always tried to keep from feeling that some men were prejudiced against me in any way."[33]

The other women in Barnes' class were Ila Tippitt, Gladys Shannon, and Helen Huff. Tippit was an attorney for Swift & Co. for thirty years,[34] while Shannon, who lived to be 102 years old, spent her career as a probate and income tax lawyer.[35] Huff worked for the Fort Worth and Denver Railroad and was licensed to practice before the Interstate

Commerce Commission.[36] Reports indicate that women who attended privately operated schools as part-time students at this time scored equally well on the bar examination as did full-time students from university-related law schools.[37] The increase in the number of private schools, which had night classes and were less expensive to attend, also allowed more women to study law. Ultimately, there was a slight rise in the number of female attorneys in Texas during the depression years, unlike in other states that reported fewer women completing their law studies and becoming licensed attorneys.[38]

Given the stock market crash in 1929 and the acceleration of the Great Depression, women were faced with another discriminatory measure. In an effort to reduce government personnel, Congress passed an act stipulating that any married woman living with her spouse would be the first to be dismissed, and married women would get the lowest consideration for future employment in civil service.[39] This, obviously, made government jobs less available for married women lawyers.

By 1930 there were seventy-five women lawyers in Texas, as compared to 6,571 men.[40] Most women continued to work alone, offering a wide range of legal services under the umbrella of general office practice. Women who studied law during this time took advantage of the range of law schools available to them, picking the school that best suited their economic and personal needs. As a result, women lawyers became a diversely educated group who, on graduation, entered an increasingly stratified legal profession. They looked for employment in law offices, tried their hands at solo practice, or found positions in the business world of banks, real estates offices, and insurance agencies. Some considered themselves lucky if they found a job as a stenographer or a law clerk; others were unable to find work at all. Now that the vote had been won, there was not even a remnant of a women's rights movement to press for equality for working women. Professional organizations such as the National Association of Women Lawyers had little influence in the male-dominated field of law.[41]

During the Depression, poverty law, or defending the poor, became a viable practice because of the economic downturn in the country. It was not a defined specialty of law at that time, but there was a need for it. Legal aid offices were supposed to attract young male lawyers looking for experience, but men avoided the low pay and the stigma attached to the field. As a result, women became the backbone of legal aid offices. They were attracted to the field not only because it offered them employment but also because of their concern for social justice. Women lawyers were often seen as "righting wrongs" endured by consumers, the poor, the old, the young, among whom many were women.[42] As historian Eleanor Flexner wrote, "In seeking those who most needed their services they inevitably found . . . women at the bottom of the heap."[43]

While women comprised a significant portion of the clientele of female lawyers, they were not necessarily the dominant part of their practices. Studies have shown that women chose lawyers based on a number of issues: social class, political sympathy, the cost and availability of legal service, and the complexity of the legal matter. In fact, women chose their lawyers much as men selected theirs.[44] Women lawyers were realistic in realizing that their income would be greater if they had a mixed clientele, and income was of central concern to women who needed both to survive financially and to gain professional autonomy in the legal field.

It is somewhat surprising that women would see a law career, with all of its hurdles, as a desirable pursuit. Flora Salado had personal obstacles in addition to those posed by the profession itself. Salado, however, was determined to change her life. During the Depression she and her family lived in St. Louis where Salado was an isolated housewife with three young children. Typical of many women at the time who were completely dependent on their husbands, she did not drive, and she could not write checks. When her husband lost his job during the Depression, Salado worked in a department store for fifty cents a day and sold cosmetics door to door. The family moved to Dallas in 1932, and in 1936 Salado was hired to sell tickets to the Texas Centennial celebration. She had to purchase the tickets in advance at a cost of $300. A judge whom she had met agreed to lend her the money. She had great success in selling the tickets. The judge was so impressed with her energy and ambition that he encouraged her to study law at one of the evening law schools. It took her four years while working by day in a law firm. On November 11, 1941, Flora Salado was sworn in by Judge Sarah Hughes. She was forty-one years old and the mother of three teenagers. Her advice to others was, "Don't wring your hands . . . go after it!"[45]

Even after bar associations indicated they were willing to admit female attorneys, many of these women felt they were not truly welcome at meetings and other activities. By 1940 twenty-one women were working as lawyers in Houston.[46] Yet the role of women in the local bar association remained limited, and they did not enjoy the privilege of full participation that male lawyers experienced. Women attorneys in Dallas experienced a somewhat easier entrance into the local bar association. Helen Viglini was elected to membership in 1920 by a unanimous vote. On the day she was elected, a toast entitled "Women and the Law" was offered at the meeting.[47] By 1936 the Dallas Bar Association listed sixteen women on its membership roster,[48] yet women were not always welcome at events. Sarah Menezes related the story of how men attending a conference with her tried to keep her from meetings in rooms where the men would be drinking. Rather than admit that they did not want women in their gatherings, they insisted this was being done for her protection.[49] It appears that bar associations in smaller communities opened their membership to women more readily than those in urban areas. It is also apparent, however, that women lawyers in many locations felt the need to establish their own associations. This was done in the years ahead.

During the 1930s, more and more women were practicing law

across the state. These included Hallie Harper in Amarillo;[50] Erma Elaine Baker in Brownwood;[51] Vida Lutrell Carmichael in Cameron County;[52] Mary West in Crystal City;[53] Ulala Burnett in Cisco;[54] Lillian Fagg Sisco in Collin County;[55] Effie Harper in Conroe;[56] Louisa Terrill Pearson,[57] Margaret Brown[58] and Corrie B. Fitzsimmons[59] in Corpus Christi; Sarah Daniels,[60] Regina Urbish,[61] and Alice Windsor[62] in Dallas; Minnie Ramsey Robey[63] in Eastland; Annie Justice Swaim in Eden;[64] Mamie Woods[65] and Opal Banks[66] in Fort Worth; Martha Lipscomb in Gainesville;[67] Artie Fultz Davis in Grimes County;[68] Mary Nan Bonham,[69] Stella Rudersdorf,[70] and Esther Spohn Scruggs[71] in Houston; Edna Cobb Smith in Lubbock;[72] Kathleen Brannon in Marshall;[73] Beulah Duensing in Plainview;[74] Kathleen Joerger Lindsey in Rosenberg;[75] Morinne Taylor Perkins in Rusk;[76] Lanette Heilbron Glasscock in San Antonio;[77] Frances Fullerton in Taylor;[78] Ellen Victery in Teague;[79] Fannie Gray Clegg in Trinity;[80] Ophelia Thaxton in Waco;[81] Elizabeth Suiter in Winnsboro;[82] and Gladys Lebethel Tatum in Wichita Falls.[83] The statistical profile of these women does not differ in much detail from those of the lawyers in 1925. The greatest changes were that fewer women were receiving their legal training by reading in a firm and fewer married women were practicing with their husbands. Both of these trends would continue to diminish over the ensuing decades.

In the meantime, however, important changes were taking place in the process of being licensed to practice law in Texas. The University of Texas diploma-privilege rule was abolished in 1935.[84] All applicants for admittance to the bar were now required to take the bar examination. In 1938 the Dallas Law School merged with Southern Methodist University School of Law and agreed to conduct an evening division on campus for those students who needed to work at full-time jobs while attending law classes.[85] This action left the Houston Law School as the only longtime proprietary school still in operation, but by 1945 it had closed.[86] The proprietary schools served an important function during their existence, but their closing marked the start of a more consistent approach to legal training. Reading the law at a firm was still an acceptable practice, but it required thirty hours per week for four years.[87] These changes resulted in more women attending established law schools that, by now, required a three-year course of study preceded by sixty hours of college credits.[88]

Occasionally, one of the requirements for being licensed was waived, as in the case of Jean MacMullen Holloway, who is listed in the record books as the youngest person ever to pass the Texas Bar. After graduating from the University of Texas at the age of seventeen in 1929, Holloway married an attorney and studied in his office in Brownwood. At the age of nineteen she successfully petitioned the Texas Supreme Court for permission to take the bar examination on the grounds that she was married and therefore not legally a minor. She was admitted to the bar in 1930. Holloway's career was a varied one: she was a member of the Women's Air Force Service Pilots during World War II, the first editor of the University of Texas Press, the author of two books, a teacher at Huston-Tillotson College, and a practicing lawyer in Austin.[89]

Another university-affiliated law school was established in 1934 when St. Mary's University absorbed the San Antonio School of Law, which had been formed by the San Antonio Bar Association in 1927. Classes had met at night in empty courtrooms at the Bexar County courthouse, and tuition was $10 per month for the thirty-six-month course. In order to foster higher standards of legal education, the San Antonio Bar Association Board of Governors negotiated with St. Mary's University to take over the school.[90] A formal standardized curriculum was then established for aspiring lawyers in the Alamo City. When classes began in the fall of 1934, thirty-one students enrolled for the evening division, including thirteen freshmen. Second- and third-year students transferred from the San Antonio School of Law.[91] Among the first students were two women. School records indicate that one of those, Mary Agnes Aird, graduated in 1936. There is, however, another woman, Patricia "Patty" Huth Gillis, who could be considered St. Mary's first female graduate. Gillis graduated in 1935, a year before Aird, but is sometimes erroneously reported as a graduate of the San Antonio School of Law instead of St. Mary's. In any event, Mary Agnes Aird and Patricia Huth Gillis were the first two women to graduate from the newly organized school.[92]

With the advent of World War II in late 1941, millions of men went off to fight, and women were urged to help the war effort by replacing men in the workplace. Three million women across the country answered the call. Most took jobs in the war plants, building airplanes, tanks, and guns. Movie newsreels and the press glorified them as patriotic "Rosie the Riveter." Other women joined the military. While women had previously been told by child-rearing experts to stay home and care for their children, they were now being told their children were better off when their mothers worked outside the home.[93] Signs of change appeared as well in the legal profession. As enrollment dropped in law schools overall, women were encouraged to attend to help maintain tuition income. Therefore, the number of women in Texas law schools increased slightly. Furthermore, in the absence of men there were a few additional openings for jobs in the legal field.

When Pearl Harbor was bombed on December 7, 1941, scores of young men immediately joined the military. Three of those enlistees happened to be the briefing attorneys for the Texas Supreme Court. In the widespread absence of male attorneys, women were suddenly considered satisfactory replacements. Although there was a shortage of women law graduates at the University of Texas at the time, most had not been able to find jobs in the legal field. Consequently, it was not difficult to find three qualified female lawyers. Mary Kate Parker, Ione Stumberg, and Virginia Grubbs, all law graduates from the University of Texas, were hired to fill the positions of briefing attorneys with the stipulation that they must give up the job when the men returned from military duty. Parker had graduated with highest honors from law school in 1934 at the age of nineteen. Stumberg had graduated second in her class in the 1937 class. Having married and become a mother, she was not practicing law in 1941 when the vacancy occurred in the offices of the Texas Supreme Court. The youngest of the triumvirate was Virginia Grubbs Noel, a 1942 graduate who married a month after assuming the job. She had worked her way through law school in the attorney general's office as a legal secretary, as a file room clerk, and finally as editor of the attorney general opinions.[94]

As the war stretched into years—a reality most of the country did not anticipate—a second shift of briefing attorneys was hired. Beth O'Neil, a University of Texas law graduate in 1944, worked as a briefing attorney from October 1944 until April 1945. Mel Ruth Ramsey, a 1945 graduate, worked from March 1945 until November of that year. Ramsey remembered, "At first they gave us very little to do. Then, they let us read opinions of the courts of civil appeals for review. Finally, Chief Justice Alexander let me do some briefing for him."[95] But, true to its word, the court returned the positions to male attorneys after the war. The women, indeed, had been merely temporary replacements.[96] Records show, however, that the Texas Supreme Court's backlog of cases declined during those years.

After this unprecedented experience, where did these women journey next in their legal careers? Mary Kate Parker Wall remained with the Texas Supreme Court as secretary of the court at an increase in salary and then served again as a briefing attorney for the court. In 1949 Wall joined the attorney general's office where she was a member of the team assigned to *U.S. v. Texas*, 339 U.S. 707 (1950), commonly known as the Tidelands case. She later worked in the Texas Legislative Council, specializing in election law legislation. Ione Stumberg did not return to practicing law until after her husband's death. She worked first in the law library at the University of Texas and then became an assistant attorney general. In 1971, Stumberg accepted a position with the Texas Senate to review proposed legislation to ensure its compatibility with existing laws. She continued in this role for seventeen years, retiring at the age of eighty-five. Stumberg's daughter later commented, "Had she been born thirty years later, she would have had a very different career. But she was never bitter or upset about it, but accepting." Virginia Grubbs Noel joined the Houston firm of Baker Botts Andrews & Wharton, where she practiced in the field of railroad litigation and was reportedly the first woman to try a case for the firm. Noel remained there for three years and then taught part-time at the University of Houston Law Center until the birth of her fourth child, after which she left the active practice of law. Beth O'Neil did not practice after the war in either Texas or New Mexico where she had moved. Mel Ruth Ramsey worked in the University of Texas law library until her husband graduated from law school. The couple then established an office in Hereford, specializing in tax law.[97] Whether these women's experiences at the Texas Supreme Court had an impact on their careers is not known, but they cracked open doors for women coming along behind them.

A woman who did not experience an open door because of absent male lawyers was Hermine Dalkowitz Tobolowsky, who graduated from the University of Texas School of Law in 1943. There, one of her professors, insistent that women should become wives and not lawyers, had given his female students a list of eligible bachelors, hoping to divert them from studying law.[98] Tobolowsky first interviewed with a firm in Houston where she was informed that if they employed her, she would never see the clients who would be told the legal work had been done by the firm's male lawyers. Tobolowsky refused the job offer. Next she interviewed for a clerking position with the Texas Supreme Court. When she appeared for her interview, the chief justice, without ever looking up from the papers on his desk, told her quite emphatically that no woman had enough sense to do that job.[99] Discouraged, Tobolowsky returned home to San Antonio where she was hired by

Lang, Cross, Beard & Ladon despite the fact she insisted on receiving the same salary as the firm's male associates. She remained with the firm for four years before opening her own office. After marrying, Tobolowsky moved in 1951 to Dallas where she again had her own practice.[100] Having experienced these discriminatory practices, Tobolowsky's consuming passion became acquiring equal rights for women under the law.

Another law graduate in the University of Texas class of 1943 initially followed a different path from Tobolowsky. Dorothy Ann Adams Kinney had the blessing of her father—longtime Potter County judge—to study law. He insisted, however, that his daughter must learn shorthand and typing as a sure means of getting a job. Following her graduation, Kinney journeyed to Washington, D.C., where she found a job in the U.S. Treasury Department. After returning to Texas, she worked in the attorney general's office before marrying and moving back to her hometown, Amarillo. Kinney's attorney husband was hired by a firm, but she could not find a position due to a potential conflict of interest posed by her husband's practice. She eventually opened her own office where she specialized in probate, estate planning, and tax law until 2001, when her health failed. According to her daughter, she was an excellent typist all of her life and, thanks to her father's advice, used that skill extensively in her career.[101]

World War II did not bring radical or permanent changes for women pursuing law careers. The progress made during the war years quickly eroded as men returned home to the jobs they held before the war. Mothers were now being told their children might become juvenile delinquents if they worked outside the home. And although World War II did open some doors for women, the number of female lawyers did not significantly increase during the next few years. The 1940 census reported 132 women lawyers in Texas, while the 1950 census figures climbed to only 224.[102] More women gravitated toward salaried government positions during those years. While white women found it difficult to find jobs once they completed their education, minority women had yet to break the barrier created not only by gender discrimination but also by racial prejudice.

In a state like Texas with a booming oil and gas industry, it was inevitable that the legal departments of petroleum companies would enlarge their staff of attorneys. When Barbara Finney graduated from the University of Texas in 1942, she was hired by the Houston firm of Baker Botts Andrews & Wharton and was placed in the corporate law section of the firm. Although her tenure at Baker Botts was brief, Finney's experience there served her well when she was hired in 1952 by Humble Oil & Refining Co. She remained there for thirty years, ending up in the trial division.[103] Finney joined Ruth Boren Bivin, a 1936 University of Texas law graduate who had started at Humble Oil as a legal secretary in 1937 and was promoted to staff attorney in 1950.[104] Finney and Bivin were the only two women lawyers at Humble Oil for many years. Oil companies had actually been receptive to hiring women lawyers as early as 1930. Among those who found their niche in the energy sector, as had Alice Drysdale Sheffield back in 1918, were Mae Ament with Vacuum Oil,[105] Kate Harding Bates Parker with Gulf Oil,[106] Elizabeth Odom with Phillips Petroleum,[107] Margaret Clark with Byrd Frost Oil Operators,[108] Billie "Willie" Fuller with Pan-Am Oil,[109] Ora Lois Mahoney with Phillips Drilling,[110] Ruth Lovett Davis with Sun Oil,[111] Myrl Holt Farrington with Continental Oil,[112] Josephine Verain with Venus Oil,[113] and Josephine Jameson with Tidewater Oil.[114]

Following World War II, two new law schools opened in the state. Both were located in Houston. In 1946 a law school was opened at what was then called Texas State University for Negroes,[115] later renamed Texas Southern University. One year later the University of Houston Law Center opened.[116] Lois Prestage Woods entered Texas Southern University law school in 1948 along with two other women. Woods remembered that the others soon dropped out because trying to combine their family responsibilities and law classes became too heavy a burden for them. Woods continued, however, graduating in 1951 as the only female in the class and Texas Southern University's first female law graduate. In an interview years later, she remembered that she did not experience discrimination from the male students because all of them felt as though they needed to succeed in this new law school. For that reason they tried to encourage one another.[117] Woods did feel that some of the professors were not totally sympathetic toward female students. She remembered that one would ask her each time they met, "Are you still here?" Since her interest was in labor law, she worked for a local labor union after graduation. Although Woods stated emphatically that her legal education was like a "shield of protection" to her, she never practiced law. After receiving a master's degree in education and curriculum writing from Syracuse University, she spent fifty years in the classroom, including stints at both Texas Southern University and the University of Houston.[118]

The year after Wood's graduation, Rita Keenan was the first woman to graduate from the University of Houston Law Center. Keenan had the distinction of being a military veteran like many of her fellow law students, for she had served in the Women's Air Corps during the war. Keenan was known to declare that she went to law school to be a lawyer, not a woman lawyer. Her son Christopher later recounted her experience the first time she went to court. A judge turned to her and said, "So you are a lawyer. Another woman came into my court but she was only carrying her husband's brief case, and she never came back either."[119] Keenan was not to be deterred because, in her son's words, "She was a soft spoken woman, but a real fighter—tenacious and dedicated to her clients." Rita Keenan practiced law until her death in 1981.[120]

Although female faculty members were almost nonexistent at the time, Virginia Grubbs Noel taught legal bibliography part-time at the University of Houston Law Center from 1947 to 1955. Other women lawyers who have been identified as teaching in law schools during those early years, in addition to Lucy Moore and Helen Hargrave at the University of Texas, were Sarah T. Hughes at Jefferson School of Law in 1924 and the Dallas School of Law in 1936–38; Juliet Sedberry at North Texas School of Law in Fort Worth in 1940–41; Margaret Harris Amsler, who began her very long tenure at Baylor in 1940; and Mattie Beryl Montgomery, who was Baylor's law librarian in 1940–41.[121] When the war years caused a shortage of faculty at Southern Methodist University law school, Judge Sarah Hughes was a part-time instructor, teaching a course on contracts and one on evidence between 1942 and 1944.[122] Female faculty would not become a common sight on law school campuses for decades.

Some barriers still existed for women in obtaining a legal education. Pat Smith applied to the Southern Methodist University School of Law in 1946 after graduating from Texas Tech University. She was refused admittance to day classes presumably because she was a woman. Determined to become a lawyer, Smith enrolled in the evening classes and, on the basis of her academic record, was permitted to transfer to the day school after one semester. Graduating in 1949, Smith opened her office as one of the first women to practice in Lubbock and soon married a fellow attorney.[123] Pat Smith Moore would post some impressive achievements in her career in the years ahead.

Geraldine Browder Tennant graduated from the University of Texas law school in 1949, one of nine females in a class of 185 students. Browder was stimulated by the "sink or swim" atmosphere she found there and reported that, as far as she could tell, there were no distinctions drawn between men and women in class. Unfortunately, the same could not be said for job hunting. Unable to find a full-time position in Fort Worth, her hometown, Tennant moved to Houston when she was offered a "semi-legal" job with a "semi-legal" salary. Eventually her career as a civil and corporate attorney flourished, along with a family of three children.[124] Her road to a seat in the judiciary began when she became a probate law assistant to the Harris County Judge, then referee for the Harris County Juvenile Court, and finally a district court judge, where she served for twelve years.[125]

Tennant's roommate at law school, Frances "Sissy" Tarlton Farenthold, had been exposed to law at a young age by her father, a Corpus Christi attorney. She credited the confidence that took her through law school to her undergraduate years at Vassar College, explaining, "You have to speak up in a classroom in a woman's college."[126] Nevertheless, she recalled her law school days as "vicious" and remembered that friends took bets on how long she would last. All bets were lost, and on graduation Farenthold joined her father's law firm.[127] Then, faced with the dilemma of balancing family and career, she left the active practice after she married and had five children. Farenthold had been reared to believe in social reform and active participation in government, so when she lost a child in 1960, she sought activity to combat her grief. That activity was Democratic politics.[128] This road would take her to the statehouse and beyond.

Women continued their journey one step at a time. It frequently seemed, however, that they took one step forward and then two steps backward. By the mid-twentieth century, women lawyers were far from reaching their goal of equality. Yet their determination to succeed and their desire to make a difference in the legal profession "kept them after it," as Helen Hargrave had proclaimed twenty-five years earlier.

Notes

1. *The Houston Lawyer*, 38 (January-February, 1986): 41–43.

2. *Bench and Bar of Texas* (Austin: Horace Evans Publisher, 1937), Vol. 1, 55.

3. *The Houston Lawyer*, 41. Before immigration law was considered a legal specialty, Joyce Burg was practicing it. During the early years of World War I, she filed affidavits of sponsorship for many German Jews after finding sponsors for them. Burg followed the same procedure for those fleeing Communist China some years later.

4. Debbie Mauldin Cottrell, "Helen Hargrave," *Handbook of Texas*, 3:461; Helen Hargrave Papers 1919–1978, Special Collections, Tarlton Law Library. Hargrave studied law library architecture and interior arrangements as part of her library studies. She contributed design ideas for both the University of Texas law library and the law library of the Texas Supreme Court. Hargrave also helped organize the law library at Texas Southern University.

5. Charles Alfred Mackenzie, "A History of the Baylor University School of Law from the Lectures of Abner S. Lipscomb through the Deanship of Abner V. McCall" (master's thesis, Baylor University, August 1988).

6. *Derry*, 182.

7. *Texas Bar Journal* 40, 9:977.

8. Mackenzie thesis. Women represented 44% of Baylor's total law school enrollment for 2006–07.

9. Barbara Bader Aldave, "Women in the Law in Texas: The Stories of Three Pioneers," *St. Mary's University Law Journal*, 25:1 (Summer 1993): 296.

10. Ibid., 297.

11. Ibid., 298.

12. "A Chronological History of South Texas College of Law," htpp://www.stcl.edu/o1welcome/chronological_history.html. (accessed November 8, 2004). South Texas School of Law changed its name to South Texas College of Law during World War II. In 1967 it ended its forty-four-year association with the Houston YMCA and began operating as a private, nonprofit educational institution.

13. *Annual Year Book*, 1928, South Texas School of Law, 8.

14. *Annotations*, Vol. 25, No. 8, April 1997.

15. Vertical file, Special Collections, Fred Parks Law Library, South Texas College of Law. Women represent 47.7% of the school's total enrollment.

16. Payne, *Dallas*, 150.

17. *Dallas Morning News*, March 6, 1947; Payne, *Dallas*, 151.

18. Joseph W. McKnight, "Erin Bain Jones," *Handbook of Texas*, 3:980.

19. Robyn Cloyd, telephone interview with author, July 6, 2007.

20. *Houston Chronicle*, November 16, 2002, 38A.

21. Women currently represent 47.6% of the total enrollment of the Dedman School of Law at SMU.

22. "Our Place in History: A Celebration of Women in the Law at the University of Texas School of Law," *Texas Journal of Women and the Law*, 8:333–334.

23. "Stewart Title Celebrating 100 Years of Service," Commemorative Brochure, 1993 printing.

24. *Bench and Bar*, 133.

25. Ibid., 164.

26. *Texas Bar Journal*, 54, 7:905.

27. Ibid., 54, 1:80.

28. Sherilyn Brandenstein, "Ruth Brazzil Roome," *Handbook of Texas*, 5:673. Ruth Brazzil Roome, who achieved notoriety in 1925 as one of the justices on the all-women Texas Supreme Court, gave up law soon afterwards. Although she married and divorced within two weeks, she kept her married name. Roome moved to central Texas where she dealt in real estate and for a time was postmistress in Bandera.

29. Kathy Day, correspondence to author, November 25, 2005.

30. Arnold, 44.

31. Ibid., 53.

32. Ibid., 46–47.

33. Ibid., 50.

34. *Texas Bar Journal*, 59, 1:89.

35. Arnold, 46.

36. Ibid., 53; *Texas Bar Journal*, 33, 4:315.

37. Hedda Garza, *Barred from the Bar: A History of Women and the Legal Profession* (New York: Franklin Watts, 1990), 101.

38. Women lawyers in Texas numbered seventy-five in 1930, while the 1940 figures showed a modest increase to 132 women, according to the U.S. census reports

for those years.

39. Cott, 452–53. The federal government's 1932 Economy Act, although controversial, was not repealed until 1937. A Gallup Poll in 1936 indicated that 82% of the public agreed that wives should not work if their husbands were employed. George Gallup observed that he had "discovered an issue on which voters are about as solidly united as any subject imaginable—including sin and hay fever" (453). Leaders of the Business and Professional Women's clubs declared this was a blow to all working women and to marriage itself. Women in government work, including attorneys, had to choose between a job and a husband.

40. *Fifteenth Census of the United States Taken in the Year 1930*, Vol. IV, Occupations by States (Washington, D.C.: Government Printing Office, 1933), 1569.

41. Garza, 101.

42. Ibid., 105–06.

43. Morello, 108.

44. Drachman, *Sisters in Law*, 187.

45. *Texas Bar Journal,* 54, 8:974.

46. Eric L. Fredrickson, *A Commitment to Public Service: The History of the Houston Bar Association* (Houston: Gulf Publishing Company, 1992), 79.

47. Payne, *Dallas*, 129.

48. Dallas Bar Association Directory 1936, Houston Metropolitan Research Center, Houston Public Library.

49. Payne, *Sarah T. Hughes*, 126.

50. *Texas Bar Journal*, 15, 1:84.

51. *Texas Bar Journal,* 19, 9:748.

52. *Texas Bar Journal*, 4, 8:397.

53. *Who's Who*, 102.

54. *1935 Martindale*, 911.

55. *Texas Bar Journal,* 36, 8:851–852.

56. *Texas Bar Journal*, 36, 8:851.

57. *Who's Who*, 73.

58. Allen Wood, *The Early Bench, Bar and Practice of Law in Corpus Christi* (Corpus Christi: Corpus Christi Bar Association, 1996); *Texas Bar Journal*, 32, 11:883. Margaret Beulah Brown began reading the law at the age of forty-eight after the death of her attorney husband. She was admitted to the bar in 1934 and soon became a partner in Brown and Ward. Maintaining her practice until 1969, Brown was described by her male law partner as "one of the few [women] who actually practiced in the courtroom and in the office."

59. *Bench and Bar*, 71.

60. Payne, *Dallas*, 166.

61. Ibid.

62. *Texas Bar Journal*, 21, 10:273.

63. *Texas Bar Journal*, 32, 9:814.

64. *Texas Bar Journal*, 44, 9:1276.

65. *1930 Martindale*, 887.

66. Ibid.

67. *Who's Who*, 55.

68. Kathy Day, correspondence to author, November 25, 2005.

69. *Bench and Bar*, 30.

70. *Who's Who*, 81.

71. *Derry*, 308.

72. *Texas Bar Journal*, 33, 6:542.

73. *Bench and Bar*, 33.

74. *Texas Bar Journal*, 43, 5:490.

75. *Chi Omega Eleusis*, Fall 2006, 14.

76. *Texas Bar Journal*, 37, 5:496.

77. *Who's Who*, 41.

78. *Texas Bar Journal*, 38, 9:1068.

79. *1930 Martindale*, 912.

80. *Texas Bar Journal*, 41, 4:467.

81. Betty Ann McSwain, ed., *The Bench and Bar of Waco and McLennan County 1849–1976* (Waco: Texian Press, 1976), 233.

82. *Texas Bar Journal*, 28, 2:77.

83. *Who's Who*, 95.

84. Huber and Myers, 514.

85. Newton and Newton, 171.

86. Houston Law School Collection, Houston Metropolitan Research Center, Houston Public Library. Houston Law School was founded by the attorney son of the first dean at the University of Texas School of Law, John Townes, Sr. It had the advantage of having noted Houston lawyers as adjunct faculty members. During its thirty-year existence, the school graduated 650 students. Remarkably, the tuition was never raised, remaining at $7.50 per month. The military draft during World War II and the growing presence of South Texas College of Law drained Houston Law School of its students, and it was finally forced to close.

87. Huber and Myers, 516–17. The practice of reading in an office to satisfy educational requirements was abolished in 1973. In reality, it had almost completely disappeared by then.

88. Ibid.

89. Judith N. McArthur, "Jean MacMullen Holloway," *Handbook of Texas*, 3:667. Noted attorney Leon Jaworski is frequently mentioned in legal publications as being the youngest person ever admitted to the Texas Bar. There, actually, have been women, including Jean MacMullen Holloway, who were admitted at the age of nineteen, as Jaworski was. As noted in chapter 1 of this book, Irene Brown may have been only eighteen when she was admitted.

90. Brandon, 52. The only requirement for enrolling at St. Mary's was sixty hours of college credit. The requirement for receiving an LL.B. degree was seventy-two hours of work. Tuition was $5 per semester hour. The school had only evening classes until 1946; in 1971 the school reverted to day classes only.

91. Newton and Newton, 166.

92. Professor Vincent Johnson, correspondence with author, April 2, 2007. Women represent 44% of the school's total enrollment.

93. For more on the 1940s and what the decade meant for women, see Judy Barrett Litoff and David C. Smith, eds., *American Women in a World at War: Contemporary Accounts from World War II.* (Wilmington, Delaware: Scholarly Resources Inc., 1997); Susan M. Hartmann, *American Women in the 1940s: The Home Front and Beyond* (Boston: Twayne Publishers, 1982).

94. Judge Mark Davidson and Kent Rutter, "Texas Supreme Court Goes to War: Texas Women Respond to the Court's Call to Duty," *Texas Bar Journal,* 65, 1:20–21.

95. Ibid., 22.

96. Ibid., 20.

97. Ibid., 23–24.

98. *Texas Bar Journal,* 55, 1:13.

99. Ibid.

100. *Handbook of Texas Online* s.v. "Tobolowsky, Hermine Dalkowitz," http://www.tsha.utexas.edu/handbook/online/articles/TT/fto49.html (accessed March 6, 2007).

101. Julie Atterbury, telephone interview by author, June 29, 2007. The U.S. Treasury Department was the first government agency to hire women professionals, according to an article in the *New York Tribune* in 1886. That employment was a matter of necessity during the Civil War to fill the vacancies created by the enlistment of employees. This was likely true during World War II as well. The Treasury Department seemed to take the lead among government agencies in being open to women employees. (Morello, 197).

102. *Sixteenth Census of the United States, Taken in the Year 1940,* Vol. II, The Labor Force, Pt. 5 (Washington, D.C.: Government Printing Office, 1943), 477.

103. Barbara Finney, correspondence to author, October 17, 2006; Interview with Barbara Finney by Eric Fredrickson, October 1, 1990, copy in Houston Bar Association Archives.

104. *Texas Bar Journal,* 63, 10:918–19.

105. *Texas Bar Journal*, 34, 11:1123–24.

106. *Texas Bar Journal*, 40, 2:256.

107. *Texas Bar Journal*, 37, 11:1211.

108. *Texas Bar Journal*, 47, 6:729.

109. *Texas Bar Journal*, 64, 2:202–203. Some women spent their entire career with one industry, as did Billie "Willie" Fuller in the oil and gas field. She was with Shell Oil Corporation 1934–42, Pam Am Oil 1942–44 and 1946–54, and Hudson Oil Company 1954–72. Fuller spent two years in the Women's Army Corps during World War II.

110. *Texas Bar Journal*, 2, 1:29.

111. *Derry*, 91.

112. Ibid., 170.

113. *Texas Bar Journal*, 55, 7:889.

114. *Texas Bar Journal*, 32, 10:813.

115. Carroll G. Robinson and Patrice D. Carrington, "Houston's Law Schools: Stepping Stones to the Legal Profession, Thurgood Marshall School of Law," *The Houston Lawyer* (September-October 1995), 39–41.

116. G. Sidney Buchanan, "Houston's Law Schools: Stepping Stones to the Legal Profession, University of Houston Law Center," *The Houston Lawyer* (September-October 1995), 39, 41–43.

117. Lois Prestage Woods, video interview by Ellen Elkins Grimes, 2001. Woods had been refused admittance to South Texas College of Law. When she was able to enroll in law courses at Texas State University for Negroes, she felt an obligation to succeed. The founding of the law school had been filled with controversy. Heman Sweatt, a black postman in Houston, applied in 1947 to enter the University of Texas law school in Austin. In order to avoid a court test, the Texas legislature appropriated $3 million for the creation of a separate university for blacks, one that would also contain a $1,000,000 law school. When the law school was completed it consisted of the basement rooms in the Supreme Court Building, a very limited library, and a few part-time instructors. At this point the U.S. Supreme Court declared segregation in education unconstitutional and found that Sweatt should be admitted to the regular University of Texas law school. Nevertheless, rather than admit Sweatt to the

Austin campus, a new school was established in Houston. One of its components would be a law school. A year later the college was established, and in 1957 its name was changed to Texas Southern University. Sweatt was eventually admitted to the University of Texas School of Law, although he never graduated. Because of the controversy surrounding the law school, its first students undoubtedly felt pressure to succeed in obtaining their legal education. Lois Wood's experience seems to indicate that there was less discrimination directed toward women at TSU, at least from male students. The Thurgood Marshall School of Law currently has the largest proportion of women students (54.2%) in the state.

118. Ibid.

119. Bonnie Gangelhoff, "Rita Keenan," excerpt from University of Houston History, 18.

120. *Texas Bar Journal*, 44, 8:1025. The University of Houston Law Center—given the name Bates School of Law in 1969 for Col. William B. Bates of the law school's founding committee—currently counts females as 49% of its total enrollment.

121. Mark W. Lambert, former special collections librarian at South Texas College of Law, provided this information, as found in "Law School Registration" and "Notes and Personals," *The American Law School Review* (Saint Paul, Minn.: West Publishing Co., 1902–1947).

122. Payne, *Sarah T. Hughes*, 96. As her contribution to the war effort, Hughes did not accept payment for teaching. She also declined the school's offer of gasoline rationing coupons.

123. Judith N. McArthur, "Patsy Smith Moore," *Handbook of Texas*, 4:823.

124. *Texas Journal of Women and the Law*, 8, 33:336–339.

125. Ibid.; *Texas Bar Journal*, 68, 7:766–67.

126. Patricia Lasher and Beverly Bentley, *Texas Women: Interviews and Images* (Austin: Shoal Creek Publishers, 1980), 46.

127. Jones and Winegarten, 152.

128. Lasher, 45.

CHAPTER THREE

Jumping Hurdles

I'VE ALWAYS TRIED TO RISE ABOVE IT. I'm sure I've tried to rationalize some of it away. The water isn't fine, but you can walk in it,"[1] reflected Charlye O. Farris as she talked from the perspective of an African-American woman about her journey in law. Farris grew up in Wichita Falls, where she graduated from high school at the age of fifteen. Three years later she earned a degree from Prairie View A&M College. After teaching for a year, she pursued her interest in law and in 1953 graduated from Howard University School of Law. Returning to her native Texas, Farris was admitted to the bar, making history as the first African-American woman licensed to practice law in the state.[2] She opened a solo practice but discovered she had more obstacles to overcome. "I did have a few problems with jury members," Farris recalled. "Some jury members did not like the fact that I was a black woman. I had to tell them, 'You have the right to resent the fact that I am black, or that I am a woman, but you have to try this defendant honestly. Don't resent them.'"[3] And there were other problems. The Wichita County courthouse's only "Colored" bathroom was in the basement, and the building had no elevators.

A ten-minute recess was hardly enough time to make a trip from the fourth floor to the basement and back again, especially if Farris needed that time to confer with her client, so the male judge offered Farris the use of his bathroom on the fourth floor during the trial. She remembers that kind gesture, which was in contrast to the treatment she usually experienced in the 1950s. To this day, Farris remains the only African-American woman attorney in Wichita Falls, having practiced there for more than fifty years.[4]

Although the Reconstruction period after the Civil War resulted in some gains for black Americans, freedom for black women meant less than it did for their husbands and brothers. A study of black professionals in 1973 concluded that "black females have had less access to the more prestigious institutions of higher education and have been more disadvantaged with respect to graduate and professional education."[5] Nowhere was this truer than in the legal profession.

Nationwide, the first black woman lawyer was Charlotte Ray, a Howard University law graduate, who was admitted to practice in the District of Columbia in April 1872. In spite of her legal training and her keen mind, Ray could not attract enough clients to maintain a practice. The rise of black women lawyers was painfully slow. Women who were willing to fight the dual battles of racism and sexism had few, if any, role models. In 1918 Iowa's Gertrude E. Rush was the only black woman lawyer west of the Mississippi River. By the 1940s there were only fifty-seven black women lawyers in the entire United States.[6] Charlye Farris became the first black woman in Texas to become a lawyer when she was admitted to the bar in 1953.

The process of integration remained a slow one. Hampered by strict segregation laws which prevented blacks from attending all-white institutions, a black woman did not graduate from a Texas law school until 1954. Gloria Bradford of Houston received her degree at the University of Texas School of Law after graduating from Prairie View A&M College, where she had participated in debate and oratorical contests. She practiced law with the firm Dent, Ford, King & Wickliff and became the first African-American woman to try a case in Harris County district court.[7]

Farris and Bradford did not remain the only African-American female lawyers in the state. In 1956 they were joined by Hattie Elam Briscoe, a graduate of St. Mary's University School of Law. Briscoe remembered being told during her first semester in law school that women had no business being there. She responded, "I am a woman, I am in law school, and I am going to become a lawyer."[8] To finance her studies, she worked as a clerk-typist at Kelly Air Force Base and took classes at night. Although Briscoe ranked first in her class of twenty graduates, no valedictorian was named, presumably to prevent a valedictory address by an African-American woman. Failing to secure a job in the Bexar County district attorney's office, Briscoe hung her shingle outside a second-floor walkup over a barber shop. For the next twenty-seven years she was the only black female lawyer in Bexar County. Briscoe practiced criminal defense, family law, and probate law until she retired at the age of eighty-one, still in her original office.[9] In Dean Barbara Aldave's tenure in the 1990s, St. Mary's acknowledged Briscoe's scholastic achievements and, to compensate for the refusal to recognize her years earlier, set up a scholarship in her name.[10]

When she was admitted to the bar in 1959, Barbara Jordan became the fourth African-American woman to be licensed in Texas. Jordan attributed her desire to study law to a speech given by a female judge during her high school years. Her father discouraged her ambitious plans by insisting that "lawyering is no profession for a girl to be in." Jordan, however, was not to be deterred. Like Farris, she chose to attend law school outside Texas, entering Boston University School of Law, where she was one of six women—only two were black—in the class of six hundred freshmen.[11] After graduation she returned to Houston to practice law. She later recalled that she had only enough money to print a stack of business cards, so she set up an office in her parents' dining room. Her first client was a fellow church member who wanted a will prepared by a lawyer. Jordan was finally able to open an office above a drugstore in her Fifth Ward neighborhood. She entered the political arena when she began registering black voters during the 1960 presidential campaign. She realized that she could use her legal training in trying to create change through new legislation.[12] Her subsequent political career would be filled with historic accomplishments.

Despite the lowering of some discriminatory barriers, the entrance of women into the legal profession in the 1950s was slow. The years after World War II brought unprecedented prosperity. Americans believed that everyone could live the good life, which included a stay-at-home wife, children, a house, a new car, and the latest appliances. At the same time, other developments—the Cold War and the atomic bomb among others—created a sense of anxiety. The country's leaders assured the public that everything was normal and that there was nothing to worry about. Unfortunately for professional women, part of this normalcy was a heavy emphasis on rigid gender roles in which men worked and married women were expected to be wives and mothers and to stay at home with the children. In reality, however, more women were moving into the work force for both personal satisfaction and increased income for their families to be able to afford the "good things of life." Yet the public frowned on women filling jobs other than the traditional female ones—teacher, nurse, secretary—and discouraged women from competing with men.[13] Women found prejudice mounting against them in the legal profession. They were told that they would be outnumbered by men, that it would be nearly impossible to get a job in a firm, and that law, after all, was a man's profession. A 1958 government publication advised women lawyers to concentrate on "real estate and domestic relations work, women's and juvenile legal problems, probate work, and patent law," which reflected "the wisdom of insiders about areas in which women were apt to find work."[14] What the article did not say was that women lawyers were likely to make only 60 percent of their male colleagues' salaries.[15]

Many women felt the same pressures in the classroom. While they had struggled earlier only to be admitted to law school, they now felt the need to work harder and to make better grades than male students in order to find places in the legal profession after graduation. In keeping with the conservative climate in the 1950s, women lawyers were not overtly feminist. However, women's enduring the hardships of legal education and entry into the profession was itself a feminist statement that laid the groundwork for both the women's movement of the 1960s and the deluge of women entering law schools in the 1970s.

Beverly Tarpley, the only woman in the class of 1951 at the University of Texas School of Law, later reflected, "There were so few of us that we did not represent the threat that the greater numbers which came later did. I knew that I would be expected to recite on the chapter on rape in my criminal law class . . . In that day, such subjects were not discussed in polite company, and this was a daunting and embarrassing experience. However, I viewed it as a rite of passage. I thought then, and I think now, that he [the professor] was trying to teach me how to handle a delicate subject in a professional manner."[16] She landed a job after graduation with a trial firm in Abilene where she was second chair for an older male attorney. Her salary was $200 a month.[17] Tarpley claims the distinction of being the first woman lawyer from Texas to argue a case before the U.S. Supreme Court. Only twenty-seven years old at the time, she described the experience as "extremely intimidating."[18]

Not all students were young. Some women entered law school after pursuing a different career or after raising a family. Marian Boner earned undergraduate and advanced degrees in physics from the University of Texas in the early 1930s. At the age of forty-six she decided to begin a second career, returning to the university to enroll in law school. After graduating second in her class in 1955, Boner became a reference librarian at the University of Texas Tarlton Law Library and as an associate professor taught courses in legal research and writing. In recommending Boner for an associate professorship, Dean Page Keeton stated, "As a scholar she has established herself quantitatively and qualitatively."[19] In 1972, Boner was appointed first director of the Texas State Law Library, where she remained until her retirement. Her book *A Reference Guide to Texas Law and Legal History* is considered a definitive legal reference source.[20]

Although she had wanted to be a lawyer since reading Clarence Darrow's autobiography in high school, Mary Joe Durning Carroll did not begin her legal studies until she turned thirty in 1944. Balancing her jobs as a mother and as associate editor of the *Handbook of Texas,* she was able to take only one or two classes a semester.[21] She graduated with honors eleven years later and joined the Austin firm of Looney, Clark & Moorhead (later Clark, Thomas & Winters) where she became a partner in 1968. Carroll disliked being called a "woman lawyer" and frequently said that she was a woman who happened to be a lawyer.[22] She is believed to be the first woman in Texas who advanced to partner in a major firm. Her last appearance as a litigator was in the Texas Supreme Court in 1994, just after her eightieth birthday.[23]

The classic example of a woman balancing motherhood and a law career was Louise Raggio. After receiving her undergraduate degree from the University of Texas and doing graduate work in Washington, D.C., she married a lawyer and had two children. At the suggestion of her husband, Raggio applied to Southern Methodist University law school in 1947. She felt unwelcome and later explained, "I was reminded that law was a male profession, that the rough-and-tumble charges and countercharges of the courtroom were no suitable contest for a lady, that if I *were* admitted (and my qualifications were better than any other candidate) I would only be taking up space that could be occupied by a man who would *do something* with his degree."[24] Raggio, however, was determined and forged ahead. After a difficult pregnancy and the birth of her third child, she dropped out of school briefly before reentering and graduating in 1952. Raggio remembered the Texas Bar examination as one of the "most horrible experiences" of her life. On a day when the temperature registered above 100 degrees in Austin, she and her typewriter were assigned to a tiny niche in the hallway behind the House chamber. Properly attired for a woman in 1952—including wearing a girdle, hose, and high heels—she sweated through three days of answering questions. With great relief she passed, but finding a job was even tougher.[25] Facing the same discrimination as so many other women, Raggio, unable to find a job, practiced from her home until she was hired as an assistant district attorney in Dallas County.[26] In 1956, Raggio joined her husband's firm that he had opened in 1955.[27] Louise Raggio would become an expert in marital and family rights in the years ahead.

Women were seldom encouraged to practice criminal law. There was a widespread perception among the public and male attorneys that women were soft and passive and would not be able to handle tough criminal cases. Still, a law professor at South Texas College of Law decided that Nettie Joe Kegans fit the mold of a criminal lawyer and suggested that she enter the field. After receiving her license in 1957, Joe (as she was called) barged straight into a field dominated by men.[28] Her first obstacle was in renting an office. The building manager insisted that Kegans' husband must sign the lease since married women were not permitted to sign contracts. Outraged, Kegans marched over to a judge she knew and, as she later recalled, had her contractual disabilities removed. She got the office and for nineteen years handled all kinds of criminal cases from it until she was named to a criminal courts bench.[29]

A real pioneer among women practicing criminal law was Gladys Melton. After receiving her law degree from Jefferson School of Law in Dallas in 1933, she remained in Dallas and established her practice. In 1957 Melton was elected president of the Dallas County Criminal

Bar Association. She was further recognized two years later when that organization named her Criminal Lawyer of the Year, citing "her leadership as president . . . her service to indigent defendants, her work for better public relations, and her ethical practice of law."[30]

Following the passage in 1920 of the Nineteenth Amendment to the U.S. Constitution, which granted suffrage to women, there was little agitation for expanding women's rights. Women lawyers, however, were concerned about the ineligibility of Texas women to serve on juries, and the issue came to the forefront in 1934 when Sarah Hughes coauthored a proposed constitutional amendment to correct this inequity. Although the proposal was rejected, Hughes became a strong advocate for such an amendment. Women attorneys joined in the campaign. They recognized women being denied jury service as true gender discrimination and knew that it could easily impact a woman's appearance as an advocate in a courtroom occupied by a male judge, all male attorneys, and an entirely male jury. Hughes continued to lead the charge for women jurors by reminding the public that only three classes of people—criminals, lunatics, and women—could not sit on juries in Texas. Even this argument did not alter the situation. By 1945 the legislature had voted down the proposition six times, and Texas remained one of only seventeen states excluding women from juries. After a long struggle, however, victory was finally achieved in 1954 when voters approved the proposal by a margin of 57 percent. Texas was one of the last seven states in the nation to extend jury service to women.[31]

Although another discriminatory barrier to true equality had been removed, women law graduates still had difficulty securing jobs in established firms, especially those in urban areas. Law firms continued to shun women. In 1956, however, one of Houston's largest firms hired Lois McDade Watson as its first female lawyer. Records show that Watson was restricted to collecting small debts and was forced to do her own typing. She was even assigned occasionally to the typing pool with the firm's secretaries. After eight years Watson left the firm. The same firm hired several more women during the next few years, but none of them remained very long. When they realized that they would not advance within the firm, they found employment elsewhere.[32] Women were still being discouraged in pursuing a legal career. As a result, the 1960 census reported only one hundred more female lawyers in the state than were reported in 1950.[33]

When Suzanne Geiss Robbins graduated as the only woman in her class at the University of Texas in 1961, the placement department in the law school refused to take her application for seeking employment, telling her it would be a waste of their time and her time, because "no firm will hire a woman." Robbins recalled, "I decided to become a C.P.A. in order to be more competitive against the boys." She attended Baylor Business School for her accounting degree, and in 1964 she clerked for Judge Adrian Spears of the U.S. District Court in San Antonio. With that experience under her belt, she joined Peat Marwick Mitchell and Co. in Dallas in the dual role of attorney and C.P.A.[34]

Some women entered the legal profession almost by accident. Ruby Kless Sondock never intended to become a lawyer. She enrolled at the University of Houston law school because she wanted to be "the best legal secretary in town."[35] A friend going through a divorce urged Sondock to change her goal and to become a lawyer. Even though she had fifteen hours remaining toward her degree, Sondock decided to take the bar exam. After passing the exam and graduating, she went job hunting, and although interviews were hard to secure in 1961, she landed one that materialized into a part-time job. Sondock later talked about her good luck since she was able to work on interesting cases and even argued one before the Texas Supreme Court in her first year of practice. She eventually opened her own office, never imagining the role the high court would play in her life in the years ahead.[36]

Unlike Sondock, Camille Hutson-Dunn knew she wanted to be

a lawyer from the time she worked as a "gofer" in her father's law office and accompanied him to court in Orangeburg, South Carolina. Hutson-Dunn was admitted to the South Carolina Bar after only one year of law school and joined her father in his practice. She later entered the University of Michigan law school, graduating in 1951. After marrying and moving to Houston, Hutson-Dunn was admitted to the Texas Bar in 1963.[37] A piece of advice that her father gave her was to "have your back pockets full"—or always be fully prepared. She took that advice to heart and became board certified in family law. Hutson-Dunn was concerned that she might burn out as a family lawyer if she couldn't keep herself from becoming too emotionally involved in cases. Her theory was that "you can't be a good attorney if you lose yourself in your emotions." Hutson-Dunn also admitted that it was terribly difficult to balance her family life and her professional career. For that reason, she practiced part-time and did pro bono work until her children were older.[38]

The roster of the Houston Bar Association in 1962 is illustrative of how some women in Texas used their legal education at that time. There were twenty-seven women listed as members. Fifteen were in solo practice, with four of those working from their houses; five were employed by corporations; three practiced in firms, but only one of these was with a major firm; two practiced in offices with their husbands; and two were undetermined as to area of practice.[39] The ways in which women used their legal education had changed little since the 1930s.

A study conducted in 1965 detailed the kinds of jobs women lawyers were finding as they entered the job market. There were the "assured" jobs—those waiting in family firms or available through some personal connection. There were the "protected" jobs—those known to be relatively open and less discriminatory—such as legal jobs in the government. Finally, there were the jobs of "seekers"—those who went out in the market as men did, looking for the best possible things.

Most women in the 1960s gravitated toward the "protected" jobs because they seemed more like a sure thing.[40]

Sometimes women decided to completely change directions in their vocational pursuits. Reba Graham Rasor had a career in journalism before she decided to become a lawyer. She was also married with children when this decision was made. Nevertheless, Rasor entered law school at Southern Methodist University, where she graduated in 1966 after juggling classes, motherhood, and housework. When the new graduate took the bar exam, she tied with one other applicant for the highest grade. Rasor spent the next five years teaching legal writing and research at Southern Methodist University law school. After a period as a solo practitioner, Rasor joined the firm of Raggio and Raggio in Dallas.[41] During these years, she used her journalism background to educate the legal community as well as the public about the new Texas Family Code that Louise Raggio and the Family Law Section of the State Bar were writing.[42] This was another example of a woman combining her skills in accomplishing a significant goal.

Two years after Charlye Farris became the first African-American female lawyer in Texas, Edna Cisneros was admitted to the bar as the state's first Hispanic female lawyer in 1955.[43] Although the entrance of both African-American and Hispanic women into the legal profession was slow during the next decade, the number of Hispanic women exceeded that of African-Americans. The 1970 census reported twenty-nine "Female Lawyers of Spanish Language" in Texas, the largest number in any state except for California and New Mexico. Although they represented a small minority when compared to the 571 white females in the profession, their numbers would increase in the years ahead.[44]

One of the twenty-nine Hispanic lawyers was Adelfa Callejo, whose childhood dream was to be a lawyer. She saved enough money over five years to afford one semester's tuition at the Southern Methodist University law school. After ten years of night classes and part-time work, she earned her law degree in 1961 when she was thirty-seven years old. Unable to find employment as an attorney, she offered to work for a dollar a year for the Dallas Bar Association's Legal Aid Society. The organization turned her down. Callejo later explained, "Many people handle discrimination in different ways—I handled mine with anger. I opened up my own practice and learned very quickly that the key to success was money. If I was going to be an effective advocate of human rights, then I had to become a millionaire . . . so that is what I proceeded to do . . . The representation of minority lawyers is lacking. We still do not have enough Hispanic attorneys, much less Hispanic women attorneys."[45] Callejo's husband joined her in practice, and their office handled criminal, family, personal injury, worker's compensation, and immigration law. Having grown up in poverty, she believed that her drive to make millions was fueled in part by her desire to have the power to be an advocate for the disadvantaged.[46]

Irma Rangel took a different path in her quest to help the disadvantaged. Like Callejo, Rangel was in her late thirties when she graduated from St. Mary's University School of Law in 1969. Having been a school teacher and principal for fourteen years before studying law, Rangel then pursued a varied legal career. She was an assistant district attorney in Nueces County, partner in a Kingsville firm, Robstown city attorney, and finally a solo practitioner. It was in the Texas legislature, however, that she was able to more fully address the inequities that minorities in Texas experienced, especially in their quest for an education.[47] Rangel credited her parents with instilling in her the importance of the struggle for a better life "not just for ourselves, but for all people."[48]

Another law school, the eighth in the state, opened in 1967. Texas Tech University School of Law was one of four new state-supported law schools in the United States established during the late 1960s. Located in Lubbock, the school was distant from the other law schools in Texas.[49] Texas Tech's first class enrolled seventy-two students, of whom six were women. They were Leota Alexander, Barbara Benson,

Joan Blanscet, Dennis Fullingim, Mary Hall, and Ruth Kirby. Three of these women—Benson, Blanscet, and Fullingim—completed their degree requirements in December 1969, having accelerated their graduation by one semester by attending summer classes and thus becoming Texas Tech's first female law graduates. Alexander, Hall, and Kirby graduated in 1970 with their original classmates. Kirby had the highest cumulative grade average in her class.[50]

Still, women were being met with hostility when they entered law school. Not only did they comprise a small segment of the classes, but they faced many of the same dilemmas that the women in earlier years had confronted. Should women speak out in the classroom like their male classmates, or should they sit quietly as "ladies"?[51] Should they choose the visibility of courtroom practice or the privacy of office practice? What should the proper woman lawyer wear, especially in the courtroom? Could they marry and have families like male lawyers or did they have to sacrifice having families? Women were still bearing the burdens placed on them by society. A woman was expected to be modest, unassuming, and intuitive. Yet, as a lawyer she needed to be bold, assertive, and decisive. Women lawyers were confident they could be all of these things, but the public still expressed doubt.[52] As a result, their journey continued to be a difficult one.

Pregnancy proved a problem for many female lawyers because it was viewed as a barrier to public appearances of any kind. It also reinforced the belief that women who were mothers could not possibly give adequate time or attention to their jobs as lawyers. If women succeeded in getting job interviews, they would often be asked whether they intended to marry or have children. Occasionally they were even asked how many children they planned to have.[53]

Some women found themselves married and pregnant while they were still in law school. Surrenden Angly recalled that she had a six-month-old child when she began classes at the University of Texas. During her first week in school she realized that she was pregnant again. When Dean Keeton learned of Angly's pregnancy and realized that her children would be only fifteen months apart in age, he insisted that she would never be able to complete law school under those conditions. Angly argued that she could, and their agreement was that there would be no exceptions made for her. Angly became a part-time student but, nevertheless, graduated in 1967.[54]

Gayle Albritton was also pregnant as she completed her law studies at the University of Texas. Before the Law Day banquet that spring, she was asked whether she would prefer not to come forward to accept her award since she was in the "family way." When she was sworn in a few months later holding her two-month-old son, the scene was such a novelty that a photographer asked her to pose with one of the Texas Supreme Court justices.[55]

One of the most difficult aspects of both law study and early employment for women was a lack of mentors and role models. Having someone to guide and encourage them would have made their paths less stressful. As Judge Mary Lou Robinson recalled, "When I began practicing law, there were no women out here to be mentors . . . Back then, girls didn't [go to law school]. Now, I am a mentor . . . . "[56] Louise Raggio has frequently told how much support she received from Judge Sarah Hughes when she began her difficult pursuit of becoming a lawyer. Not only did Hughes encourage Raggio along the way, but she also helped Raggio get her first job as an assistant district attorney by recommending her to the Dallas County district attorney's office.[57] Dorothy Shuberg Owens had the good fortune as a twenty-two-year-old to work for her aunt, Anna Sandbo, Austin's first woman lawyer, who was both mentor and role model for Owens.[58] Suzanne Geiss Robbins discovered that mentors could very well be men. She credits Dean Page Keeton of the UT law school and Judge Adrian A. Spears, the federal judge for whom she clerked, as being "fabulous" mentors to her.[59]

Women also lacked the experience of bonding with other female students. They were still few in number, and most campuses did not provide a place for women to gather. A student in the 1960s explained, "[a]ll the women in the law school would lunch in the little room connected to the women's restroom—we were told the school was built for men."[60] Another agreed, "Yes, we spent time in the ladies' room. But many times, if you were in there and you were just really down, somebody else would come in, sit down, talk with you. Just kind of get you pumped back up."[61] This bonding led to more organized networking among women female students, which in turn evolved into formal organizations once they were practicing attorneys.

Kay Bailey Hutchison and Sarah Ragle Weddington were two of seven women in a class of more than 400 graduates in 1967.[62] Hutchison earned her law degree at the University of Texas through a program which at that time allowed undergraduates to enter law school without first earning a degree. Hutchison, like many other female graduates, could not find a job in the legal field. She decided to look in another direction and was hired by a Houston television station where she covered politics. Her assignments in the state legislature led her to conclude that Texas needed a stronger two-party system. In 1972 she ran as a Republican for a seat in the House and was elected.[63] This would prove to be only the first step in Hutchison's political career.

Weddington is best known for having successfully argued *Roe v. Wade* before the U.S. Supreme Court just four years after she graduated from the University of Texas School of Law. Weddington had a strong desire to change society because of the world in which she grew up. She described it as a time when social and legal restrictions forced women into narrower roles than ones they longed to occupy. "We were told 'Women don't,' 'You can't,' 'That would be too strenuous for you,'" Weddington remembered. She decided to become a lawyer and to work for equal legal rights for women.[64] Almost immediately after opening her own practice she joined with a Dallas lawyer, Linda Coffee, on the *Roe* case to defend their client's right to have an abortion. Coffee, a University of Texas graduate and former clerk to Judge Sarah T. Hughes, filed the case in Dallas County.[65] When *Roe v. Wade* moved to the U.S. Supreme Court, Weddington argued before the nine justices in 1971 and again in 1972. In January 1973 Weddington and Coffee learned that they had won the case. The Supreme Court held that the United States Constitution guarantees to women a right of privacy that includes the decision of whether to continue or terminate a pregnancy. Weddington is thought to be the youngest person to argue a U.S. Supreme Court case successfully.[66] During the judicial process, the *Houston Post* ran an article that ended with the comment, "If their day in court proves anything, it certainly proves that genteel Southern ladies can indeed be very good lawyers."[67]

Joan Tarpley was influenced to become a lawyer during her two-year assignment in West Africa with the Peace Corps. She came to the conclusion that a career in law would combine her two passions—talking to people and providing assistance to them. She thought when she applied to Southern Methodist University School of Law that, as an African-American, she would encounter racism. That did not prove to be true and in 1968 Tarpley was the first African-American woman to graduate from Southern Methodist University, placing in the top 10 percent of her class. Her greatest obstacle was in finding a job. Like others before her, she was only offered a position as a law librarian. Yet Tarpley was determined to practice law. Her determination would help her in blazing new trails in the years ahead.[68]

Women came to realize that discriminatory practices would continue unless they were confronted. They also realized that they might have to fight their own battles. In the years ahead Iris Hefter Robinson would take on gender bias, another issue that was of great concern to women lawyers. Yet Robinson had the same difficulties in the 1960s as her sister attorneys. She graduated from South Texas College of Law in 1967, ranked third in her class. When she went job hunting, she was told to "go to D.C. if [you] want to be a trial attorney with the government because we're not hiring any women here." Discouraged, Robinson accepted the only job she could find—bookkeeper for a law firm. Seven years later she became a member of the firm, and shortly thereafter she became a shareholder. She never forgot, however, the bumpy road she had traveled.[69]

When women were able to get job interviews in the private sector, they knew that salary would be an issue. Inevitably, they were offered less than a male with the same qualifications interviewing for the same position. One newly licensed woman reported, "The lawyer interviewing me said they paid beginning associates $800 so they would offer me $700."[70] Some women were bold enough to negotiate for equal compensation, while others were so glad to get a job that they acquiesced and took the lower offer. It was not until the passage of the Equal Pay Act on June 10, 1963, (effective one year later) that it became illegal to pay women lower rates for the same job as men were doing strictly on the basis of their sex. The Act prohibited employers from discriminating between men and women by paying different wages for work that "requires equal skill, effort, and responsibility," and is "performed under similar working conditions."[71] Exceptions must be lawfully based on something other than gender. Although this was a step forward for all women in the workforce, the burden of proof remained a barrier for women, including those in the legal profession.

The year after the Equal Pay Act was passed, another act confronted gender discrimination. Title VII of the Civil Rights Act of 1964 made it unlawful for an employer to discriminate with respect to hiring, firing, compensation, or other terms of employment on the grounds of "race, color, religion, sex, or national origin." The original bill, focused on race, was amended to include "sex" at the initiative of a Southern opponent of the legislation who hoped this action would trivialize the bill and thus defeat it. His plan backfired when the amendment passed.[72] The part of the law applying to sex discrimination was not taken too seriously, but resistance to enforcing this law gave added impetus to the emerging feminist movement.[73] Female lawyers would find themselves in the middle of this issue in the approaching decade.

Since Texas is a community property state, laws stipulate that property acquired or earned during marriage belongs equally to the husband and to the wife, but as late as 1967 the husband was in control of everything. Only in death could the wife bequeath her half of the property to her children or anyone else of her choosing. If a couple sold their community property, she had to sign the deed and swear before a notary, with her husband not present, that she had voluntarily affixed her signature. A wife could not borrow money in her own name. She could not make bond without her husband's signature. If she wanted to start a business, she had to file a lawsuit asking to have her disabilities removed. If her husband refused to join in the suit, it was rejected. Disabilities of coverture were removed for mercantile and trading purposes but not for professional ones.[74] This restriction meant that all married women lawyers were practicing illegally because the laws made their husbands accountable for everything they did.

Married women had long despaired of their status as second-class citizens. Although a committee of the State Bar had addressed the situation by drafting a bill to take away some of the disabilities of coverture of property rights for married women, the legislature took no action when the bill was introduced and the bar committee was dissolved.[75] But the issue did not fade away. When Louise Raggio was named chairperson of the State Bar's Family Law Section in 1965, she convinced the newly elected State Bar president to assign the Marital Property Bill to her section. Two years and seven drafts later, the bill was ready to work its way through the legislative process. Against all odds, the bill was passed by both the house and the senate. Governor John Connally signed it into law in June 1967. Married women in Texas could now legally conduct their own affairs, including the practice of law.

The Family Law Section of the bar was then handed an even larger assignment—revising all of the family laws in the state of Texas. Louise Raggio chaired the Bar's Family Code committee, which began an overhaul of various state statutes concerning marriage, custody, family, adoption, and divorce. This effort took seven years. Enacted in three sections between 1967 and 1974, the Texas Family Code was hailed as the first unified domestic relations law code in the world and became a model for other jurisdictions.[76]

Between 1920 and 1970, the number of female lawyers in the state remained less than 4 percent,[77] but the next decade would see a surge in the number of female lawyers. Much had occurred in the 1960s that impacted women's lives—increase in life expectancy, development of the birth control pill, increase in the number of divorces, increase in the number of single women, proposal of the Equal Rights Amendment, and the beginnings of the feminist movement.[78] In the legal profession, the long-simmering issue of discrimination would come to the forefront. As the modern era for women lawyers began, the pathway remained rocky. It would require the dedicated efforts of many for women to acquire level footing on their journey.

Notes

1. *Texas Bar Journal*, 54, 11:1194.

2. Sherilyn Roberts, "Charlye Ola Farris Ahead of Her Time," *Eclipse*, January-February 2006, 41.

3. "First black female lawyer in Texas shares her story with students," *Law News*, Texas Wesleyan University School of Law, March 1, 2005.

4. Roberts, *Eclipse*, 41; *Texas Bar Journal*, 66, 8:646. Farris recalled that in order to take the bar exam she needed recommendation letters from five lawyers. Not knowing any lawyers, black or white, in Wichita Falls, she finally found a former judge who introduced her to enough people to procure her letters.

5. Morello, 144.

6. Ibid., 148.

7. Baade Collection; *The Society Page*, Vol. 3, No. 1, 4 (University of Texas School of Law Office of Student Life, Fall 2006).

8. Veronica Salazar, "First Black Woman Lawyer Hits Her Stride, "*Express News* (San Antonio), March 25, 1984, cited in Ruthe Winegarten, *Black Texas Women: A Sourcebook* (Austin: University of Texas Press, 1996), 183–84.

9. Harriet Elam Briscoe Papers 1937-1997, Manuscript Collection 7, University of Texas at San Antonio, http://www.lib.utsa.edu/Archives/Manuscripts/ms67.html (accessed November 8, 2004).

10. *Texas Lawyer*, Vol. 14, No. 11, 1, 8. Brandon, 80–82. Briscoe later recalled that she had a very lonely existence in the legal community until Judge Carol Haberman welcomed her into a circle of colleagues who became friends (82).

11. Morello, 169.

12. Mary Beth Rogers, *Barbara Jordan: An American Hero* (New York: Bantam Books, 1998), 77–78. See J. Clay Smith Jr., ed., *Rebels in Law: Voices in History of Black Women Lawyers* (Ann Arbor: University of Michigan Press, 2000) for a collection of essays by black women lawyers about their efforts to ensure equal justice and equality under the law for all persons.

13. The 1950s were not good years for women who dared to break out of the domestic sphere and enter the professional arena. For a view of life for women in the 1950s, see Joanne Meyerowitz, ed. *Not June Cleaver: Women and Gender in Postwar America, 1945–1960* (Philadelphia: Temple University Press, 1994); Brett Harvey, *The Fifties: A Women's Oral History* (New York: HarperCollins Publishers, 1993).

14. Epstein, 81.

15. Sarah Anne Cutler, "Mrs. Ward Cleaver, Esq.: Women in the Legal Profession in the 1950s OR How to Succeed in Law When You May Not Rock the Boat (and There is No Seat for You), Georgetown University Law Center, http://www.law.georgetown.edu/glh/cutler.htm (accessed October 6, 2006).

16. *Texas Journal of Women and the Law*, 8:339–340.

17. Brian Bethel, "Abilene attorney blazed legal trail," *Abilene Reporter News*, July 31, 2005, Section 1 AA.

18. Ibid., 3.

19. Roy M. Mersky, "Marian Oldfather Boner," *Handbook of Texas*, 1:632.

20. Ibid.

21. Ibid., 992.

22. Julia A. Woods, Ashley Craddock and Regan Marie Brown, *Austin Lawyers: A Legacy of Leadership and Service* (Birmingham, Ala.: Association Publishing Service, 2005), 121. Carroll disliked being called a "woman lawyer" because she did "not consider the practice of law to be a sexual activity."

23. Tracé Etienne-Gray, "Mary Joe Durning Carroll," *Handbook of Texas*, 8:992.

24. Louise Ballerstedt Raggio with Vivian Anderson Castleberry, *Texas Tornado* (New York: Citadel Press, 2003), 111–12.

25. Ibid., 131–32.

26. Ibid., 145–46.

27. Ibid., 161.

28. John Makeig, "No-nonsense Judge Joe Kegans, 69, pioneer for women, dies," *Houston Chronicle*, January 7, 1997, 12A.

29. Presentation given by Judge Joe Kegans and attended by author, June, 1995.

30. *Texas Bar Journal*, 22, 9:577.

31. Payne, *Sarah T. Hughes*, 97–100, 139–40, 147–49, 178–79.

32. John H. Crooker Jr. and Gibson Gayle Jr., *Fulbright & Jaworski: 75 Years (1919–1994)* (Houston: Fulbright & Jaworski L.L.P., 1994), 120; Harold M. Hyman, *Craftsmanship and Character: A History of the Vinson and Elkins Law Firm of Houston 1917–1997* (Athens, Ga.: The University of Georgia Press, 1998), 394.

33. Smith, *Rebels in Law*, Chart C2, 288.

34. Suzanne Geiss Robbins, correspondence to author, November 9, 2006.

35. *Texas Bar Journal*, 55, 1:98.

36. *Texas Bar Journal*, 61, 1:87.

37. Ruth Williams Cupp, *Portia Steps Up to the Bar: The First Women Lawyers of South Carolina* (Raleigh, N. C.: Ivy House Publishing Group, 2003), 89–90.

38. Judge Camille Dunn, video interview, December 18, 1996, Houston Bar

Association Archives.

39. Houston Bar Association Directory 1962, Houston Metropolitan Research Center, Houston Public Library.

40. Epstein, 89–90.

41. *Texas Bar Journal,* 37, 5:421–422.

42. *Texas Bar Journal,* 58, 5:520.

43. Enstam, *Handbook of Texas,* 6:1049.

44. Smith, Chart C3, 290.

45. *Texas Bar Journal,* 53, 9:1053.

46. Norma D. Tabares, "Adelfa Callejo," Stanford University Law School, Fall 1999, http://womenslegalhistory.stanford.edu/papers/CallejoA-Tabares99.pdf (accessed March 5, 2007).

47. Teresa Palomo Acosta and Ruthe Winegarten, *Las Tejanas: 300 Years of History* (Austin: University of Texas Press, 2003), 190.

48. "Irma Rangel," http://www.twu.edu.twhf/tw-rangel.htm (accessed March 5, 2007).

49. Richard Amandes, "The History of the School of Law of Texas Tech University," *Texas Tech Law Review* 1 (1969–70), 37–39. The nearest law school, the University of New Mexico, was 300 miles away in Albuquerque, New Mexico.

50. Dean Walter Huffman, correspondence to author, March 31, 2007. Females currently comprise 45% of the total enrollment at Texas Tech's law school.

51. In the article, "Of Ivory Columns and Glass Ceilings: The Impact on the Supreme Court of the United States on the Practice of Women Attorneys in Law Firms" (*St. Mary's Law Journal* 28:546 n. 95), Nancy L. Farrer includes some theories advanced by other authors on why women's participation in law classes tended to be less than that of the men. They were: (1) women were less comfortable speaking in class, (2) professors tended not to call on women, and (3) women did not feel compelled to dominate conversations as much as men.

52. Epstein, 268–69, 273–74, 278–79.

53. Mona Harrington, *Women Lawyers Rewriting the Rules* (New York: Penguin Books, 1993), 19. In 1939 a survey revealed that 76% of all women lawyers in the

United States had no children. Ten years later 70% had no children. Only 9% had as many as two children. These lawyers seemed to place career ahead of motherhood and, sometimes, even marriage. That has changed, but more recent studies have shown that women lawyers tend to have fewer children than other professional women.

54. *Texas Journal of Women and the Law*, 8:343, 346.

55. Gayle Albritton, correspondence to author, October 4, 2006.

56. *Texas Bar Journal*, 68, 3:243.

57. Payne, *Sarah T. Hughes*, 180.

58. *Who's Who*, 72.

59. Suzanne Geiss Robbins, correspondence to author, November 9, 2006.

60. *Texas Bar Journal*, 55, 1:12.

61. *Texas Journal of Women and the Law*, 8:349.

62. Jones and Winegarten, 159, 162.

63. Ibid., 158.

64. Ibid., 162. Weddington, like others, had difficulty finding a job. She recalled that firms would regularly fly male students to interviews, but refused to do the same for females. The head of the UT law placement office finally told firms that they could not use the school's facilities for interviews unless they treated both sexes the same. Weddington said that she was flown to Dallas for an interview, but she did not get the job. The senior partner told her that they had to cuss out young lawyers to train them and they couldn't do that to women. (Cited in Woods, Craddock and Brown, 121–22.)

65. Payne, *Sarah T. Hughes*, 307–08.

66. Jones and Winegarten, 162–63.

67. Payne, *Sarah T. Hughes*, 405.

68. Kim Higgins, "Joan Tarpley: The Embodiment of Empowerment," *Eclipse*, January-February 2006, 49.

69. Molly Glentzler, "Women with a Career," *South Texas College of Law Quarterly*, Summer 1995, 8. As chair of Women and the Law Section of the State Bar,

Robinson played a key role in the work of the Texas Gender Bias Task Force, which made sexual harassment during litigation an aggrieved offense.

70. Karen Ann Bernat, "What's Wrong with a Lawyer in a Mini-Skirt?" *Towne Hall Notes*, December 1969, 3-4.

71. Equal Pay Act, http://en.wikipedia.org/wiki/Equal_Pay_Act_of_1963 (accessed March 22, 2006). While the Equal Pay Act protects both men and women, the original intent of Congress was to establish pay parity for women. It was not until 1972, however, that the law was amended to include women in an executive, administrative, or professional capacity.

72. Woloch, 512–13.

73. Epstein, 94–95. The Equal Employment Opportunity Commission was created to aid in enforcement of Title VII of the Civil Rights Act. A series of amendments broadened the provisions to include any employer with fifteen or more employees, as well as state and local governments, agencies, and educational institutions. Legislation defined law school placement offices as employment offices and thus made them targets for suits.

74. Enstam, *Handbook of Texas*, 6:1046–49. See also Jean Stuntz, *Hers, His, and Theirs: Community Property Law in Spain and Early Texas* (Lubbock: Texas Tech University Press, 2005).

75. Raggio, 174–77.

76. Ibid., 178–86; Payne, *Sarah T. Hughes*, 376–77; Elizabeth Vrato, *The Counselors* (Philadelphia: Running Press, 2002), 44.

77. Epstein, 4. Nationally, the growth of women lawyers remained rather static from 1910 to 1960. In 1930 the number was 2.1% and rose to 2.4% by 1940. In 1950 the proportion of women increased to 3.5%, but then fell to 3.3% in 1960. During these years Texas' ratio of women to men compared with these figures or was slightly below them.

78. See Sheila M. Rothman, *Woman's Proper Place: A History of Changing Ideals and Practices* (New York: Basic Books, Inc., Publishers, 1978), for a discussion about the changing concepts and patterns of women's lives and the debate over feminism that was erupting in the 1970s.

CHAPTER FOUR

Forging Ahead

IN 2000 CATHY LAMBOLEY BECAME GENERAL COUNSEL for Shell Oil Corporation and found herself in a position to help advance the careers of women lawyers. She welcomed the opportunity to open doors that had been closed to women. Lamboley never thought about becoming a lawyer while she was attending the University of Wisconsin. As she studied to become a teacher, her idealism blossomed. When the Vietnam War heated up, Lamboley became an antiwar protestor and was tear-gassed several times. After graduation, she began teaching until a beloved relative suggested that she attend law school. Taking his advice, she entered the University of Texas law school and joined Shell Oil Corporation on her graduation in 1979.[1] Lamboley moved up through the ranks and, by refuting the notion that women always hit a glass ceiling, she attained the position of senior vice president, general counsel, and corporate secretary of Shell Oil. Lamboley's idealism and sense of fairness once again surfaced. Not only did she work to promote women within the walls of Shell, but she developed an initiative through which all of Shell's outside legal service providers must report on the diversity within their firms. As a result, the number of both women and minorities not only at Shell but also in other companies increased dramatically under Lamboley's watchful eye.[2] This kind of support had not often been present for women lawyers in corporate America. It was encouraging to know that one woman's advocacy could alter the career aspirations of so many others.

Ann MacNaughton's love of learning and passion for helping people engaged her, too, in the civil rights and antiwar efforts of the tumultuous 1960s. She remembers vividly where she was when she learned of President Kennedy's assassination in 1963, but she knew nothing about the Gulf of Tonkin Resolution Congress adopted the next summer or the rapidly escalating Vietnam War it enabled, when she left home to study languages at Indiana University in 1966. She knew and applauded the Voting Rights Act of 1965 but was oblivious to the brutality of "Bloody Sunday" in Selma, Alabama, that led up to it. Stunned, outraged, and disgusted when greeted by town police wielding billy clubs at the Indiana University business school while waiting with others for an announced campus debate about the use of napalm in Vietnam, she was bussed to the Bloomington jail, learned to sing "We Shall Overcome," and came home to Houston where she became active in civil rights, antiwar, and planned parenthood efforts. After college she became a social worker until what she learned about the impact of U.S. property laws on women and families impelled her to enter law school in 1973. Night students could not work on law review, so MacNaughton quit her job as a social worker and worked her way through school as the University of Houston's women's advocate. Even though she graduated in the top 10 percent of her class, prestigious Houston firms were hiring few women attorneys, even those who were law review editors. MacNaughton accepted a position in an oil and gas company that she charged with gender discrimination a few years later, leaving the company to complete MBA studies. Despite the bumpy road, she went on to achieve success as a corporate attorney in what was then an almost exclusively male oil and gas industry. A measure of the extent to which gender bias eroded over those decades was evident when she reconnected in the 1990s with the general counsel she charged with gender-based discrimination in the 1970s and persuaded him to join with her in writing the model dispute resolutions clause for international oil and gas contracts.[3]

The 1970s seemed to be a turning point for women in law. The number of women in law schools tripled in many locations as attention riveted on the judicial system as the pivotal point for the resolution of divisive civil rights, women's rights, and other social issues.[4] The shocking events of the 1960s—assassinations, shootings on college campuses, riots at a national political convention, the war in Vietnam—led into the decade of the 1970s, where women not only entered law school in larger numbers but became active in addressing social issues confronting them. As men were drafted for the Vietnam conflict, law schools once again needed to fill their classrooms. Like during World War II, women were being recruited to enroll. Government officials and women's groups were encouraging women to seek legal careers. Equality of opportunity resolutions were adopted both by the Association of American Law Schools and by the American Bar Association.[5] Law school placement offices now had a duty to ensure equal employment opportunities for their female students.

The revitalized women's movement was a strong contributing factor for the increase in women law students. As women organized to demand their birthright as citizens and persons, the Equal Rights Amendment (ERA)—first introduced in 1923 and reworded to its current form in 1943—became the central symbol of the struggle. It stated: "Equality of rights under the law shall not be denied or abridged by the United States or by any state on account of sex."[6] Politicians supported organized women's voices in a way that they had not done since the battle for the ballot fifty years earlier. The ERA passed the United

States Senate and then the House of Representatives, and on March 22, 1972, the proposed Twenty-seventh Amendment to the Constitution was sent to the states for ratification.[7]

Support for the ERA was by no means unanimous among women. Some objected to it because it would override protective measures given to women in jobs, for example, requiring night work or heavy lifting. Opponents also feared that equal rights would mandate women's involvement in military combat.[8] Supporters of the ERA argued that such protective covenants actually restricted women from seeking many jobs. They wanted equality across the board without any protective covenants, which they regarded as discriminatory. Even though an extension of ten years was granted for getting the necessary thirty-eight votes from the states for ratification of the amendment, it failed by receiving only thirty-five votes. The amendment has been before every session of Congress since 1982, but it has yet to be ratified.[9]

Just eight months after the Texas legislature ratified the ERA, Texas voters endorsed the state Equal Rights Amendment that had been fifteen years in the making. Hermine Tobolowsky, representing the Business and Professional Women's clubs, had testified before a Texas Senate committee in support of a bill that would expand married women's right to control their property. When some senators responded to her testimony with amusement, Tobolowsky decided that the B&PW should campaign for a constitutional amendment rather than depend on changes in individual laws. B&PW members, led by Tobolowsky, campaigned across the state, forming coalitions with influential women's groups.[10] Their activities continued in spite of the opposition of some legislators who still argued for protective legislation for women. Even when the Family Code was passed in 1967, the women of the B&PW did not relent and reintroduced their proposed amendment. Finally their hard work paid off when the state ERA was passed by the legislature and endorsed by Texas voters in November 1982.[11] In recognition of her hard work, Hermine Tobolowsky became known as the "Mother of the Texas Equal Rights Amendment."[12]

Although the number of women in Texas law schools increased, some conditions had not changed. When Harriet Murphy entered UT law school in 1966, she was the only black student. She later recalled, "[A]fter I arrived, I felt that I was expected to carry on my shoulders the burden of 25 million blacks . . . I resented any implication that I was to be some kind of example." Murphy, however, worked to remedy the situation. She and some white students together began actively recruiting black students. By the time Murphy graduated, she was no longer the only black law student.[13]

Other women faced different problems in getting their legal education. Janis Jack lived 225 miles from the school she attended. Although she was married and had a small child, she flew from Corpus Christi to Houston twice a week to attend classes at South Texas College of Law. Her determination to get a degree was spurred no doubt by a professor who asked her why she was in law school since her husband was well able to support her. Jack kept her hectic schedule until she graduated in 1981 and began her practice in Corpus Christi.[14]

In speaking of law school in the 1970s, Myra McDaniel admitted, "[I]t was the best of times, and it was the worst of times. We certainly were harassed because there were enough of us to harass."[15] Male students did not seem to take the fifteen women in the class seriously because many of them were married and had children. McDaniel, who entered law school at the age of thirty-nine, was told that she must be doing this for "fun." When the women of the class of 1975 went out to find jobs, they were met with discrimination head-on. Even after they were in the workplace, according to McDaniel, sexist and racist remarks abounded all around them.[16]

When Chris Elizalde entered the University of Texas law school in the late 1970s less than a third of the class was made up of women, but she recalled that women were a large enough minority that they could no longer be ignored. She added that she never experienced any overt discrimination in class from her professors. "I had one woman professor throughout my law school career," Elizalde explained. "All the rest were men. But they were wonderful men, for the most part."[17] In speaking of one particular professor she noted, "He called us all by our last names, no mister or miss. And if he wanted to refer to us collectively, he'd call us people . . . He had taught me a whole lot more than I ever believed."[18] When she graduated, Elizalde found just the position she was seeking—staff attorney for the Texas Association of School Boards.[19]

Lynne Liberato's goal when she decided to go to law school in the late 1970s was to improve her skills as a journalist; she had worked at the *Huntsville Item,* the *Commerce Journal*, and a Houston television station. She was employed in public relations for Shell Oil Company while attending South Texas College of Law. "After I got there [law school], I stopped thinking of myself as a journalist and started thinking of myself as a future lawyer," recalled Liberato.[20]

Unlike Liberato, Linda Addison went to law school because it was a family tradition. Her father and a grandfather were lawyers in Poland. But Addison also had another reason for studying law. Her parents were Holocaust survivors and, as Addison explained, her parents' experience illustrated what happens when the rule of law goes awry. She also admitted—in a lighter vein—that she was attracted to a career in law, as were others in her generation, by television's ace attorney Perry Mason. Addison graduated from the University of Texas School of Law in 1976 and joined the law firm of Fulbright & Jaworski.[21]

Sometimes the path to becoming a lawyer was a long, circuitous one. Alice Dwyer always wanted to be a lawyer, but her father thought teaching would be a more appropriate endeavor for his daughter. Dwyer dutifully began her studies with this goal in mind. Her work on a doctoral degree was interrupted by marriage, the death of her supervising professor, and the birth of a daughter after a difficult pregnancy. Dwyer returned to El Paso and spent the next ten years teaching history and government. However, the dream of becoming a lawyer was still alive. In 1967 she entered Southern Methodist University law school, graduating three years later. She practiced with other attorneys and then in her own office until she joined El Paso Natural Gas, where she worked in contracts and administration. Even after her retirement in 1990 Dwyer assisted her attorney brothers until their poor health forced the closing of their offices. El Paso attorney Lucy Zavala has called Alice Dwyer "a pioneer and my hero." Zavala explained, "Alice successfully competed in a man's world, and she opened doors for me and other women who followed in her footsteps."[22]

In spite of the growing number of women graduating from law school and the fact that they were no longer considered a novelty, finding a job was still not easy in spite of the pressure exerted by the Equal Employment Opportunity Commission. It was particularly difficult when a woman sought a job in a large firm. Melinda Harmon graduated from the University of Texas in 1972 and then clerked for U.S. District Judge John V. Singleton. When Harmon went job hunting, she found that most large firms were reluctant to hire a woman lawyer. Even if you were hired, she noted, "There was no guarantee that anybody was going to treat you like a real lawyer when you got there."[23] Instead, Harmon joined Exxon Corporation, where she became a trial attorney in the litigation section.[24]

Gayle Albritton can attest to the attitudes regarding the presence of women associates in large firms at that time. When Albritton graduated, she began searching for a job in Dallas. The member of a firm who interviewed her said, "You have great credentials and I would love to hire you, but my senior partner would never hear of hiring a woman." Albritton took a job, instead, on the tax staff of Price Waterhouse and later engaged in private practice as the first female lawyer in Rockwall, Texas.[25]

Some women at Southern Methodist University law school became increasingly disturbed by what they perceived to be continuing discrimination against female lawyers. They were greatly concerned about their lack of opportunities in the legal profession, particularly in the hiring of women as clerks and as associates within firms. The Southern Methodist University Association of Women Law Students showed a large measure of courage in 1975 when they decided to address this issue. The students were joined by four anonymous female practitioners in Dallas who feared reprisals should they be identified. The group brought complaints of discrimination before the Equal Employment Opportunity Commission, which granted them permission to sue. Several out-of-court settlements were agreed on, but the greatest accomplishment was that Dallas firms became more receptive to hiring women lawyers. The downside was that none of the five students, who became known as troublemakers, were hired. Some even left Texas in order to pursue careers in law.[26]

Even as women questioned equal employment policies, more opportunities seemed to open for them. Jane Yount worked first with a firm in Houston after her graduation from South Texas College of Law. As she became an expert in international oil and gas law, she joined Conoco Inc., where she supervised all of their contracts in the Eastern Hemisphere. She then worked as senior attorney with Cities Service Co. In 1976 she was named "One of the Top 100 Corporate Women in the U.S." by *BusinessWeek* magazine. In 1976 Yount was the first woman to receive the Distinguished Alumni Award from South Texas College of Law. At the time of her death, she was with Marathon Oil Company.[27]

Like Yount, other women found corporate law an attractive field. Barbara Quackenbush and Andrea Bryant, however, tried other careers first. When Quackenbush was growing up in Alabama, her father insisted that she become a secretary because jobs would always be available for good secretaries. After finishing college, she moved to Houston and followed her father's advice by finding a job in the Texas Medical Center working for one of the most prominent physicians there. Along the way, a colleague suggested that Quackenbush might enjoy law. She enrolled at the University of Houston Law Center and took classes at night. In 1975, with degree in hand, she was hired as an associate by a major firm in Houston. After several years she decided to shift gears, ultimately becoming an attorney in the real estate division of Exxon Corporation. Quackenbush thought this seemed like a good fit for her interests and skills.[28]

Andrea Bryant began working in Washington, D.C., as a programmer for IBM. After several years of employment, Bryant was sent by her company to Georgetown University School of Law where she, like Quackenbush, attended night classes while continuing in her job. She graduated in 1978, moved to Austin, and became a patent attorney for the IBM office there. Bryant later commented that her employers had a very good equal opportunity program in which they leveled the playing field for everyone. She felt that she had certainly benefited from IBM's climate of affirmative action.[29]

Even when a woman was hired by a firm, she was not guaranteed a long, successful career with it. Many firms in the 1970s felt obliged to hire women—at least, a token woman—but they were still reluctant to advance them within the firm.

Vinson & Elkins, a Houston firm, hired a succession of women lawyers in the early 1970s. Law graduates from the University of Texas, the University of Houston, and Yale University, they all proved to be fully professional, and each gained the respect of her colleagues. To the firm's credit, they were assigned legitimate work instead of being placed in secretarial or librarian slots. Yet it was sometimes performing work that male associates did not want. The first female associate hired was assigned to "blue sky"[30] work. After eight years of almost unrelieved labor in that area and amid no signs of future promotion, she left.[31] The second female associate was also a trained accountant. Assigned to the wills, trust, and estates group, she quickly gained the confidence of clients with whom she worked. She, too, however, saw no prospects of promotion and left after eight years to join another firm.[32] Two other women were hired in that period, and while both appeared to be headed for partnerships, they left after four years and moved into academic law positions.[33]

In 1973, Carol Dinkins, the next woman hired by Vinson & Elkins, followed a different path from that of her predecessors. Dinkins had wanted to be a lawyer since her teen years when she helped in the office of her father, the only attorney in Mathis, Texas. By the time she graduated from the University of Houston Law Center, she had a husband and two young children. Despite having been an editor of the University of Houston law review, Dinkins was not guaranteed a job. She accepted the invitation of one of her professors to conduct federally funded research in a new legal field, environmental law. When she completed two years at this task, Dinkins knew she had found her specialty. During her interview with Vinson & Elkins, she let the firm know that she was not interested in a "mommy track" position and that she wanted to eventually become a partner. Dinkins was hired. Just seven years later she achieved the partnership for which she had worked.[34]

Occasionally a woman was actively recruited by a firm. That was the experience of Doris Rodriguez in Houston, where women still represented a minuscule number of associates in the larger firms. Rodriguez not only graduated near the top of her class at the University of Houston, but she also had prior experience with the Department of Housing and Urban Development. She accepted the offer of Andrews Kurth because it was "a great law firm, had great work, had nice people [and] just seemed to be comprised of a different kind of person."[35] When Rodriguez became a partner in 1987, she was the first Hispanic woman to make partner in any major Houston law firm.[36]

Other women negotiated their roles within firms. Kay Grimes began working at Cox & Smith in San Antonio after graduating from St. Mary's in 1988. At that time, attorneys had two options—associate or partner. After working for one year as an associate, Grimes asked to become a staff attorney, which meant working reduced hours on a nonpartnership track. Her firm was resistant to the idea, but after being presented with Grimes' research on the subject, they relented and approved her request. This practice, which was unique at the time, has become a more common procedure in many firms. Grimes has experienced a varied career in which she worked for a large firm, was a trial attorney for the Equal Employment Opportunity Commission, practiced employment law from a home office during her child-rearing years, and is currently in-house counsel for one of her longtime clients, Lone Star Bakery, Inc. Grimes explained, "I had my first child while in my third year of law school, and that has always served me well in setting career perimeters."[37]

Still other women joined established firms and then went out on their own. Carleen Rhodes Lewis followed this path. After graduating from the University of Virginia Law School in 1984, Lewis moved to Houston and joined the firm of Sewell and Riggs. Four years later she and a male colleague founded the firm of Goforth Lewis. In her law practice Lewis was dedicated to defending the rights of consumers. She is recognized as being among those who began the litigation against Vioxx and other related drugs. Lewis, along with two colleagues, was trial counsel for the first Vioxx case.[38] Sadly, her promising career was cut short when she died at the age of fifty-one.

Hilda Tagle reflected on the dilemma of deciding which path to follow after graduating from law school. She said, "As a woman and minority I had a tendency to gravitate towards public service. Justified or not, I felt that a big firm was not going to want me since I was not in the top ten percent of my class, not Anglo, and not male. I really admire these young lionesses today that start with a big firm. They went out there and put themselves on the line, and did not let fear stand in the way."[39]

As in the past, there were women who opened solo practices.

Although the earliest women lawyers sometimes had no choice but to open their own offices and practice alone, by the 1970s many women preferred building their careers as solo practitioners. Barbara Runge opened her own office after graduating from Texas Tech School of Law in 1973. She acquired two female associates during the next few years, but in 1981 she chose to resume her solo practice. Runge, a family law specialist, says that law is a wonderful profession for a woman because it is challenging and rewarding. She explains, "Every day in my life I have been given the opportunity to help people who are in crisis and who are in what is probably the most traumatic time of their lives."[40]

Five other women decided to blaze a trail in another direction. Zinetta Burney, Algenita Scott Davis, Joan Edwards, Shelvin Hall, and Haroldeen Hartsfield formed their own law firm in Acres Homes, a minority community in Houston that was lacking in basic services. Their firm is believed to be the first all-female black firm in the state. Although it did not remain all-female, the firm, according to Burney, continued to strive to create diversity in the legal industry.[41]

By the 1980s women were entering the partner track in some firms. Still the number of female partners in large firms climbed slowly in comparison to the number of women graduating and entering the legal profession.[42] The real power in a firm comes from being a rainmaker—someone who brings more work to the firm than he or she can do. Traditionally, rainmaking was conducted through male networking between attorney and client. Quite often the settings for such activity were the golf course, sporting events, and after-hours socializing. Women have been forced to devise other methods of bringing in business, in part because of the demands on their time by family.[43]

Although women had long sought equality with male attorneys, they realized that it was going to be difficult to enter the profession under the same rules. Trying to balance family responsibilities and career demands became a nearly herculean task for many women. The profession was forced to make adjustments for women with families.

Maternity leave came into play, as did the creation of part-time positions.[44] Barbara Quackenbush and Beverly Tarpley found they needed to take advantage of these new accommodations. Quackenbush, the first Vinson & Elkins associate to have a baby, recalled that the firm willingly agreed to her maternity leaves, although she does remember that they were minimal in length of time.[45] Tarpley explained that her Abilene firm gave her a great deal of support in her dual roles and was willing to limit her travel while her children were young.[46] While these policies made it easier for women to balance career and family, they made it less likely that these women would rise to positions of power if they practiced in large firms. Instead of the glass ceiling being the only barrier to advancement, now it was the "maternal wall," as it was sometimes called.[47] Demanding hours, inflexible schedules, and emphasis on billable hours placed a burden on women who were the primary caregivers of children. One solution was to place women in a track where they would not achieve as much but they would be able to have a family. The reality, however, was that women were abandoning careers in law firms and in the legal profession, generally, at a higher rate than men.[48]

A recent positive development has been the advancement of women to the position of managing partner in a firm or to a place on the firm's management board. Harriet Miers was one of the first women in the state to head a firm when she became a managing partner of Locke Liddell & Sapp in 1999. Miers, a 1970 graduate of Southern Methodist University School of Law, clerked for U.S. District Judge Joe E. Estes after graduation and was the first female hired by Locke Purnell Boren Laney & Neely (later Locke Liddell & Sapp) in Dallas. Miers, a top litigator in the longtime firm with clients like Microsoft and the Walt Disney Company, rose to become a partner in the firm.[49] Yet the selection of a woman as managing partner of a firm is a rare occurrence. In 2000, only 5 percent of the managing partners of large firms nationwide were women. And in 2002, despite women having previously been selected as managing partners of their firms, not one of the twenty-five largest firms in Texas had a female managing partner.[50]

The glass ceiling, which has seemed firmly in place when managing partners are chosen at the larger firms in the state, has cracked a bit. Demetris Sampson can attest to that. Sampson knew she wanted to be a lawyer when she was eleven years old because she saw it as a way to help people. She speaks of her parents as "terrific role models." She credits Judge Louis A. Bedford, the first African-American judge in Dallas, as her mentor in the legal profession. After receiving her J.D. degree from the University of Texas, she earned her master of laws in taxation from Southern Methodist University. In 1987 Sampson joined a firm (now Linebarger Goggan Blair & Sampson) where she became the first African-American woman to work as a partner in a majority law firm in Dallas. She ultimately became the managing partner. Reflecting on her career, Sampson said, "When you grow up African-American and female . . . regardless of the profession, you learn from the time you're a child that you have to be better to be as good. You have to apply yourself and not be mediocre but to always strive for excellence."[51]

Lisa H. Pennington earned a rare achievement in 2001 when she became managing partner of the Houston office of Baker & Hostetler, an international firm with sixty local attorneys. At that time, she was the only female managing partner of a firm listed among the one hundred largest law firms in Texas. A 1983 graduate of the University of Texas School of Law, Pennington focused her practice on representing management in employment law and tried cases at every level of the judicial system.[52] When she became managing partner, Pennington worked on the premise that happy lawyers are productive lawyers. Realizing that women have responsibilities outside the office, she strived to create an atmosphere more conducive to combining family and work. This included giving praise for jobs well done, providing the tools needed to succeed, and having open communication when problems appeared.[53]

More recently, Jerry Clements was named firm wide managing partner for Locke Liddell & Sapp. Clements had been on Locke Liddell's management committee for nine years and had led the firm's litigation section for five of those years. And even though a major firm is usually managed from its largest or initial office, she is being allowed to lead the firm of nearly 400 lawyers from Austin, rather than from Dallas or Houston. Clements noted that twenty-first century technology will allow her to run the firm remotely, along with air travel between cities. Clements also remarked, "I'll be glad when it's no longer newsworthy when the managing partner of a major law firm is a woman."[54]

In 1992 Texas Wesleyan University School of Law was added to the wide array of schools in Texas educating future lawyers. It evolved from the Dallas–Fort Worth Law School that opened in 1989 and offered night classes to a broad segment of students.[55] After three years of operation, the school had proved that a night school could be successful, but administrators felt it would be more viable if it were connected to a university. They approached Texas Wesleyan University's Board of Trustees, which enthusiastically received the proposal. Thus on August 1, 1992, the Texas Wesleyan University School of Law opened.[56] The school graduated its first class in 1994. Its facilities remained in Irving until space was acquired in downtown Fort Worth in 1996.[57]

For most of the twentieth century, women faced a solid barrier in becoming law school professors. In 1970 there were only thirty-three women who were full professors in law schools in the entire United States. Of these, one was a director of research and nine served as librarians. Thus, in reality, there were only twenty-three full professors teaching in an accredited law school in 1970.[58] Women held other positions such as registrar, admissions officer, or librarian without faculty rank. Women usually occupied lower academic rank on the faculty because they were less likely to be on a tenure track, and they were more often assigned to the courses men avoided: family law, trusts and estates, and legal research and writing.[59]

Margaret Amsler, who retired in 1972, found this to be true when she began her teaching career at Baylor in the 1940s. Amsler taught contracts, agency and partnership, corporations, commercial transactions, real property, personal property, bills and notes, insurance, and surety and mortgages. As Amsler explained, "These were the courses the men didn't want to teach. [The Baylor president] once told me that they were the courses that just didn't have much sex appeal."[60] Amsler was the first woman to receive full professor status in Texas and the third in the United States. At the time of her retirement, Amsler had served the longest tenure of any Baylor Law School faculty member.[61]

Although a few women were considered part-time or adjunct professors, only Margaret Amsler was a full-time professor.[62] Two things occurred that would spur the hiring of more female professors. In 1967, President Lyndon Johnson issued an executive order that prohibited sex discrimination in employment and mandated all recipients of federal contracts to take affirmative steps to hire and promote women.[63] Then, in 1972, the American Bar Association passed a resolution urging law schools to "make substantial efforts to recruit, hire, and promote women professors."[64] Once affirmative action guidelines were established, law schools may have become nervous about possible sex discrimination suits. Between 1967 and 1975 the number of women law professors grew at a faster rate than women lawyers as a whole.[65]

The qualifications for becoming a professor of law in a highly ranked school were considered to be threefold: having a brilliant academic record in law school; serving on law review; and clerking for a judge of outstanding reputation, preferably in a federal court.[66] Women had no difficulty in achieving the academic credentials. In fact, women frequently held the top rankings in their class, and many also served on the law review. Clerking for a judge, however, was more difficult. It wasn't until the 1970s that women could even aim for such an experience. Since most judges were men, they tended to select male law graduates as their clerks. When the number of women on the bench increased, so did the number of female law clerks.[67]

Texas law schools slowly began adding women to their faculties. In 1971 Texas Tech hired its first woman, Ruth Kirby, who ranked first in her graduating class that same year. Kirby taught at Texas Tech for four years. Annette Marples, an honors graduate of Texas Tech, joined the faculty in 1973 and taught until her retirement in 1992. During those years Professor Marples served as both assistant and associate dean. Marilyn Phelan, who joined the faculty in 1974, still teaches and holds the Paul Whitfield Horn Professorship, the highest academic honor conferred on faculty members by Texas Tech University. Professor Phelan also served as associate dean of the law school and for six years was general counsel for the university.[68]

St. Mary's University School of Law considers Frances Sawyer Henke its first female faculty member. Sawyer was appointed as librarian in 1947 and was also a lecturer in legal bibliography for fifteen years. A library job has been a common assignment for women on law school faculties over the years. It was also a common procedure to combine a woman's teaching assignment with some administrative duty as St. Mary's did after their appointments in the early 1970s. Phyllis C. Harper was assistant dean and assistant professor of law, Sue M. Hall served as director of placement and alumni relations as well as assistant professor, Teresa B. Phillips was both an associate law librarian and associate professor, and Shirley W. Butts was an associate professor of law before being named to an appellate court.[69] Bonita K. Roberts was the first woman to receive tenure at St. Mary's, and Ana M. Novoa was the first Mexican-American woman to receive tenure there.[70]

Betty Dohoney, like the professors at St. Mary's, combined administrative duties with classroom teaching. Dohoney, a graduate of Baylor Law School, began teaching at her alma mater in 1972. She remained on the faculty for sixteen years with seven of those years as a full-time professor. During some of that time she also served as assistant dean.[71]

A listing of South Texas College of Law faculty reveals that Sheryl Bolton Johnson was the first woman faculty member, in 1972–73, and Ramona Freeman John taught in 1973–74. Both were part-time faculty members. Georgia Miers, a 1961 graduate of South Texas, was the first woman law librarian, serving from 1961 to 1965. No other women's names appear until 1977, when Joan Heisler, Beverly A. Spencer, and Lyn Beatrice Adams were listed as faculty members. There is no indication of the courses they taught. Heisler and Spencer were adjunct faculty, and Adams was an associate professor.[72]

Irene Merker Rosenberg joined the faculty at the University of Houston Law Center in 1974 and became its first female tenured professor. Rosenberg, a graduate of New York University College of Law, came to Houston from New York City, where she practiced as an attorney with the Juvenile Rights Division of the Legal Aid Society and became nationally known as a scholar in juvenile justice. Rosenberg is still teaching at the University of Houston, where she developed two new courses in the law school curriculum: juvenile justice and legal analysis.[73] Rosenberg was joined on the faculty in 1977 by a former student, Jacqueline Lang Weaver, who teaches, among other courses, oil and gas law and policy and environmental law. Weaver, coauthor of the leading treatise on Texas oil and gas, remains on the University of Houston faculty.[74]

The University of Texas had given faculty status to librarian Helen Hargrave in the late 1920s.[75] However, not until 1974 was a woman hired for a full-time faculty position other than librarian. That woman was Barbara Bader Aldave, who received her J.D. degree from the University of California at Berkeley, where she was in the top 1 percent of her class and was admitted to Order of the Coif. Aldave came to the University of Texas after teaching at both the University of Oregon

School of Law and at her alma mater, the University of California. During her fifteen years at the Austin campus, Aldave rose to the rank of professor, teaching business associations, law and literature, constitutional law, and securities regulations. Aldave made history in 1989 when she became the first woman to head a Texas law school. St. Mary's University made her dean of its law school, a position she held for nine years. Aldave left St. Mary's in 1998 and returned to the University of Oregon School of Law where she had begun her teaching career.[76]

Academic history was repeated in Texas in 2000 when the University of Houston Law Center named Nancy B. Rapoport as dean and professor of law. Rapoport received her J.D. degree from Stanford Law School, after which she clerked for a judge on the Ninth Circuit Court of Appeals. Before coming to the University of Houston, her career included practicing bankruptcy law in San Francisco and serving as associate dean for student affairs as well as professor of law at Ohio State University. She then moved to the University of Nebraska College of Law to become dean and professor of law. As dean of the Bates College of Law at the University of Houston for six years, Rapoport oversaw the hiring of fifteen trained and tenure-track faculty members, the first curriculum revision in twenty years, a new strategic plan, two new centers, and a significant increase in fundraising and alumni support. Rapoport, a nationally recognized leader in curriculum development, unexpectedly resigned in 2006 over differing views for the future of the school. She is now the Gordon & Silver, Ltd., Professor of Law at the William S. Boyd School of Law at the University of Nevada. Rapoport has written *How Legal Education Fails Law Students*, in which she makes a strong case for change in educating law students today.[77]

While Texas has had only two women serve as deans of law schools, there were thirty-six female deans nationwide in 2006.[78] The number of women in academia in Texas compares favorably with national figures: women comprise 35 percent of law school faculties in

Texas while women make up 38.2 percent of faculties nationwide.[79] Among Texas schools, Thurgood Marshall School of Law at Texas Southern University has the highest percentage of women faculty members at 48 percent, while the University of Houston Law Center has the lowest at 23 percent. Only 40 percent of the full-time women faculty members in the state, however, hold the rank of professor.[80] Law students today will at least experience having a woman professor, unlike those students in the 1950s and 1960s who had never even seen one. Female faculty members have also been instrumental in introducing new courses on women and the law and on sex discrimination.

A large number of women have served as adjunct professors of law at schools. Many have been innovative in establishing new programs. Justice Bea Ann Smith taught law at the University of Texas as an adjunct professor from 1982 to 1989 and has continued to teach since 1997 while in private practice and during her tenure on the Third Court of Appeals. Smith was a leading force in establishing the law school's judicial internship program in which judges supervise students who intern for a semester with the Third Court of Appeals, the Texas Supreme Court, and the Texas Court of Criminal Appeals, as well as with federal judges, the Travis County Probate Court, and the State Office of Administrative Hearings. The program has expanded to include judges outside the Austin area. Asked about the benefits of these internships, Smith said, "I always stressed to students that the best part of their internships would be the improvement in their writing skills. And I think we lived up to our part of that bargain."[81]

Presenting legal information in a clear and concise manner was the goal of Michol O'Connor when she took a new direction in her career in 1992. O'Connor, a 1973 graduate of the University of Houston Law Center, had worked in almost every aspect of the law—briefing attorney for the First Court of Appeals, assistant district attorney in Harris County, assistant U.S. attorney for the Southern District, a solo practice, and associate in an established firm. In 1988 O'Connor was elected to the First Court of Appeals, where she served as a justice for twelve years. Her vast experience took her in a new career direction in 1992. O'Connor's goal of presenting legal information in a clear and concise manner led her to found Jones McClure Publishing. The company provides practicing attorneys with books on various fields of substantive and procedural law. O'Connor explained that this unusual legal pursuit emerged from the early years in her career when she realized that many legal documents were difficult to comprehend, thus preventing lawyers from acquiring knowledge needed for their casework. She hopes that her books have changed that reality for many in the profession.[82]

In 1990 Texas claimed 10,679 female lawyers, a little less than a third of the state's total lawyers. Women comprised 41 percent of the state's law school students.[83] Although much had changed in the past few years, students reported that some things were unchanged. A study was conducted in the early 1990s by interviewing women attending thirty law schools across the country, including the University of Texas and Texas Tech University. The women reported that they were no longer reminded constantly that they were taking the place of men, but said they still received demeaning comments and their concerns were often ignored. Others reported that there were few opportunities to connect with their female classmates on common issues of interest.[84]

A group of first-year female students at the University of Texas, seeking a way to work together toward a common goal, founded the *Texas Journal of Women and the Law*. As Elyse Rosenblum recalled, "[We] were looking for an intellectually comfortable and challenging home at the law school. We met in the library and talked about different ideas for starting a journal. We argued about many things: the mission statement, how to fund our project, the name."[85] But in the end, as Rosenblum explained, the journal became more than just a law journal. It became the central focus of these women's law school experience. In the process, the women proved they were not wasting space in law school. Rather, they had created something of lasting value that would help other women find their place more easily. The *Texas Journal of Women and the Law* continues to inspire dialogue about legal, social, and political issues affecting women—their rights, their bodies, their careers, their families. The staff believes that the journal's use of independent inquiry into feminist issues will raise awareness among the public and accelerate reform in the lives of Texas women.[86]

A lack of bonding among women students was a concern of Judge Carolyn Clause Garcia when she discovered in 1991 that women were being discouraged from networking and supporting other women. Garcia started a mentoring group for female students at South Texas College of Law. She explained, "They were teaching women law students that they shouldn't include on their resume that they were members of women law groups; that they wouldn't be hired; that they would be scrutinized as being wide-eyed and liberal."[87] Garcia added that she was shocked that feminism would be portrayed as having such a negative impact. In reality women were proving that they were effective communicators, both in a courtroom setting and in written briefs. Yet some of the stereotypes associated with women still existed and were often perpetuated to keep women in the background.[88]

Women lawyers in Texas have greatly increased in the past two decades, but one family has set a record of its own—seven female lawyers on the branches of their family tree. This story begins with Miriam Barrier Hall, who was admitted to the bar in 1926 after graduating from the University of Texas. Hall practiced for several years with her husband in Harlingen. Three of Hall's nieces studied law, also at the University of Texas—Barbara Hinds Finney, Patricia Hinds Spearman, and Mary Pearl Hall Williams. Finney had a thirty-year career as a trial attorney with Humble (Exxon) Oil Company, while Spearman practiced law in San Angelo, served as a municipal judge there, and later taught at North Carolina Central Law School in Durham. Williams was a longtime Travis County judge whose two daughters, Shelley Williams Austin and Stephanie Williams, graduated from the University of Texas School of Law. But that is not the end of this family saga. Finney's granddaughter, Jessica Bartlett, has completed her first year at the University of Illinois Law School. This family has provided its own role models for succeeding generations of women lawyers.[89]

A defining moment in history came in 1981 for women—not just for those in the legal profession, but for all women in our country—when Sandra Day O'Connor was named to the U.S. Supreme Court. Texans were proud to claim Justice O'Connor as one of their own, since she was born in El Paso and received most of her education as a young girl there.[90] Women were inspired to see a woman placed in such a high position of honor and responsibility.[91] Women in the legal profession were encouraged that women were being recognized as capable of sitting on our nation's highest court. All women have benefited greatly since that historic occurrence a quarter of a century ago.

Studies have shown that a sizeable percentage of women go to law school because they are interested in social justice, not for status and money. Sylvia Ann Law, former president of the Society of American Law Teachers, has said, "Women are attracted by the perception that law shapes social relationships and if you understand it, you can build, say, a better health care system, or a criminal justice system, or bring more equity to family law."[92] Women have brought a unique perspective to the law profession, whether they were the pioneers of yesterday or those in the twenty-first century.

Notes

1. *Texas Bar Journal,* 67, 10:889.

2. Mary Flood, "She knows diversity's more than lip service," *Houston Chronicle,* May 13, 2007, D1, 5.

3. Ann MacNaughton, interview by author, June 15, 2007.

4. Dusky, 21.

5. Epstein, 55.

6. Roberta W. Francis, "The History Behind the Equal Rights Amendment," http://www.equalrightsamendment.org/era.htm (accessed April 12, 2007). Alice Paul, leader of the National Woman's Party, the more militant wing of the suffrage movement, introduced the original version of an equal rights amendment at the 75th anniversary of the Seneca Falls Women's Rights Convention of 1848. It read: "Men and women shall have equal rights throughout the United States and every place subject to its jurisdiction." In 1943 Paul rewrote the amendment in its present form. Although it was presented in every session of Congress, it never received strong support until the civil rights movement erupted.

7. Ibid.

8. Ibid. Opponents also claimed that the amendment would deny a woman's right to be supported by her husband, privacy rights would be overturned, and abortion and homosexual marriages would be upheld. Other opponents were advocates of states' rights and fundamentalist religious groups. For a discussion by women lawyers on the pros and cons, see *Texas Bar Journal*, 26:1004, 1005, 1074–76, 1078–79.

9. Dusky, 261.

10. In the 1970s the B&PW organization was the strongest channel through which women worked in raising awareness of laws discriminating against women and in taking action to change those laws. As women were elected to lawmaking position and governing bodies and as women bar associations formed, the B&PW ceased to be as important to women in the legal arena. It had been, however, the strongest ally in promoting women's rights for half a century, http//en.wikipedia.org/wiki/Business_and_Professional_Women.html.

11. Sherilyn Brandenstein, "Texas Equal Rights Amendment," *Handbook of Texas,* 6:326.

12. *Texas Bar Journal*, 55, 1:13.

13. *Texas Bar Journal*, 53, 9:1050.

14. *South Texas College of Law Quarterly*, Summer 1995.

15. *Texas Journal of Women and the Law*, 8:349.

16. Ibid.

17. Ibid., 351.

18. Ibid., 352.

19. Ibid., 353.

20. Mary Alice Robbins, "More Women Move Into Firm Management," *Texas Lawyer*, November 11, 2002 (reprint).

21. Ibid. Women frequently mentioned that they were inspired to become lawyers after watching Perry Mason on television. It was no accident that a male lawyer became their role model, since for decades "lady lawyers" had usually been portrayed in the media as attractive women more interested in matters of the heart than those of the courtroom, where they appeared young, naive, and inexperienced. They were frequently featured in comedy roles because women lawyers were not taken seriously at that time. By the late 1970s—perhaps in deference to the women's movement—the image of women lawyers improved somewhat in the media, especially on television. They were now portrayed as being competent, tough-minded, cool, dauntless, and ardent advocates. However, they were always cast in supporting roles. In 1981 the role of a savvy assistant public defender in "Hill Street Blues" finally made a woman lawyer the leading character. See Ric Sheffield, "On Film: A Social History of Women Lawyers in Popular Culture 1930 to 1990," *Loyola of Los Angeles Entertainment Law Journal*, Vol. 14, 1993, pp. 73–114.

22. *El Paso Bar Bulletin*, May 2005, 5–6.

23. Hyman, 394.

24. Ibid.

25. Gayle Albritton, correspondence to author, October 4, 2006.

26. Payne, *Dallas*, 277; Raggio, 193.

27. *Texas Bar Journal*, 54, 11:1256.

28. Barbara Quackenbush, interview by author, March 29, 2007.

29. *Texas Bar Journal*, 53, 9:1052.

30. Blue sky laws are statutes that provide for the regulation and supervision of securities offerings and sales and are intended to protect citizens from investing in fraudulent companies. These laws acquired their name in the Unites States Supreme

Court case *Hall v. Geiger-Jones Co.*, 242 U.S. 539 (1916), when the court discussed "speculative schemes which have no more basis than so many feet of blue sky." *Hall*, 242 U.S. at 550.

31. Hyman, 394–95.

32. Ibid., 395–96.

33. Ibid.

34. Ibid., 397–99.

35. Eric L. Fredrickson, *Andrews & Kurth: The first 100 years of excellence* (Houston: Andrews & Kurth L.L.P., 2002), 107.

36. Ibid., 107–108.

37. Kay Grimes, correspondence to author, September 11, 2006.

38. *Houston Chronicle*, June 7, 2006, B5.

39. *Texas Bar Journal*, 53, 9:1052. Hilda Tagle began her legal career working in the city attorney's office in Corpus Christi. She later was an assistant county attorney for Nueces County. In 1980 Tagle entered private practice. Five years later she was appointed to a Nueces County Court at Law, the first step in her judicial career.

40. Caroline Marciano, "Keeping Up with Past Presidents: Barbara Runge," *Newsletter of Association of Women Attorneys*, April 2006, 5.

41. *Texas Bar Journal*, 53, 9:1053–54.

42. The national figure for female partners in law firms was 2% in 1980. By 1991 it had risen to 10%, and in 2002 women held 17% of the partnerships.

43. Harrington, 29.

44. Ibid., 31–32, 238. Harrington argues that the single most difficult barrier against women advancing in the legal profession is the issue of bringing up children. The system is not designed to integrate the two demands on women: work and family. Until this is done, Harrington declares that more women will opt out of the profession.

45. Quackenbush interview.

46. *Texas Journal of Women and the Law*, 8:342.

47. Timothy O'Brien, "Up the Down Staircase: Why Do So Few Women Reach

the Top of Big Law Firms?" *The New York Times,* March 18, 2006, Business Section 1, 4. Interestingly, some women in the nineteenth century were attracted to law because, in their opinion, the work schedule could be flexible. A young woman lawyer in Illinois even thought it was good for one's health to "spend a day in bed when the occasion demands."

48. Ibid.

49. Michael Fletcher, "Quiet but Ambitious White House Counsel Makes Life of Law," *Washington Post,* June 20, 2005, http://www.washingtonpost.com/wp-dyn/content/article/2005/06/20/AR2005062001161.html (accessed September 10, 2007).

50. Robbins. Others mentioned in the article were Laura Franze with Akin, Gump, Strauss, Hauer & Feld in Dallas; Kimberly Yelkin in the Austin office of Gardere Wynne Sewell; Tracie Renfroe with Bracewell & Patterson (now Bracewell & Guiliani) in Houston; Lynne Liberato with Haynes and Boone in Houston; Jerry Clements with Locke Liddell & Sapp in Dallas; Marie Yeates in the Houston office of Vinson & Elkins; and Linda Addison with Fulbright & Jaworski in Houston. From 1996 to 2000 Myra McDaniel was the managing partner of Bickerstaff, Heath Smiley, Pollan, Kever and McDaniel in Austin. According to *Perspectives* (Spring 1999), McDaniel was the first African-American woman in the nation to become the managing partner of a major firm.

51. Haley Shapley, "Demetris Sampson: A Servant to All," *Eclipse,* January-February 2007, 47.

52. Robbins.

53. Mary Sit-DuVall, "Managing Partner Brings Others Along," *Houston Chronicle,* February 7, 2004, 1C, 5C.

54. Monica Perrin, "Locke names managing partners for Texas, Houston," *Houston Business Journal,* October 20–26, 2006, 14A.

55. Arnold, 64–68.

56. Arnold, 70. Texas Wesleyan University School of Law opened the 1997–98 session with an enrollment of approximately 40% women. When asked what women offer the legal community, Associate Dean Malinda L. Seymore replied that they bring "such important trends as the recognition of women's issues as legitimate areas of study and the different viewpoints that women offer, especially related to media-

tion law." (77) The current enrollment of women is 51.7% of the entire school's enrollment. See DeLoggio Achievement Program: Women in Law School, http://www.deloggio.com/choosing/women.htm (accessed August 5, 2007).

57. Arnold, 72–73.

58. Epstein, 220.

59. Dusky, 92. Women professors rarely taught the courses with the reputation of being the most intellectually challenging and prestigious, such as constitutional law. Such courses brought more opportunities for publishing and public speaking, which translated into a higher income.

60. Aldave, 298.

61. Ibid., 295.

62. Ibid., 298. Although Amsler was an instructor or associate professor from the very beginning of her teaching career, she did not obtain the rank of full professor until 1955—fifteen years after she began teaching. History of the Baylor Law School Faculty, http://law.baylor.edu/History/Faculty.htm (accessed March 15, 2007).

63. Epstein, 220.

64. Ibid., 221.

65. Ibid., 220–23. In a study conducted in 1976, lawyer/sociologist D. Kelly Weisberg found that the proportion of women law faculty in twelve top-ranked schools, including the University of Texas, was only 4.8%.

66. Epstein, 220; Dusky, 95. Dusky adds a fourth component to the requirements: working for a couple of years for a prestigious law firm or a public interest organization such as the ACLU or Legal Aid. U.S. Supreme Court Justice Ruth Bader Ginsburg is a good example. Justice Ginsburg attended one elite law school, Harvard, and graduated from another, Columbia. She tied for first place in her graduating class, made law review, and clerked for a federal court judge. When she could not find a job with a law firm, she taught a few courses at Columbia, which helped her get a teaching job at Rutgers Law School. Then in 1972 Ginsburg was appointed as the first woman professor at Columbia. (Epstein, 228)

67. Epstein, 246. Justice William O. Douglas appointed the first female clerk on the U.S. Supreme Court in 1944. No others were appointed until 1966. By 1980 fifty-two female clerks had been appointed, although during this time not every justice

chose even one woman. Epstein concluded that justices considered "liberal" have more often chosen women as clerks than those labeled "conservative." Yet President Ronald Reagan appointed the first woman to the U.S. Supreme Court. Justice Ginsburg has indicated that slightly more than half of her clerks at any given time are women.

68. Dean Walter Huffman, Texas Tech University School of Law, correspondence to author, March 31, 2007.

69. Professor Vincent Johnson, St. Mary's University School of Law, correspondence to author, April 2, 2007.

70. St. Mary's University School of Law Faculty, http://www.stmarytx.edu/law/index.php/go=fac_novoa (accessed May 27, 2007).

71. History of Baylor Law School Faculty, http://law.baylor.edu/history/faculty.htm (accessed May 22, 2007).

72. Listing of Library Staff, 1952–96; Listing of South Texas College of Law Faculty 1923–85, Fred Parks Law Library; correspondence with South Texas College of Law Special Collections Librarian.

73. University of Houston Law Center Faculty, http://www.law.uh.edu/faculty/main.asp?PID=37 (accessed May 22, 2007).

74. Ibid., http://www.law.uh.edu/faculty/main.asp?PID=45 (accessed May 22, 2007).

75. Hargrave is discussed in chapter 2 of this book.

76. University of Oregon School of Law Faculty, http://www.law.uoregon.edu/faculty/aldave (accessed April 27, 2007).

77. University of Houston Law Center Faculty, www.law.uh.edu/faculty/main.asp?PID=35 (accessed May 22, 2007).

78. Association of American Law Schools Statistical Report on Law School Faculty, 2005–2006, Table 2B, http://www.aals.org/statistics/0506/0506_T2B_tit4_8yr.html (accessed May 22, 2007).

79. Ibid.; figures compiled by author.

80. Compiled by author using both correspondence and online statistical information from each of the nine law schools in the state.

81. *The University of Texas at Austin School of Law, News and Events*, November 10, 2006, http://www.utexas.edu/law/news/2006/111006_smith.html (accessed July 1, 2007).

82. Justice Michol O'Connor, telephone interview by author, June 30, 2007.

83. Smith, Appendix C, Chart C5, 297. The number of female lawyers had tripled in the last decade. Of these, 818 were Hispanic, 573 were black, and 137 were from other ethnic groups. While the number of minority women had increased, 98% of the lawyers were white.

84. Dusky, 29–30.

85. *Texas Journal of Women and the Law*, 8:358.

86. Ibid., http://www.utexas.edu/law/journals/tjwl/ (accessed June 3, 2007).

87. Debra Beachy, "In the door, but not in charge," *Houston Chronicle*, November 9, 1994, E1, 4, 5.

88. Ibid.

89. Patricia Spearman, correspondence to author, September 30, 2007; Barbara Finney, correspondence to author, October 17, 2006, and March 29, 2007; J. C. Hall, telephone interview by author, March 29, 2007.

90. Joan Biskupic, *Sandra Day O'Connor: How the First Woman on the Supreme Court Became Its Most Influential Justice* (New York: Harper Collins, 2005), 16–21. Although Justice O'Connor's home was on the Lazy B Ranch in the Gila River Valley of Arizona, she spent the school months with her grandmother in El Paso, returning home for the holidays and the summer months. In El Paso, she attended Radford School for Girls and Austin High School from which she graduated at the age of sixteen.

91. In 1949 India Edwards, Executive Director of the Women's Division of the Democratic National Committee, lobbied for a woman to be appointed to fill at least one of the two vacancies on the U.S. Supreme Court. President Harry Truman seemed amenable to the idea, but the two nominations eventually went to men. The sitting court had complained that a woman on the court would prevent them from taking their robes off, putting their feet up, and discussing cases as they always had in the past. *See St. Mary's Law Journal*, 28:529.

92. Dusky, 26.

Chapter Five

Serving the Public Interest

IN 1916 WHEN SARAH MENEZES MADE THE HIGHEST SCORE on the bar examination, the legal community was effectively alerted that women could become a force within the profession. Although the lofty accomplishment did not result in her immediate employment, Menezes was finally hired by a Dallas law firm to manage its office staff. She later recalled, "It was considered an exceptionally fine job for a woman. I had my name on the door and that was really something in those days. I was very proud. They had several young [male] lawyers and didn't really need me although they occasionally sent me to the courthouse on errands."[1] In 1925 Menezes was hired as the first female lawyer in the United States Attorney's Office for the Northern District of Texas—another accomplishment of note. She remained in that position until 1933.[2]

Government practice tended to be a protected environment for women lawyers. These positions, considered to be for the public good, provided job security and did not require the incumbents to look for business. Most of the cases could be handled during normal work hours. Furthermore, women did not face the discrimination that existed in the private sector. These advantages appealed to women and frequently outweighed the reality that their wages in the public sector would likely be less than those in private establishments.

In spite of Menezes having acquired a job as an assistant U.S. attorney, no more than one woman worked in the Dallas office at any given time during the next fifty years.[3] The first woman on record as an assistant U.S. attorney for the Southern District of Texas was Lou Nora Spiller, who was admitted to the State Bar in 1944 after graduating from George Washington University School of Law and doing postgraduate work at Columbia University. Spiller remained in the U.S. Attorney's Office for several years after being hired in 1947.[4]

By the 1960s, positions as assistant U.S. attorneys became more available to women. Four colleagues in the Houston division of the Southern District decided to utilize the experience they had received there to form an all-female law firm. Mary Sinderson, Anna Stool, Mary Daffin, and Angela Flores represented diversity in ethnicity, age, and legal education. Their common thread was that they had been associated with the U.S. Attorney's Office for tenures ranging from four to thirteen years. In an interview conducted on the opening of their firm, they reflected on their legal careers and how they became lawyers. Flores, who came from a family of lawyers and had planned since childhood to study law, explained, "I like the advocacy forum. I've always been pretty outspoken." A premed student before she switched to law, Stool reflected, "Being in school in the sixties raised my consciousness, and I realized that one way you could effect change was in the system." Daffin admitted that she had never fostered ambitions to be a lawyer, but her husband and brother-in-law were both lawyers for whom she had done research. She said that they encouraged her to study law because she had "a knack for research." Sinderson had been the senior litigation officer for the U.S. attorney in Houston—one of only thirty in the country—and had entered law school when she was twenty-nine and the mother of two small children. As to her reasons for becoming a lawyer she explained, "I'm very analytical and the law suited my temperament . . . the law is also the last bastion of the generalist. If you're a lawyer, you have to know something about everything. It's a continuous learning experience." They were unanimous in their agreement that the federal courthouse was a great training ground and an exciting place to practice.[5]

Not until 1993 was a woman named U.S. attorney in Texas. Gaynelle Griffin Jones, a former appellate judge then practicing with the firm of Vinson & Elkins in Houston, was appointed by President Bill Clinton to fill the position of U.S. attorney in the Southern District of Texas. Jones, a graduate of Boston College School of Law, had seventeen years' experience as a prosecutor, as both an assistant district attorney and an assistant U.S. attorney.[6] Jones remained in the office for four years, during which she managed a staff of 130 lawyers in six offices covering an area of forty-three counties.[7]

The Northern District of Texas received its first female U.S. attorney in 2002 when President George W. Bush appointed Jane Boyle to the post. Like Jones, Boyle had prosecutorial experience, both as an assistant district attorney and as an assistant U.S. attorney. Before becoming U.S. attorney, she had spent twelve years as U.S. magistrate in the Northern District. Boyle remained in the post of U.S. attorney until President Bush appointed her as a U.S. district judge in 2004.[8]

When President Lyndon B. Johnson launched the War on Poverty in 1964, community action programs were set up in many cities. In 1966 the U.S. Supreme Court ordered a mandatory federally funded public defender system. Within a few years, the number of lawyers available to represent poor defendants rose more than six fold across the country. Until then no course on poverty law had ever been taught at a law school. By the late 1960s dozens of courses were being offered to meet the needs of the many students anxious to serve as public defenders.[9]

Marjorie A. Meyers was one of those attracted to this field. Meyers earned her J.D. degree from the University of Pennsylvania, after which she became an assistant federal public defender, a post she held for sixteen years. In 2004 the Fifth Circuit Court of Appeals appointed Meyers as public defender for the Southern District of Texas. She was the first woman attorney to hold this position.[10]

Although their ascent to these high government offices was slow, women had found a variety of opportunities in government service during their early years on the legal scene. World War I created some jobs for these aspiring lawyers, although the records describing their duties are sparse. Women attorneys hoped, as did the suffragists struggling for the right to vote at the same time, that their wartime service would broaden their acceptance into the legal field. While the suffragists won victory in attaining partial voting rights in Texas in 1918 and complete suffrage with the passage of the Nineteenth Amendment in 1920, most women attorneys still found doors closed to them.

Women realized that they could gain valuable experience in prosecutorial offices where they were able to work on cases independently and gain knowledge that would take years to acquire in a private office. In the course of this work, they could interact with police, defense lawyers, judges, and jurors. In the past, women were thought to be unsuited or incompetent to handle even pretrial negotiation, much less to bring in an indictment and conviction in the courtroom. Courtroom appearances were met with disapproval from most male lawyers since the appearance of a woman lawyer in the courtroom had such negative connotations. Nevertheless, some male district attorneys hired women to work in their offices. In the beginning, they were probably kept in the background and seldom participated publicly in a trial. One of the earliest assistant district attorneys was Helen Viglini, who was hired in Dallas County in 1920. Viglini had been admitted to the bar in 1919 after studying in a law office. Her experience as an assistant district attorney stood her in good stead when she opened her own office, which she maintained for forty years. It likely helped her, too, when she was the first woman to argue a case before the Texas Supreme Court.[11] Viglini's hiring did not immediately open the district attorney's door for other women, but gradually others filled this position. Mildred Douglass followed Viglini in the Dallas office,[12] while Louisa Terrill Pearson joined the Nueces County office in Corpus Christi.[13] In 1936 the Harris County office hired two women, Joyce Burg and Louise Callaway, a recent South Texas School of Law graduate.[14] Burg later recalled her tenure in the district attorney's office by explaining, "I didn't stay long because after six months he [the district attorney] called me in and said, 'I have to list you as a secretary because there's another lawyer that we need to hire.' And this was a night school lawyer, and I thought, I went to the University of Texas and I said, 'I'm not going to stay.' He was going to cut my salary. The $25 didn't bother me too much, but I put my hat on—in those days we always wore hats—and I never went back."[15]

Over the next several years women found places in the state's prosecutorial system in defiance of the still-prevailing attitude that women had no place in a courtroom or dealing with court-related matters. After all, with a minuscule number of women on the bench and no women on juries, the courtroom was still a male domain. In spite of the continued prejudice against female trial attorneys, Eva Bloore Barnes became Tarrant County's first assistant district attorney in 1945.[16] Naomi Harney was hired in Potter County a few years later,[17] while Ann Gann was the first in Cameron County[18] and Emma Garrett McMillan was the trailblazer in Brazoria County.[19]

By 1955, women were sitting on juries. Louise Raggio, as Dallas County's lone female prosecutor in the early 1950s, tried a case before an all-woman jury, believed to be the first in the state. She recalled that the women sat there with fixed jaws and steely eyes, listened to the testimony, and within minutes returned a guilty verdict, thereby refuting the commonly held belief that women would be too soft-hearted to convict a defendant.[20] As the years passed, other women made their marks as assistant district attorneys in their areas: Jean Wallace in Midland County,[21] Norma Fink in Bexar County,[22] and Elizabeth Nowlin Craver in Lubbock County.[23]

When Shirley Butts joined the district attorney's office in Fort Worth, she was the second woman to occupy that position. She was assigned to the civil service section of the office which dealt primarily with juvenile cases. Her assignment was greeted by the other assistant district attorneys and the judges with a lack of enthusiasm. Butts remembers vividly her first day in court when she was told to meet another staff attorney at the courthouse. She appeared carrying files about which she knew nothing. Her colleague never appeared, as this was a setup used to initiate new attorneys in the office. The judge was not happy with this new attorney, regardless of the circumstances. Butts said later that the experience taught her to never appear in court unprepared. Butts, eventually, was put in charge of the civil section. During her tenure in the district attorney's office, she appeared before every court in the civil courts building, learned how to tailor her practice to suit each individual judge, and came to appreciate the critical importance of getting along with the court clerks. Her experience proved to be invaluable when she later became a judge.[24]

Discrimination frequently followed women into the courtroom. As Marta Rosas once explained, "The most noticeable discrimination I have run into since starting to practice law was when I prosecuted a particularly difficult child custody case filed against a woman for abducting her kids. One of the jurors after the trial ran into the defense lawyer and said that during voir dire she had thought that I could not be any good since I was filling two quotas—that of a woman and a minority—but subsequently decided she was wrong. I am sure she was not the first to feel that way." Rosas, in contrast to the experiences of other minority women, said that she did not encounter discrimination in her classes at Texas Tech, although she was one of only three Hispanic females in a class of nearly two hundred.[25]

It was not until 1957 that a woman became a district attorney, when Edna Cisneros assumed that position in Willacy County.[26] In spite of the ever increasing number of female assistants, the glass ceiling so often imposed on women kept the number of female district attorneys low. The office was still considered a male domain when Amy Adams became the first woman in the state to defeat a male candidate in a contested election for district attorney. Adams was the sole assistant in the Parker County office in 1986 when the district attorney unexpectedly resigned. She was appointed to act as district attorney for six months until an election could be held to fill the unexpired term. Her opponent was a well-funded male whose family was widely connected in the area. Adams was young and virtually unknown in the county. Furthermore, she was not politically involved and had never thought about running for office. After a whirlwind campaign, Adams—against all odds—was victorious. Her success in winning that office and remaining there after two subsequent elections was regarded as strong encouragement for the growing number of women who aspired to legal careers. Female district attorneys, however, are still rare in Texas.[27]

Women encountered more success in filling the position of county attorney, although that process was also slow. Nellie Gray Robertson was the state's first female county attorney when she held that position in Hood County from 1918 to 1925.[28] The caption under Robertson's photograph in the 1918 University of Texas yearbook was prophetic, as it read, "Nellie expects to be the first female county attorney in Texas."[29]Among the women who held the office during these early years were Artie Fultz Davis in Grimes County,[30] Catherine L. Miller in Bee County,[31] Annie Justice Swaim in Concho County,[32] Naomi Harney in Potter County,[33] and Anna Ramírez in Webb County.[34] Harney was elected to the post in 1961 and resigned in 1974 to seek a county court at law judgeship. She had previously worked as an attorney for the city of Amarillo and as assistant district attorney in Potter

County. At the time of her resignation Harney commented, "The field [of law] is wide open for women in governmental, corporate, or private practice on her own." Then she added, "A woman must work harder to prove herself as she must in any profession."[35]

Marsha Floyd did not need to prove herself, but she worked diligently to ensure that the Harris County attorney's office was not stripped of its constitutional powers. In 1983 when the County Commissioners Court created the Harris County Toll Road Authority—constituting itself as the Board of the Authority—it hired outside counsel to represent the county. The county attorney filed suit to prevent the commissioners from acting as the board and usurping the powers of the county attorney's office. Floyd was the lead attorney on the case and, after years of litigation, she prevailed. As first assistant county attorney in the late 1980s, Floyd brought another case to a successful conclusion. When the state forced Harris County to keep state prisoners at the county's own expense, the county sued and won to recover millions of dollars owed them by the state. The judgment was so large that the governor called a special session of the legislature to pass legislation that would punish Harris County unless it made a more favorable settlement with the state. Floyd proved that a woman could be a successful litigant, no matter how tough the battle. As one of her colleagues said, "She made law with her brain and hard work." Floyd was also instrumental in establishing the Government Lawyers Section of the State Bar of Texas.[36]

The difficulty of balancing family and practicing law was one that confronted women in government positions just as it did for those in other areas of the legal profession. Mary McKerall's experience showed that a supervisor who recruited women and sought to make them an integral part of the staff could make the difference in creating equality in the work place. McKerall had joined the Harris County attorney's staff in 1974 as the only female in an office of thirty-two males. When she was named a deputy division chief in 1983, McKerall announced that she was expecting her second child and asked if that would be a problem. The answer was a resounding "no." McKerall added that the staff of women attorneys reached 50 percent of the entire staff by the late 1980s and that many of these were young mothers. Unfortunately, not every government attorney worked in such a favorable environment.[37]

Women were city attorneys in smaller communities across Texas as early as 1934. Some of the first were Edwardine Couch in Bonham,[38] Emma Webb in Elgin,[39] Fannie Gray Clegg in Trinity,[40] Willie Zac Drummond in Mission,[41] Martha Lipscomb in Gainesville,[42] and Agnes Sagebiel in Fredericksburg.[43] They were followed by Morinne Taylor Perkins in Rusk,[44] Bettie Jo Stock in Portland,[45] Emma Garrett McMillan in Angleton,[46] and Maria Luisa Slaughter in Abilene.[47] In 1977 the city of San Antonio named Jane Macon as the first woman to lead its legal staff. A graduate of the University of Texas School of Law, Macon served in this capacity until 1983 when she joined a local firm.[48]

Iris Jones, a Texas Southern University graduate who had previously been an assistant attorney general and a civil litigator with two Austin firms, rose in the ranks to head the city of Austin's legal department where she supervised a staff of fifty in-house attorneys and also managed outside counsel relationships for the city. When asked at that time to share her thoughts on being a black female attorney, Jones replied, "I remember walking into meetings and clients would look at me so distinctly ('she's young, she's black, she's female, and she's *short*') and then they would say 'You are our lawyer?' . . . Because of the high visibility of my position . . . [i]t is a good opportunity not only to act as a role model, but to get the community accustomed to the idea that a minority woman can deliver good legal services and provide a professional image."[49] Jones moved to another position with the city of Austin when she became the city's first police monitor, serving as ombudsman between the police department and the community on matters of racial issues.[50] Jones, who confided that she was inspired by Barbara Jordan, added, "It is encouraging . . . to break new ground because I know others will follow."[51]

During the early 1930s President Franklin D. Roosevelt implemented his New Deal program, creating the largest federal government in history. Roosevelt, the first president to appoint a woman to his cabinet,[52] also supported the inclusion of women lawyers in the Department of Justice.[53] This encouragement by the federal government spurred the hiring of women in state offices as well.

The Texas attorney general's office, in particular, was receptive to hiring women. Hattie Henenberg became one of its first female employees when she was hired as an assistant in 1929. She remained there for two years. In 1932, Henenberg worked as a volunteer in the election campaign of Franklin D. Roosevelt and John Nance Garner, encouraging women nationwide to support the Democratic candidates. Her successful campaigning propelled her to Washington, D.C., where she spent several months as a special assistant to the U.S. attorney general.[54] These years also produced additional assistant attorneys general in Austin. Minnie Ramsey Robey, considered one of the earliest women in West Texas to pass the bar, closed her practice in Eastland on the death of her attorney husband and joined the appellate division of the Texas attorney general's office.[55] Effie Wilson Waldron[56] and May Yelderman,[57] both Austin lawyers, and Erma Elaine Baker of Brownwood[58] were added to the staff in 1937. Marietta McGregor Payne holds the distinction of serving longer than any other woman as an assistant attorney general in Texas. Her two stints in the office spanned the years 1947–68 and 1971–76. She spent nearly her entire legal career in the attorney general's office, specializing in taxation with emphasis on matters pertaining to state inheritance taxes.[59] Payne was the only woman on staff when she was hired and later commented that "the ultimate requisites for success remain the same: a certain turn of mind, real love of the law, 'blood, sweat, and [no] tears.'"[60]

Sometimes one government position led to others. Myra McDaniel graduated from the University of Texas Law School in 1975 at the age of forty-two. Her first employment was in the attorney general's office, where she became chief of the taxation division. In 1981 she moved to the Texas Railroad Commission as special counsel. After serving as legal counsel to Gov. Mark White, she was appointed Texas secretary of state, a position she held for three years. McDaniel was not the first woman to serve in this post, but she was the first African-American female secretary of state.[61]

Carolyn Moore, a Texas Tech law graduate, has also had a varied and interesting career in government service. It began in Lubbock with defending people accused of Class C misdemeanors—mainly traffic tickets—in municipal court. Moore reported that the one hundred trials she conducted were good experience for her at the beginning of her career. After a move to Amarillo, she worked briefly for the Potter County attorney doing everything from collecting child support to prosecuting misdemeanors. Back in Lubbock, Moore worked for the Child Protective Services for ten years, where she spent long hours convincing district and county attorneys to prosecute abuse and neglect cases. While she was employed in the Lubbock County criminal district attorney's office, Moore instituted some procedures which, hopefully, would reduce specific crimes. As she worked on domestic violence cases, she required defendants to seek counseling. For those facing DUI charges, Moore established a victim impact panel that met with those convicted of drunk driving so they would know what effect their actions had on others. Moore is currently the administrative law judge with the Division of Workers' Compensation of the Department of Insurance—a job Moore says she "truly loves."[62]

Texas women also found themselves moving into positions in the federal government. In 1977 Sarah Weddington was appointed general counsel for the U.S. Department of Agriculture, the first woman to hold that position. The following year she became a special White

House adviser to President Jimmy Carter on women's issues. In this position, she fought for the extension of the time required to ratify the Equal Rights Amendment and provided Carter with names of women qualified for high-level appointments.[63]

Houston attorney Carol E. Dinkins took leave from her law firm in 1981 to become assistant attorney general for the Environment and National Resources Division of the U.S. Department of Justice. During her tenure the division implemented the comprehensive acts known as "Superfund" and created the Environmental Crimes Section. Three years later Dinkins was appointed deputy attorney general of the United States. As the second ranking officer in the Department of Justice, she was responsible for supervising investigations and litigations in many areas, including civil rights, civil claims, antitrust, tax, immigration, environmental law, and criminal law as well as enforcement agencies like the Federal Bureau of Investigation and the Bureau of Prisons. In this capacity, Dinkins oversaw the day-to-day management of more than 60,000 employees.[64] After a year as the highest-ranking woman in the federal government, Dinkins returned to Vinson & Elkins, the Houston firm where she is still a partner.[65]

Temple University Law School graduate Anna Maria Farias has spent much of her career in Washington, D.C. Farias served as special assistant/attorney adviser to the U.S. Department of Education and as legal adviser to the deputy secretary of labor under the presidencies of Ronald Reagan and George H. W. Bush. She then returned to her hometown of Crystal City, Texas, where she was the executive director of the Crystal City Housing Authority. At that time, Farias won a national award for being the only executive director in the country who was reared in public housing and came back to reside there once she was named director. After eight years at the helm in Crystal City, Farias returned to Washington, first as counsel to the secretary of the U.S. Department of Housing and Urban Development and then in HUD's Office of Community Planning and Development as deputy assistant secretary for grant programs with oversight of $6.3 billion.[66]

Karen Tandy, a Texas Tech law school graduate, became the first woman to head a federal law-enforcement agency when she was confirmed by the U.S. Senate in 2003 as administrator of the Drug Enforcement Agency. The newspaper headline announcing Tandy's appointment read, "Tough Texan to Tackle Drug War." The article, noted that Tandy would concentrate on disrupting major drug operations and targeting the more than $65 billion in profits made by drug traffickers each year. The director of the Office of National Drug Control Policy said about Tandy, "She has shown that she believes law enforcement can be proactive, not just passively waiting for someone to poison yet another child with drugs and then arrest them." Tandy began her law career as an assistant U.S. attorney, first in Virginia and then in Washington, D.C., handling the prosecution of violent crimes, drug offenders, money laundering, and forfeiture cases. She moved to Justice Department headquarters in 1990. By 2001 she was supervising the efforts of DEA, FBI, Customs, and state and local law enforcement officials—10,000 of them—in this country and overseas.[67]

Although no woman has made it to the White House as the occupant of the oval office, Harriet Miers went to Washington, D.C., in 2001 to serve as staff secretary and assistant to President George W. Bush. After two years in that position, she was appointed deputy chief of staff for policy. In November 2004 Bush named her to the post of White House counsel, the chief legal adviser for the office of the President. In this capacity, Miers worked with a staff of thirteen lawyers in cooperation with the Justice Department, providing guidance on issues ranging from the legal parameters for the war on terrorism to presidential speeches.[68] On October 3, 2005, the president nominated Miers to be an associate justice of the U.S. Supreme Court to replace Justice Sandra Day O'Connor, who had announced her intention to retire once a successor was named. Before confirmation hearings began for Miers, she asked President Bush to withdraw her nomination. Miers remained as White House counsel until January 2007 when she resigned and returned to the law firm of Locke Liddell & Sapp (now Locke Lord Bissell & Liddell), where she is a partner.[69]

Many of the preconceived ideas relating to women lawyers practicing in the public sector have proved to be faulty assumptions. Women have shown they can be aggressive, if need be, in representing the government in a trial. They have become skilled in helping persons to access government resources, especially in times of hardship or crisis. They have exhibited a willingness to work long hours when necessary, even if these schedules interrupt their family life. And, finally, it became evident as more women filled government positions that their authority was accepted by those with whom they worked. The most recent report from the State Bar of Texas indicates that 17 percent of its women members are employed as government attorneys, as compared to 11 percent of the bar's male members.[70] Sociologist Cynthia Fuchs Epstein explains that women are attracted to government work because they view it as public service and working for the public good.[71] Whether they are in courtrooms prosecuting cases, sitting behind desks preparing forms, or out in the field gathering information, women in government positions are making a difference in the lives of a sizeable segment of our state's population.

Notes

1. *Texas Bar Journal*, 35, 4:326.

2. Payne, *Dallas*, 127–28.

3. Ibid., 275.

4. *Derry*, 328.

5. Barbara Karkabi, "All-woman Law Firm: Equal Partners Working for Change," *Houston Chronicle*, April 28, 1983.

6. *Houston Chronicle*, July 20, 1993.

7. University of Houston Law Center Faculty, http://www.law.uh.edu/faculty/adjunct/main.asp?PID=2665 (accessed September 14, 2007).

8. *Texas Bar Journal,* 65, 6:493.

9. Garza, 154.

10. Azalea Aleman, correspondence to author, December 1, 2006.

11. Payne, *Dallas*, 128–29.

12. *Texas Bar Journal*, 32, 6:464.

13. *Who's Who*, 73.

14. Houston Bar Association Directory, 1936.

15. Joyce Burg, interview by Eric L. Fredrickson, October 1, 1990, copy in Houston Bar Association Archives.

16. Arnold, 47.

17. *Texas Bar Journal*, 37, 4:326.

18. *Texas Bar Journal*, 37, 5:420–421.

19. *Texas Bar Journal*, 56, 8:849.

20. Payne, *Dallas,* 276.

21. *Texas Bar Journal*, 42, 5:866–867.

22. Brandon, 85.

23. Deaths, *UT Alumni News,* Fall 2005.

24. Ellen Mitchell, "A Portrait of Senior Justice Shirley Butts," *San Antonio Lawyer*, March-April 2006, 6.

25. *Texas Bar Journal*, 53, 9:1051.

26. *Texas Bar Journal*, 20, 3:124.

27. Marvin Adams, correspondence to author, September 28, 2006.

28. *Bench & Bar*, 164.

29. *1918 Cactus*, 86.

30. Kathy Day correspondence, November 27, 2006.

31. *Texas Bar Journal*, 25, 4:342.

32. *Texas Bar Journal*, 44, 10:1276.

33. *Texas Bar Journal*, 37, 4:326.

34. Acosta and Winegarten, 253.

35. *Texas Bar Journal*, 37, 4:326.

36. Mary McKerall, correspondence to author, May 25, 2007.

37. Mary McKerall, interview by author, May 20, 2007.

38. *Texas Bar Journal*, 35, 10:1083.

39. *Texas Bar Journal*, 45, 1:129.

40. *Texas Bar Journal*, 41, 4:467.

41. *1925 Martindale*, 828.

42. *Who's Who*, 55.

43. *Derry*, 300.

44. *Texas Bar Journal*, 37, 5:496.

45. *Texas Bar Journal*, 36, 8:857.

46. *Texas Bar Journal*, 56, 8:849.

47. *Texas Bar Journal*, 58, 5:520.

48. *Texas Bar Journal*, 42, 5:864.

49. *Texas Bar Journal*, 53, 9:1055–56.

50. Professional Business Development Institute: Faculty, http://www.pbdi.org/pages/consultants.asp?Action=DrawDetail&ListingID=111 (accessed September 17, 2007).

51. *Texas Bar Journal*, 53, 9:1056.

52. Cott, 458, 464–65. In 1932 President Roosevelt appointed Frances Perkins, whose background was in social welfare, as secretary of labor. While women made unprecedented progress in being appointed to government positions, their appointments were not evenly distributed throughout the executive branch. Rather, they were concentrated in the Labor Department, with its heavy emphasis on women's

and children's affairs, and in newly created agencies where they would not be treading on ground traditionally held by males. Interestingly, the second woman to serve in a presidential cabinet was a Texan, Oveta Culp Hobby, who was the first secretary of health, education, and welfare in President Dwight Eisenhower's administration. Hobby is sometimes noted as a lawyer. Although she attended several terms at South Texas College of Law, Hobby did not graduate and was never admitted to the bar.

53. Woloch, 452–57.

54. Sherilyn Brandenstein, "Hattie Henenberg," *Handbook of Texas,* 3:561.

55. *Texas Bar Journal*, 32, 10:814.

56. *Who's Who*, 104.

57. *Texas Bar Journal*, 11, 9:563.

58. *Texas Bar Journal*, 19, 10:748.

59. *Texas* Bar *Journal*, 48, 2:237.

60. *Texas Bar Journal*, 37, 5:420.

61. *Texas Journal of Women and the Law,* 8:331–333.

62. Carolyn Moore, correspondence to author, June 29, 2007.

63. Lasher, 186–87; *Texas Bar Journal*, 41, 10:969.

64. Thora Qadummi, "Carol E. Dinkins is named one of top women lawyers," *Houston Business Journal*, May 1–7, 1998.

65. Hyman, 406.

66. U.S. Department of Housing and Urban Development, Community Planning and Development, http://www.hud.gov/offices/cpd/about/staff/bios/farias.cfm (accessed March 7, 2007).

67. Brian Rogers, "Karen Tandy, Class of '77, Appointed Head of DEA," *Texas Tech Lawyer*, Spring 2004, 7–8.

68. Harriet Miers, *Wikipedia*, http://en.wikipedia.org.wiki/Harriet_Miers (accessed February 27, 2007).

69. Harriet Miers, Returning to Locke Liddell & Sapp, Press Release, April 18, 2007.

70. Nils Greger Olsson and Dustin Kim, "Annual Report on the Status of

Women and Racial/Ethnic Minorities in the State Bar of Texas (2005–06)," State Bar Department of Research and Analysis.

71. Epstein, 112–13.

Chapter Six

Standing for Election

DALLAS ATTORNEY EDITH THERREL WILMANS, who was admitted to the bar in 1918 after studying in a law office, was elected to the Texas House of Representatives in 1922. When Wilmans was sworn in, the *Austin American* newspaper reported on the event by describing the new legislator as wearing a brown satin dress, a gray sports coat, brown shoes and hose, and a gold and gray turban. The reporter added, "She did not have the proverbial bouquet."[1] As the chamber's only "lady member," Wilmans was allowed to choose her desk. The next day she rebuked legislators at an informal gathering for making the event ridiculous instead of professional. Wilmans had conducted her campaign as an advocate for creating a domestic relations court in Dallas County, requiring health certificates before issuing a marriage license, funding state support for children whose fathers were in prison or an asylum, and raising the age of compulsory school attendance to sixteen. Only one of the five bills introduced by Wilmans—an education appropriations bill—became law, and, although she regarded being a legislator as "difficult, thankless, and unprofitable," she ran for reelection in 1924. When Wilmans lost the race for reelection, she resumed her law practice in Dallas. She ran for governor in 1926 and again in 1928 hoping to prove that women were serious candidates. Three subsequent races for the house and a congressional seat were also unsuccessful, but Wilmans had created a precedent for women officeholders in Texas.[2]

Women, viewing politics as a means of reform, had developed their own political culture. They displayed it in the private sector, however, rather than in the public one. Nevertheless, they became skilled in gaining support for their causes by using persuasion.[3] Attorney Hortense Ward had successfully used these acts in 1913 in leading the efforts for the passage of the Married Women's Property Law, which gave married women partial control over both their separate and community property.[4] Women realized that holding an elective office would enable them to participate in the process of change. Female lawyers were especially attracted to the state legislature, where laws were made to effect changes. The election of Wilmans to the Texas House of Representatives encouraged other women to run for office. As historian Ruthe Winegarten noted, "[T]heir presence has signaled the beginning of the end of the Texas Legislature as the largest and most influential men's room in the state."[5] The election of twenty-six women lawyers over the next seventy-five years would help to ensure that it never again was a body for men only.

Sarah T. Hughes was thirty-four years old when she was elected to the legislature in 1930 after spending $300 on her campaign.[6] Her opponent was Dallas attorney Helen Viglini, a sister of Edith Wilmans. Women who had fought against discrimination were not above resorting to the traditional image of proper women if it served their purpose. This tactic was used by Viglini in the race for house representative against Hughes. Viglini assumed a domestic posture in opposition to Hughes' professional one. She campaigned by saying she was "old fashioned enough to believe a woman's first duty is to her husband, home, and children." This, of course, was aimed at Hughes, who was married but, by choice, had no children. Then Viglini added, "But since I am a widow and have raised my children, I feel that I can with a clear conscience ask the privilege of representing my county in the legislature." Surprisingly, given the prevailing criticism of women placing work ahead of family, Viglini's rhetoric did not bring her victory.[7] When Hughes campaigned for a second term, her male opponent ridiculed her candidacy by saying, "We should slap her face and send her back to the kitchen."[8] Hughes, however, won and was the only woman in the house during the Forty-third Legislature. Hughes became involved in such issues as penal reform, oil proration, and public school land use. She tried unsuccessfully to introduce legislation requiring child support by noncustodial parents. Hughes also cosponsored a bill legalizing jury service for women but, ironically, she would become a judge before she could become a juror.[9] Hughes later reflected on her time in the house: "I thought that I was able to do more good for the community, and the state as well, in the legislature than in any other office I've ever had."[10] Then she added that being elected to the legislature was the biggest thrill of her career.

Only a year after she finished law school in 1937, Margaret Amsler campaigned for a seat in the Texas house. "I was trading on being a woman," she recalled. "It was summer. I wore a pink dress . . . I would get up and go to factories at six o'clock in the morning and . . . climb up in cotton gins."[11] Amsler defeated seven male opponents and became one of two women in the Forty-sixth Legislature. There were strained relations between Amsler and Governor W. Lee "Pappy" O'Daniel, who referred to her as "that woman." She became part of "The Immortal 56," a group of legislators opposed to O'Daniel's attempts to levy a sales tax by amending the state constitution. The rebellious group succeeded in defeating O'Daniel's proposal, and the amendment never went to the voters. Amsler believed her opposition to the governor caused her to lose reelection to the house in 1940. During her tenure there, however, Amsler learned how to handle some potentially contentious issues.

Aware there was friction among some legislators over which brand of beer should be served at social occasions, Amsler decided to drink only Dr Pepper, which had been developed in her hometown of Waco, Texas.[12] Amsler returned to Waco and began a long tenure as Professor Margaret Harris Amsler at Baylor's law school. As a former legislator familiar with the lawmaking process, Amsler wrote numerous bills and lobbied sitting legislators to sponsor them. Many of these were designed to change corporate law. She helped draft the Texas Business Corporation Act, passed by the legislature in 1955.[13]

UT law graduate Elizabeth Suiter—like Amsler the daughter of an attorney—served three terms in the legislature. Following in the footsteps of her father, who had been a state senator, Suiter often commented that she had grown up on the floor of the senate. Defeated in her first bid for the house in 1940, she won when she ran again in 1942 on a platform of economy in wartime and served as vice chair of the House Judiciary Committee. Suiter successfully sponsored legislation which included measures to regulate insurance companies and to clarify the name on insurance policies. She tried unsuccessfully to abolish gender-based discriminatory wage rates. Choosing not to run for a fourth term, Suiter returned to her law practice in Winnsboro, Texas.[14]

A new trail was blazed in 1966 when Barbara Jordan became the state's first black senator since 1883 and its first black woman legislator. Having lost races in 1962 and in 1964, she refused to be defined by either her race or her gender. "I'm not a black politician," she insisted. "I'm not a female politician. I'm a politician. And a good one."[15] She recognized, however, that women were not welcomed by everyone. When a senator said, "We can't have a woman in here. We don't even have a bathroom for women." Barbara Jordan replied in her unmistakable voice, "Then build one!"[16] Once she was a state senator, Jordan's primary goal was to become an insider even though she was the only female among thirty males. As Jordan explained, "We are a macho state . . . Those thirty men didn't know what to expect of me, and I certainly didn't know what to expect of them . . . [But] I knew that the best way for me to operate as a player in the Senate was to become friends with my colleagues and not to have them uncomfortable because there was a woman in their presence."[17] Nearly half of the 150 bills Jordan introduced were passed. She supported the state's first minimum wage and civil rights laws and sponsored a bill to establish a state commission on fair employment practices. Jordan was instrumental in making Texas one of the first states in the South to ratify the federal Equal Rights Amendment and to propose and secure the Equal Rights Amendment to the Texas Constitution.[18] Although Jordan was sometimes considered too conciliatory, she believed in compromise when necessary, and she learned the art of compromise well in her six years in the legislature.

The only woman in the house from 1969 to 1973 was Frances "Sissy" Tarlton Farenthold. She quickly assessed the situation after arriving and reported, "I was in the legislature about two weeks before I decided that reform had to be my major concern. I went there knowing blacks were not represented, knowing Mexican Americans weren't represented. I found that Texans weren't even represented."[19] As a new legislator, Farenthold defined herself as an advocate of civil rights, not women's rights. She initially opposed a state Equal Rights Amendment because the State Bar of Texas was against it. (The State Bar was not alone in initially opposing the Texas Equal Rights Amendment. Many women's groups opposed it on the grounds that women would lose their hard-earned protective rights. Many women believed it would be better to change those laws discriminating against women.) However, as she experienced the treatment afforded women—being refused admittance to a house committee meeting because of a club's all-male policy, discovering that the governor did not realize a woman (Farenthold herself) was even a member of the legislature, and being addressed by legislators as their "Valentine pet"—she became a strong

CLOCKWISE FROM TOP LEFT:

As a member of the Texas Senate and of the U.S. House of Representatives, **BARBARA JORDAN** championed civil rights for all minorities. While in the state senate, she served as "Governor for a Day" on June 10, 1972. Photographer: Bill Malone. Photo courtesy of Texas State Library and Archives Commission.

In 1922 **EDITH WILMANS** of Dallas was the first woman elected to the Texas legislature. An avid suffragist, Wilmans remained supportive of extending women's rights. Photo courtesy of Texas State Library and Archives Commission.

In 1968 **MARY JOE DURNING CARROLL** became a partner in an Austin law firm. This was an unusual achievement at that time for a woman. Photo courtesy of Clark, Thomas & Winters, P.C., Austin.

HILDA TAGLE was appointed U.S. District Judge for the Southern District of Texas in 1998 after serving in county and state judgeships. Judge Tagle was the first Hispanic woman named to the federal judiciary in Texas. Photo courtesy of Gov. Bill & Vara Daniel Center for Legal History, State Bar of Texas.

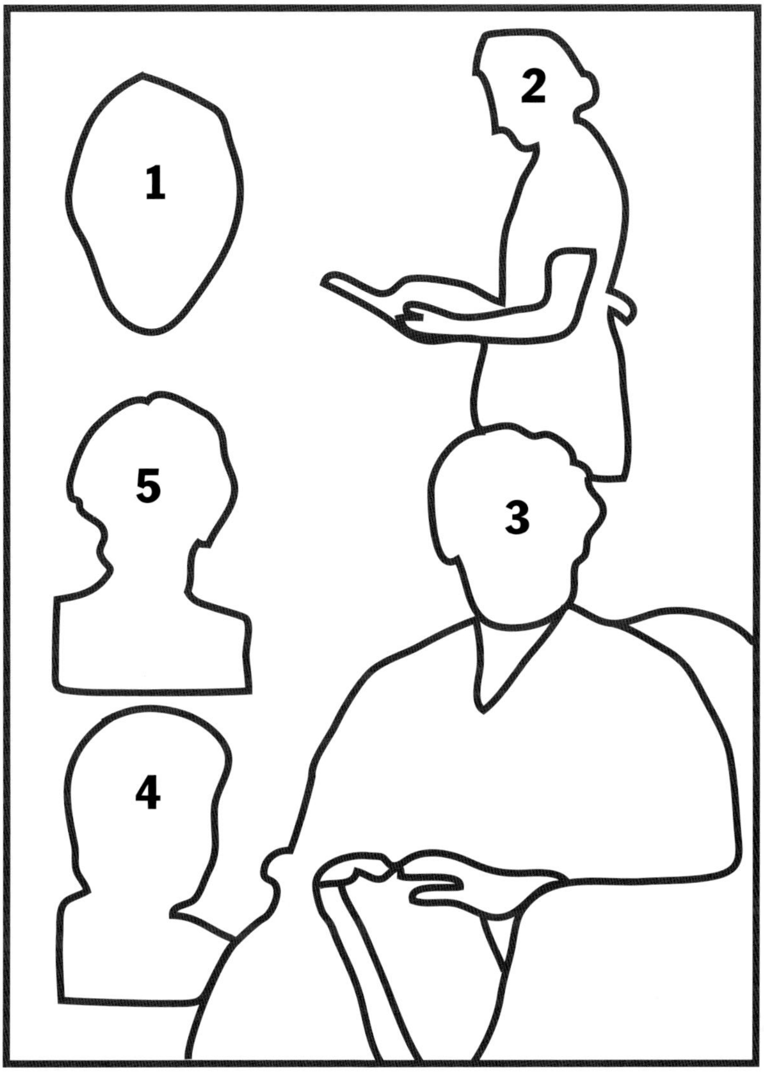

CLOCKWISE FROM TOP LEFT:

1 **ALICE DRYSDALE SHEFFIELD** graduated from the University of Texas School of Law in 1918 and began her long career with Gulf Oil Corporation. Sheffield Room in Townes Hall and the Alice Jane Drysdale Sheffield Regents Chair in Law reflect the bequest she left the school at her death. Photo courtesy of St. Luke's United Methodist Church Archives, Houston.

2 **LOUISE RAGGIO**, shown with her young sons in 1952, spearheaded the drafting and passage of the Texas Marital Property Act in 1967. All three of Raggio's sons became lawyers and practiced with their mother. From the collections of the Texas/Dallas History and Archives Division, Dallas Public Library.

3 **JUDGE SARAH T. HUGHES** sat on the bench for over forty years, first as a state district judge and then as a federal judge. For many years she advocated jury service for women, which finally became law in 1954. Photo courtesy of Dallas Historical Society. Used by permission.

4 The first female law school dean in Texas was **BARBARA BADER ALDAVE**. She became dean of St. Mary's University School of Law in 1989 after serving on the law school faculty at the University of Texas for fifteen years. Photo courtesy of Gov. Bill & Vara Daniel Center for Legal History, State Bar of Texas.

5 **JUDGE GABRIELLE KIRK MCDONALD**'s career has spanned the globe. She has served as a civil rights lawyer, a law professor, a federal judge, and the president for the International Criminal Tribunal for the former Yugoslavia. Photo courtesy of Gov. Bill & Vara Daniel Center for Legal History, State Bar of Texas.

CLOCKWISE FROM TOP LEFT:

1 **SARAH WEDDINGTON** successfully argued *Roe v. Wade* before the U.S. Supreme Court just four years after she graduated from law school. Photo courtesy of Gov. Bill & Vara Daniel Center for Legal History, State Bar of Texas.

2 In 1992 **ROSE SPECTOR** became the first woman elected to the Texas Supreme Court. She was previously a state district judge in Bexar County. Photo courtesy of Justice Rose Spector.

3 **HATTIE ELAM BRISCOE** graduated first in her class at St. Mary's University School of Law at the age of 40. She was a solo practitioner in San Antonio for more than forty years. Photo courtesy of San Antonio Bar Association.

4 **HARRIET MIERS** (left) and U.S. District Judge **MARY LOU ROBINSON** received the Sandra Day O'Connor Award for Professional Excellence in 2005. Miers, a former State Bar president, and Robinson, a federal judge since 1979, have provided strong leadership for women lawyers in the state. Photo courtesy of Gov. Bill & Vara Daniel Center for Legal History, State Bar of Texas.

5 During a career that spanned seventy years, Houstonian **JOYCE BURG** was an early practitioner in immigration law. She helped to resettle German Jews during World War II by finding sponsors for them and filing affidavits of sponsorship. Photo courtesy of Houston Bar Association.

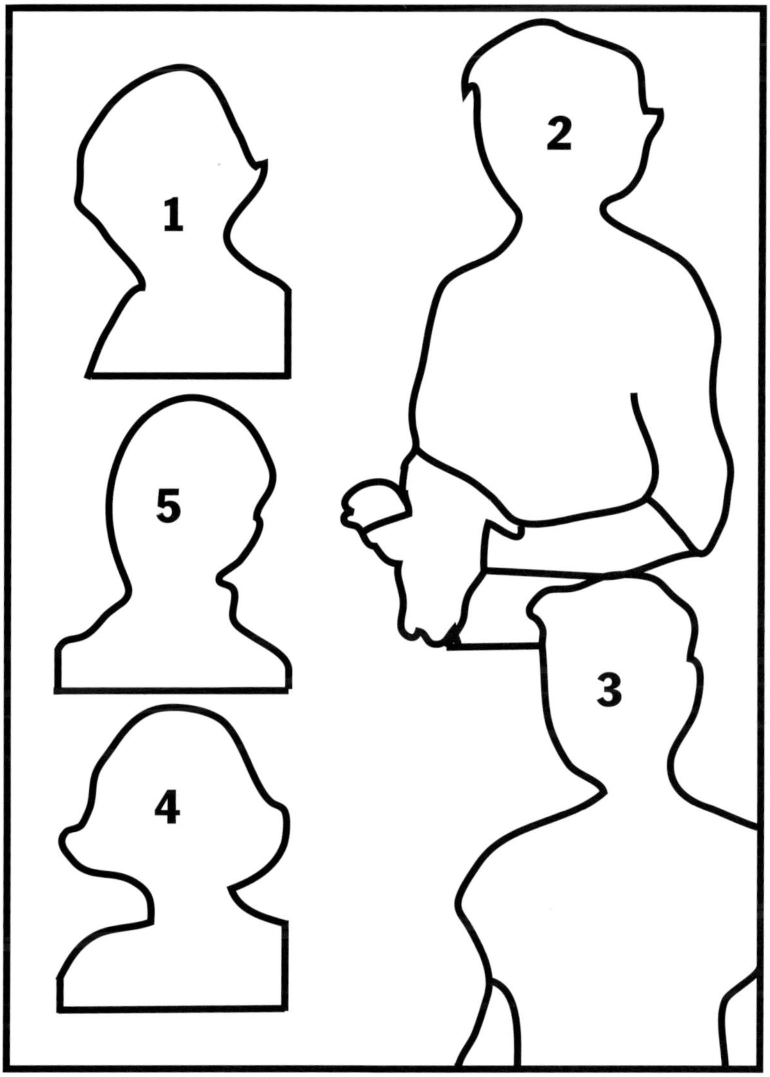

CLOCKWISE FROM TOP LEFT:

1 In 1915 **HORTENSE SPARKS WARD** became the first Texas woman admitted to practice before the U.S. Supreme Court. Ward, a strong advocate for women's rights, was responsible for the passage of legislation favoring women in the early 20th century. Photo courtesy of Gov. Bill & Vara Daniel Center for Legal History, State Bar of Texas.

2 In 1953 **CHARLYE O. FARRIS** was the first African-American woman admitted to the Texas Bar. Farris has practiced in Wichita Falls for more than fifty years. Photo courtesy of Gov. Bill & Vara Daniel Center for Legal History, State Bar of Texas.

3 Baylor University Law School Prof. **MARGARET HARRIS AMSLER** was the first woman in Texas to teach law as a full-time faculty member. Known as "Lady A" to her students, Amsler taught at Baylor from 1940 to 1972. Photo courtesy of Gov. Bill & Vara Daniel Center for Legal History, State Bar of Texas.

4 **IRMA RANGEL** became the first Hispanic woman elected to the Texas House. She served from 1977 until her death in 2003. Photo courtesy of Gov. Bill & Vara Daniel Center for Legal History, State Bar of Texas.

5 **FRANCES "SISSY" FARENTHOLD**'s career has been multifaceted: state legislator, law professor, college president, practicing lawyer, and political activist. In all her endeavors Farenthold has been a powerful advocate for reform. Photo courtesy of Frances "Sissy" Farenthold.

CLOCKWISE FROM TOP LEFT:

In 1994 **SHEILA JACKSON LEE** was elected to the U.S. House of Representatives from the 18th Congressional District. At the forefront of her concerns in Congress are immigrant, minority, and women's issues. Photo courtesy of Rep. Sheila Jackson Lee.

KAY BAILEY HUTCHISON is the first woman to represent Texas in the U.S. Senate. Hutchison's legislative career began when she was elected to the Texas House of Representatives in 1972. Photo courtesy of Sen. Kay Bailey Hutchison.

Dallas attorney **ADELFA B. CALLEJO** was one of the first Hispanic women to practice law in Texas. She has spent forty-seven years representing the underserved in her community. Photo courtesy of University of Texas at San Antonio Institute of Texan Cultures.

supporter of reform in that area.[20] As an environmentalist, Farenthold attempted to protect beaches, bays, and estuaries from pollution and commercial development. She passed an antiquities bill giving the state a share of artifacts found along the Texas coast. She tried, but failed, to prohibit nuclear power plants from being built in Texas. Farenthold was sometimes called an "advocate for lost causes" because she tried unsuccessfully to establish a governor's committee on children and youth, a family planning service, a public utilities commission, and education programs for preschool children—issues for which she would be labeled "ahead of her time." Farenthold is best known for her involvement in the "Dirty Thirty," a bipartisan group of representatives who investigated the Sharpstown stock fraud scandal, thus ending the political careers of several top officials. Farenthold, still focused on a comprehensive reform of Texas politics, ran unsuccessfully for governor in 1972.[21] After another unsuccessful run for governor in 1974, Farenthold retired from political office to teach one of the first "Women and the Law" classes offered by a Texas law school—the University of Houston—using a casebook authored by the then-not-so-well-known attorney Ruth Bader Ginsburg.[22]

In 1972 Kay Bailey Hutchison ran for a seat in the house and became the first Republican woman elected to that body. She found fund-raising difficult because of her gender. She explained, "Women couldn't get big checks from contributors. So I just worked hard getting lots of smaller checks, most of them from other women."[23] Bipartisan cooperation among women in the house resulted in the Bailey-Weddington law that ensured compensation to rape victims, protection of their privacy, and stopping authorities from treating victims as if they were guilty. In addition, Hutchison cosponsored legislation to guarantee credit rights for women and introduced an unsuccessful bill to alter the garnishment of wages for child support. Years later she observed, "My gender does not determine my ideology. Yet, as a woman in the Texas legislature, I thought of and pursued issues that men often would not think of pursuing."[24] Hutchison left the house in 1976 when President Gerald Ford appointed her vice chair of the National Transportation Board, a position she held two years before marrying and moving to Dallas.[25] Kay Bailey Hutchison, however, was not through with public office.

The year 1972 was a landmark one for women seeking legislative posts. A record six women were elected to the legislature that year. Three of these were attorneys. In addition to Hutchison, seats were won in the house by Sarah Weddington and Senfronia Thompson. Weddington was the first woman from Travis County elected, defeating a runoff opponent who referred to her only as "that sweet little girl."[26] One of the first things Weddington did as a legislator was to help change the law that restricted women's ability to get credit cards in their own name. She later recalled, "I was a licensed attorney . . . I was putting him [my husband] through law school . . . and we were basically living on my salary, and I didn't think I ought to have to have his signature . . . So I would not accept credit on that basis."[27] After the Equal Credit Bill was passed, Weddington went back and got her credit card. Weddington also cosponsored the Kidney Health Bill, which ensured Texans' access to kidney dialysis machines.[28] She joined with the other women in the house to stop schools from terminating pregnant teachers and to ensure five-year-olds' access to kindergarten. In 1978 Weddington resigned from the legislature to take a post in the Carter administration.[29]

Senfronia Thompson of Houston arrived in the house in 1973—one of the first two black women ever to serve there. She credited the positive atmosphere in 1972 with so many women running for office as the inspiration for her to jump into the fray. As a legislator, Thompson, who received her law degree from Texas Southern University and a master of laws from the University of Houston, focused on issues related to women, minorities, labor, consumers, victims of domestic violence, teachers, and the protection of civil liberties. She once said she was not in the legislature "to window dress." Thompson authored and passed the Durable Power of Attorney Act, the Uniform Interstate Family Support Act, the Sexual Assault Program Fund, and the Family and Juvenile Justice Codes. In 1999 Thompson succeeded, after twelve years, in passing her bill legalizing a limited amount of alimony, thereby ending Texas' claim as the only state in the nation without it. Senfronia Thompson has the honor of being the "dean" of women in the house, having served almost thirty-five years there.[30]

Although women were being elected in larger numbers, they remained an unusual sight in the legislature. When they were invited to official functions, the invitations suggested they bring their wives.[31] Clearly, many still thought that political office belonged to men. At the same time, male legislators often went out of their way to treat their female colleagues in ways that seemed to be flattering but were actually demeaning. On more than one occasion women legislators were sent candy to placate them for some snub.[32] A newly elected female remembered that a longtime male legislator patronized her by telling her, "Don't you worry, little lady. Don't expect to do anything great this session. Just sit back and learn."[33] Another said she looked forward to walking down the floor of the house without being called "little lady, sugar, or darlin'."[34]

In 1977 Dallas attorney Lanell Cofer, a Texas Southern University law graduate, won a special election to replace a representative who had resigned to take another government position. Cofer was influenced to study law after hearing Judge Sarah Hughes give a speech and was inspired to become involved in politics after listening to a commencement speech by Barbara Jordan. Cofer, described by other legislators as young and shy when she entered the house, assured her constituents that "experience and exposure will take care of that." Cofer supported redistricting to give minorities more representation, regulating animal shelters, increasing funding for Prairie View and Texas Southern universities, and requiring sprinklers in nursing homes. After serving five years, Cofer was defeated in the Democratic primary election.[35]

During her nine terms in the house, Betty Denton seldom had any election opposition. A graduate of Baylor law school, she was elected to the legislature in 1976 to fill the vacated seat of her husband. Denton supported interpreters for deaf students, increased benefits for retired teachers, funding for cancer research through cigarette taxes, basing auto insurance rates on driving records rather than age and gender, making generic drugs available, raising teacher pay, improving health care for senior citizens, creating a state elections and ethics commission, producing drug-free zones around schools, and stiffening penalties for selling drugs near schools. Denton was defeated in 1994 and later resumed practicing law in Waco.[36]

In 1976 Irma Rangel became the first Hispanic woman elected to the Texas House. Although she received some campaign money from the Texas Women's Political Caucus, Rangel credited the women farm workers in the state for being the most help in fund-raising. "They knew I had been involved with the farm workers' march in 1966 and that I was compassionate toward their problems and concerns,"[37] Rangel explained. She made the concerns of women, children and the poor the focus of her work. Toward this end, Rangel passed legislation to provide educational and employment programs to mothers on welfare, to create centers for victims of domestic abuse, to help grocers and wholesalers donate food to the elderly poor, to extend the absentee voting system, and to increase funding for South Texas colleges and universities. Irma Rangel died in 2003 while serving her fourteenth term in the house.[38] During her twenty-seven years in the legislature, Rangel was considered a role model and morale booster for younger Latina legislators.

Debra Danburg's road to the Texas House of Representatives differed from that of the other women who had served there. After graduating from the University of Houston Law Center, she was advised by a mentor to "learn the ropes as an insider" and became a legislative aide to a house member. During those four years she noted that she "did everything a legislator does except push the button to vote."[39] In 1981 she was elected to her own seat and hit the floor running at full speed. In her first session she rewrote the sexual assault laws of Texas. She later reflected, "Where people considered me to be somewhat strident or radical on sexual assault legislation fifteen years ago, now every guy and his dog is ready to sign on as a joint author." But she added, "[T]he year-in, year-out research, working with coalitions, working with the women who are actual victims of violence, has been done almost entirely by the women in the legislature."[40] She went on to champion antistalking legislation. Danburg rose rapidly in the leadership ranks of the house. She succeeded in securing a bill of rights for elderly people in health-care settings, a Texas Trails System to develop nature trails, regulations governing billboards, legalization of breast feeding in public, protection for endangered species, assistance for individuals with AIDS, stiffer penalties against drunken drivers, and the right of homeowners to secure loans using their home equity as collateral. She was also the go-to person to stop all antichoice bills for two decades whether in substantive committees or with valid points of order in debate on the floor.[41] After serving twenty-one years in the house, Danburg was defeated in 2002 when the lines of her district were redrawn. She then returned to full-time law practice.

After serving as one of two lawyers representing the Republican party in a state redistricting case, Patricia Porcella Hill decided to run for the legislature. A graduate of the University of Houston law school, she was elected in 1982 to represent a Dallas district. Most of Hill's legislative accomplishments were in the fields of environmental, criminal, and consumer law. Among those were the reenacting of the Air Control Board, restricting billboards in urban areas, creating new felony courts across the state, requiring insurance companies to pay for mammogram screening for women over thirty-five years of age, reforming worker compensation laws, and keeping AT&T a regulated utility. Hill decided not to run for reelection in 1991 because, as she said, "she got tired of it; same issues every session."[42] Instead, she made an unsuccessful run for Texas attorney general. When she left the house, she joined a law firm in Houston.

When Cyndi Taylor Krier was elected to the Texas Senate in 1984, she was only the sixth woman ever to serve in that body, the sole female senator during her first session, and the first woman from Bexar County in the senate.[43] On her first day, Krier learned that the senate dress code required that women wear bras, a regulation apparently directed at female journalists covering the proceedings. Krier responded by asking if male senators were required to wear any particular underwear. She had no difficulty in obtaining a reinterpretation of the code.[44] Krier, a graduate of the University of Texas, went on to introduce fifty-two bills in her first session, and twenty-seven of them passed. She considered her most significant accomplishments to have been improving collection of child support, addressing problems of child abuse and family violence, establishing juvenile courts, promoting arbitration and mediation, improving children's health care, and repealing archaic statutes that discriminated against women. Krier said her most memorable moments as a senator were not those spent passing or defeating legislation, but those helping constituents, like "the mother who needed mental retardation services for her disabled son who years later sent me his graduation picture or the owner of a small business which was about to close until the workers' compensation system was reformed."[45] Krier resigned her seat in 1992 to run for Bexar County judge.[46]

When Sue Smith Schechter, a graduate of South Texas College of Law, ran for the legislature in 1991, it was her first experience in politics. In her two terms she focused on mental health and children's issues and passed legislation to make school volunteers immune from liability, allow judges to consider sexual abuse of a child in emergency placement hearings, extend the friend of the court program for enforcing child support and visitation, waive college tuition and fees for children in foster care, and raise the age for topless dancing. She believed that female legislators' strength stemmed from their refusal to accept the mind-set of "that's the way it has always been." Because they recognized that women and children had been left out when previous laws had been passed, women in the legislature pushed for changes which would have a positive impact on the lives of children and other women. Schechter decided not to run for a third term because of the stress created by trying to balance family and public responsibilities.[47]

A record of civic leadership helped Yolanda Navarro Flores, a University of Houston law graduate, win election to the house in 1992. Flores introduced legislation to reform the electoral process, to advance secondary and higher education, and to restrict alcoholic beverage in city parks. In 1994 Flores ran for a new state senate seat instead of running for a second house term. She lost the race, but ran again for the house seat in 1996. After losing once again, Flores continued her law practice in Houston.[48]

In 1992 Susan Combs was elected to the Texas House of Representatives from Travis County. She believed that being a woman in the legislature made no significant difference. "The key is not your sex but your ability to persuade others of your view or to achieve consensus," she said.[49] In her two terms there, Combs regarded the passage of the Private Real Property Rights Preservation Act as one of her major legislative achievements. This act, which was opposed by environmentalists, permitted private property owners to collect damages from state agencies and local governments, including schools, if environmental regulations reduced property values. Environmentalists targeted Combs for defeat in her third term, but she resigned her seat a year before her second term ended to become state office director for U.S. Senator Kay Bailey Hutchison. In the 1998 elections, Combs became the state's first female commissioner of agriculture.[50] In 2006 Combs, a University of Texas law graduate, made another change when she ran for state comptroller and was elected.[51]

The 1990s produced more women lawyers in the legislature. Patricia Gray, a graduate of South Texas College of Law, represented Galveston County in the house from 1992 to 2002. During her terms she chaired the Committee on Civil Practices and the Committee on Public Health. Gray also served on the committees for corrections, environmental regulation, general investigating, and appropriations. In 1993 Vilma Luna of Corpus Christi was elected to the house. During her tenure there she served as vice chair of the appropriations, calendar, and ways and means committees. Luna resigned her post in July 2006 after almost thirteen years as a representative. Dora Olivo practiced in Fort Bend County after graduating from the University of Houston Law Center. In 1997 she was elected to the house, where she served on the public education and public health committees. Olivo worked on bills that regulated promotion of students, requirements for a high school diploma, and alternative education programs.[52]

Elections at the dawning of a new century ensured that women would continue to be elected to represent their constituents in the Texas House of Representatives. Ann Kitchen, a former assistant attorney general for consumer protection, was elected in 2001. She decided to run for the legislature because of the proactive experience she had working on two major health-care bills as a member of the Health and Human Services Commission. Issues that were important to Kitchen were transportation, public school funding, health insurance for school employees, and pipeline safety.[53] Former Comal County Judge Carter Casteel, a graduate of St. Mary's University law school, was sworn in as a member of the house in January 2003. Casteel sponsored and supported legislation that curbed lawsuit abuse, promoted economic development, overhauled the workers' compensation system, and enhanced public health and safety.[54] Veronica Gonzales, a graduate of the University of Texas law school and a McAllen attorney, was the first female elected to represent District 41 in the Texas

House of Representatives. In her first term Gonzalez was elected by her colleagues to serve as secretary of the State Democratic Caucus and also served on the Bi-National Alcohol and Drug Abuse Task Force.[55] An Alice attorney and a former assistant attorney general, Yvonne Gonzalez-Toureilles, was elected as a legislator in 2004. She was named to the House Committee on Energy Resources and the House Committee on Human Services, which was charged with the responsibility of overhauling the Children's Protective Services system. Gonzalez-Toureilles made history by becoming the first state representative to give birth during a regular session.[56] Ana E. Hernandez was elected to fill an unexpired term and was re-elected to a full term in 2006. Hernandez, an attorney at ConocoPhillips, began her career in politics by participating in the Texas Legislative Internship Program. She worked as an intern in three continuous sessions while attending law school at the University of Texas. Hernandez was a founder of Latinas on the Rise, an educational and mentoring program for young Latinas.[57]

Since Edith Wilmans' entry into the house in 1923, most people—male legislators, the press, and the public—have assumed that women legislators are interested primarily in "women's issues," which are defined as those concerns that involve women's equality under the law and that evolved from women's traditional role as caregivers in family and society: health care, education, and the welfare of children and family. Yet we know that women do not necessarily come to the legislature with a feminist agenda. In fact, some have even declined to identify with women's issues, fearing this will give them less status in the male-driven body.[58]

In reality, there is no typical female legislator. Yet, whether they call themselves conservative, moderate, or liberal, women are likely to support women's issues, perhaps because they more easily recognize the inequities present in the lives of women and children. At the same time, women—especially those who are attorneys—are particularly attuned to passing reform measures that will achieve equality for all Texans, regardless of gender, race, or socioeconomic status. In an interview, Cyndi Taylor Krier expressed her beliefs in the importance of having people in elective office who are representative of the whole population. To Krier, having women in office—no matter the level of government—does not mean they will necessarily vote differently, but they will likely prioritize issues differently and often they will present views differently.[59]

These female attorneys, undoubtedly, have made and are continuing to make an impact in the halls of state government during their tenures in the legislature. The number of women filling these positions has increased over the years, but most would agree that being a candidate for elective office is still a daunting challenge, especially in the area of fund-raising. Yet their presence is no longer a novelty as it was in the beginning. It has become an accepted fact that women are smart enough and tough enough to be lawmakers in our state.

Legislative posts, of course, do not require a law degree. That is true of many other elective offices in the state. Yet women lawyers have often sought these positions and successfully held them. One of these jobs is that of county judge, the county's top administrative official and a potentially powerful position. After serving two terms in the Texas Senate, Cyndi Taylor Krier decided she wanted her political presence to be more constructive and productive. She ran for Bexar County judge on a campaign pledge to "open the courthouse to everyone." On December 8, 1992, Krier was sworn in as the first female county judge in the history of Bexar County. During her ten years in office, she focused on developing youth, education and conservation programs, controlling government spending, and enacting a broadly based ethics measure.[60]

Before Krier served as a county judge, Barbara Culver had served as county judge in Midland County. A practitioner in Midland, Culver was elected county judge in 1962 as the first female and the first

Republican in this position. She remained in the post for fifteen years. Culver was honored when the Midland County detention center was named Judge Barbara Culver Juvenile Justice Center.[61]

In many parts of the state, the county commissioners courts have been an impenetrable male body. Such was the case in Harris County until attorney Sylvia Garcia was elected to one of the four positions in 2002. Garcia, a graduate of Texas Southern University law school, served as presiding judge of the Houston Municipal Courts for ten years. Before that, Garcia was an attorney for the Gulf Coast Legal Foundation and an administrative law judge for the Equal Employment Opportunity Commission, and she had her own law firm. In 1998 she became controller for the city of Houston, where she remained until she successfully ran for county commissioner. Garcia is not only the first woman on the Harris County Commissioners Court, but she is also the first Hispanic to occupy a seat.[62]

Women have also served as the mayors of the places where they reside. This office, like others, does not require a law degree. Nevertheless, several women lawyers have filled the position. Elizabeth Suiter was elected mayor of Winnsboro in 1963 after she left her post in the state legislature.[63] Artie Fultz Davis was Navasota's first woman mayor in 1978 to 1980,[64] while Minnie Solomonson served as mayor of South Padre Island from 1982 to 1986 after retiring from her law practice in Dallas.[65] Evelyn Lord was elected mayor of Beaumont four times. Having previously served on Beaumont's city council, she occupied the mayor's chair from 1990 to 1994 and from 2002 to 2005. Lord, who decided to become a lawyer when she served as a state senator in Delaware in the early 1960s, graduated from the University of Louisville School of Law (now Brandeis School of Law) as the only woman in a class of 108. Although Lord kept being detoured from becoming a member of the State Bar in Texas by family responsibilities and relocations, she worked as the legal administrator for the Beaumont firm of Orgain, Bell and Tucker, as vice president of Texas Commerce Bank, and was instrumental in founding Beaumont's teen court, which is named for her. Although Lord never became a practicing lawyer in Texas, she remarked, "I can truthfully say that my legal education has always stood me in marvelous stead in whatever position I found myself."[66]

Only six women from Texas have ever served in the United States Congress. Three of those have been attorneys.[67] In 1972 Barbara Jordan moved from her post in the Texas Senate to the U.S. House of Representatives, where she became the first black woman from a southern state and the first black Texan to take a seat in Congress. She was also the first Texas woman elected to Congress in her own right. During her three congressional terms, Jordan cosponsored bills establishing equal credit for women, freedom of information, a larger food commodities program for school lunches, tax credits for low-income workers, and several health programs. She also supported the extension of the 1965 Voting Rights Act to cover Mexican Americans in the Southwest in spite of the opposition of the Texas congressional delegation, the governor of Texas, and the secretary of state of Texas. After serving three terms, Jordan announced she would not seek reelection. Instead, she returned to Texas and became a professor at the Lyndon Baines Johnson School of Public Affairs at the University of Texas, teaching courses in ethics and political values.[68]

Kay Bailey Hutchison blazed a new trail in 1993 when she became the first female from Texas to serve in the United States Senate. Hutchison, a former state treasurer, has been reelected three times since her initial election to an unexpired term. She has supported the expansion of funding for breast cancer research and passed bills making stalking a federal crime and allowing full-time homemakers to save for retirement through IRAs. Other areas where she holds committee positions are homeland security, defense, and education. Hutchison is the fourth-highest-ranking Republican in the Senate, having been elected by her colleagues to serve as chair of the Republican Policy Committee in the One-hundredth Congress.[69]

In 1994 Sheila Jackson Lee, a University of Virginia Law School graduate, was elected to the U.S. House of Representatives from the Eighteenth Congressional District, which Barbara Jordan had also represented. Jackson Lee had previously served as a municipal judge in Houston and as a member-at-large on the Houston City Council. In Congress, Jackson Lee is an outspoken advocate for her stance on issues, which range from supporting affirmative action to immigrants' and women's rights. Minority issues are at the forefront of Jackson Lee's political concerns. She is the first vice chair of the congressional Black Caucus.[70] Jackson Lee, like Hutchison, is still serving in Congress.

Although no woman has ever ascended to either of the top two positions in our country, two Texas women had the spotlight on them as nominees at national conventions. In 1952, while president of the National Federation of Business and Professional Women's clubs, Judge Sarah Hughes was nominated for the vice presidency on the Democratic ticket. She found a woman to second the nomination when no man would agree to do so. The nomination, however, was just a formality because Democratic Party chair, fellow Texan Sam Rayburn, would not allow the nomination to be made unless Hughes immediately withdrew her name from consideration. Hughes later recalled, "I'm glad it wasn't finally put to a vote, because I only had two and a half votes."[71]

Frances "Sissy" Farenthold was more successful at garnering votes when she was nominated for vice president at the National Democratic Convention in 1972. Farenthold was nominated by a multiracial coalition led by the newly formed National Women's Political Caucus. She won 420 votes, coming in second to the eventual nominee, Senator Thomas Eagleton. This made Farenthold the first woman ever to receive convention votes for vice president. "That was the first time I was supported because I was a woman. I had always been supported despite the fact," she ironically commented after the convention.[72] The following year Farenthold became the first chair of the National

Women's Political Caucus, which was founded to develop a bipartisan political strategy to involve more women, minorities, and young people in electoral politics.[73]

There is no doubt that women are being elected to public office in larger numbers than ever before. Yet they are far from holding 50 percent of the elective offices in Texas—a number that would more nearly reflect the percentage of women in the general population. Why is this true eighty-five years after a woman broke the gender barrier by being elected to the Texas legislature? Women continue to face difficulties in raising money for political campaigns. They often face male incumbents better situated to utilize the party structure, whether Democratic or Republican. And, unlikely as it may seem, there is still inherent prejudice against placing a woman in a position of power, no matter the locale.

Shortly before her death, Barbara Jordan reflected on her career in the Texas legislature and the fact that many Texans were still not fully represented there. Jordan declared, "We cannot stand to have, in a democracy, any significant portion of the people who do not have a voice in what happens to them. All I know is that we as a people—black, white, Asian, Hispanic, must keep scratching the surface until we get where we've got to be, and that's all-inclusiveness for all people."[74]

Notes

1. Jones and Winegarten, 78.

2. Ibid., 77–80.

3. Women were forced to make their own rules as they entered the public stage, and they became experts at devising methods in which they could promote their own agenda. For a historical perspective on women's changing lives, see William Chafe, *The Paradox of Change: American Women in the 20th Century* (Oxford: Oxford University Press, 1991); Dorothy and Carl J. Schneider, *American Women in the Progressive Era, 1900–1920: Change, Challenge & the Struggle for Women's Rights* (New York: Doubleday, 1993); Glenna Matthews, *The Rise of Public Woman* (New

York: Oxford University Press, 1992). For a contemporary view of women in public life, see Deborah L. Rhode, ed., *The Difference "Difference" Makes: Women and Leadership* (Stanford: Stanford University Press, 2003).

4. Scott, *Handbook of Texas,* 6:818.

5. Jones and Winegarten, 11.

6. Ibid., 96.

7. Payne, *Sarah T. Hughes*, 39. Viglini was described as "small and fiery" in the *Dallas Times Herald*, April 30, 1930.

8. Jones and Winegarten, 96–97.

9. Ibid., 97.

10. Ibid., 99. Hughes would claim later that the greatest achievement of her career was the construction of a new Dallas County jail, eight years after she ordered improvements to the jail. It appears that Hughes was enthusiastic about every endeavor she undertook.

11. Ibid., 103.

12. Ibid., 103–05.

13. Ibid., 105. For her efforts in revising corporate statutes, Amsler was given the State Bar of Texas' first President's Award, given to the outstanding attorney in the state.

14. Ibid., 118–19.

15. Ibid., 6.

16. Rogers, 111.

17. Jones and Winegarten, 147.

18. Ibid., 146–47.

19. Elizabeth W. Fernea and Marilyn P. Duncan, eds., *Texas Women in Politics* (Austin: Foundation for Women's Resources, 1977), 62.

20. Jones and Winegarten, 153–54.

21. Ibid., 153–56.

22. Ann MacNaughton, interview by author, June 15, 2007. MacNaughton was a

student in the class.

23. Jones and Winegarten, 158–59.

24. Ibid., 159.

25. Ann Fears Crawford and Crystal Sasse Ragsdale, *Texas Women: Frontier to Future* (Austin: State House Press, 1998), 352–53.

26. Fernea and Duncan, 78–79. After the election was over, Weddinton's opponent was severely teased by his friends for letting a "sweet, little girl" defeat him after he had spent so much money trying to win. His answer was that she had tried to deceive the public because sometimes she wore her hair up and sometimes it was down, and that sometimes she wore short skirts and other times they were long. He could never admit that he was defeated by a better-qualified candidate who happened to be a woman.

27. Jones and Winegarten, 163.

28. Fernea and Duncan, 81.

29. Jones and Winegarten, 163–64.

30. Ibid., 176–78.

31. Ibid., 163.

32. Ibid., 154.

33. Ibid., 255.

34. Ibid., 15.

35. Ibid., 191–93.

36. Ibid., 201–03.

37. Ibid., 204.

38. Roxanne Almaraz, "Irma Rangel: Lawyer, Legislator, Educator," Stanford University Law School Women's Legal History Biography Project, Spring 2004, http://womenslegalhistory.stanford.edu/papers04/Rangel_bio-AlmarzS04.pdf (accessed March 2, 2007).

39. Jones and Winegarten, 211.

40. Ibid., 212–13.

41. Ibid.

42. Ibid., 217–18.

43. Crawford and Ragsdale, 301.

44. Ibid.

45. Jones and Winegarten, 231–32.

46. Ibid., 232.

47. Ibid., 246–47.

48. Ibid., 250–51.

49. Ibid., 252–53.

50. Ibid.

51. See list of state officeholders.

52. Jones and Winegarten, 262, 263, 267.

53. Karen Olsson, "Who Wants to be a Legislator?" *The Texas Observer*, February 19, 2001, http://www.texasobserver.org/article.php?aid=638 (accessed September 14, 2007).

54. Carter Casteel, http://www.cartercasteel.com/page2/page2.html (accessed March 9, 2007).

55. Texas House of Representatives Membership, http://www.house.state.tx.us/members/dist41/gonzales.htm (accessed March 9, 2007).

56. Texas House of Representatives Membership, http://www.house.state.tx.us/members/dist35/bio/toureilles.htm (accessed March 12, 2007).

57. Texas House of Representatives Membership, http://www.house.state.tx.us/members/dist143/bio/hernandez.htm (accessed March 9, 2007).

58. Jones and Winegarten, 15–16.

59. Crawford and Ragsdale, 305.

60. The University of Texas System, Board of Regents, http://www.utsystem.edu/BOR/profiles/Krier.htm (accessed June 29, 2007). At the time this article appeared, Krier was vice chair of the University of Texas Board of Regents.

61. *Texas Bar Journal,* 37, 5:423.

62. Sylvia Garcia, http://www.co.harris.tx.us/comm_garcia/Commissioner.aspx (accessed August 2, 2007). While Garcia was the first woman elected in her own right to a county commissioners court, before her election two other women had been appointed to replace their husbands on the Harris County court.

63. *Texas Bar Journal*, 28, 1:77.

64. Kathy Day correspondence, November 25, 2006.

65. *Texas Bar Journal*, 67, 6:493.

66. Evelyn Lord, correspondence to Deborah Penner and Ellen Grimes, January 28, 2006.

67. The others were Lera Thomas, Kay Granger, and Eddie Bernice Johnson.

68. Lasher, 102.

69. Kay Bailey Hutchison, http://hutchison.senate.gov/bio.html (accessed May 14, 2007).

70. Claudia Feldman, "Sheila Jackson Lee Goes to Washington," *Houston Chronicle*, Texas Magazine, February 19, 1995, 6.

71. Payne, *Sarah T. Hughes*, 164–68. Hughes said that she was not so naive as to think a woman could be elected vice president in 1952, but she thought women should get in the arena and fight instead of "stuffing letters and licking stamps."

72. Jones and Winegarten, 156.

73. The Women's Political Caucus became the organization most responsible for pushing women's rights. Ibid., 378.

74. Jones and Winegarten, 61.

CHAPTER SEVEN

Ascending to the Bench

IN FEBRUARY 1935, SARAH T. HUGHES WAS APPOINTED JUDGE of the Fourteenth District Court in Dallas County by Governor William Allred, who described Hughes as "capable, conscientious and courageous."[1] Since no woman had ever served in a permanent position in the state judiciary, the appointment generated a great deal of attention and no small amount of controversy. Hughes' own state senator complained, "Mrs. Hughes is a married woman and should be at home washing dishes."[2] Women throughout the state were insulted by the senator's remark and responded by mobilizing with great enthusiasm on Hughes' behalf. Her appointment was confirmed after fiery debate in the Senate chambers.[3] Judge Hughes would be reelected to the post for the next twenty-six years. During that time, however, she would have few female colleagues join her on the bench.

Women judges actually had a very auspicious beginning in Texas. In 1925 a potential conflict of interest arose that not only disqualified the three sitting justices on the court, but possibly eliminated every male member of the bar from serving as replacements. At issue was a trust and title dispute involving two tracts of land in El Paso

County and the Woodmen of the World, a fraternal organization that sold insurance to men who then automatically became members of a Woodmen lodge.[4] Nearly every male lawyer in the state in 1925 was a member.[5] At the trial-court level, plaintiff J. M. Darr and those who joined him, acting as trustees for the Woodmen of the World, were partially successful, having been given title to only one tract of land. On immediate appeal, however, judgment was reversed, granting the plaintiffs title to both tracts of land. When the case came to the state's highest court, Governor Pat Neff appointed three women—Hortense Ward of Houston, Edith Wilmans of Dallas, and Nellie Gray Robertson of Granbury—to replace the disqualified justices. Then Neff discovered that Robertson, who was to have been chief justice, and Wilmans did not have the seven years of experience required for the post. Neff sought to place Emma Webb of Elgin on the court, but she, too, was unqualified. The governor finally found qualified lawyers in Hattie Henenberg of Dallas and Ruth Brazzil of Galveston. Hortense Ward was then named chief justice.[6] Of the thirty licensed female lawyers in Texas at that time, it appears that only ten had more than seven years of service at the bar.[7]

A week before the case was to be heard, *The Dallas Morning News* reported, "All records were shattered and at least three precedents established . . . when Gov. Neff appointed a special Supreme Court composed entirely of women. It was a healthy New Year gift of recognition to the woman barrister of today. This is the first instance a woman has been appointed to sit on the supreme bench; it is the first time a higher court is to be composed entirely of women; and it is the initial case where a majority of the judges will be women."[8] Both the legal profession and the public were waiting in anticipation to see if women could, indeed, carry forth such an important task.

The court session opened on January 8, 1925. The clerk of the court was absent. According to papers in the Texas State Library, he "arrived with a cane fishing pole and a jug . . . saying . . . I'll be d___ed if I am going to nursemaid a bunch of women. I'm going fishing."[9] And he departed. The three women were administered the oath of office, which at that time required each justice to swear that she had never fought a duel. It was duly noted that none of them raised their right hands as they took the oath. The case, *Johnson v. Darr*, was heard on January 30, 1925. Four months later the all-female court affirmed the decision of the appeals court with Chief Justice Ward writing the opinion.[10] The proceedings were widely publicized as being a novelty. Ward, however, remarked, "The novelty . . . is entirely lost in the great responsibility."[11] In an appearance before the Texas House of Representatives, Ward added, "It is the ambition of the women today to break down the prejudices which men have against them in business and the professions, so that the way may be smoother for those who follow."[12] Although the female justices' capable efforts were widely considered a step in that direction, it would be almost sixty years before another woman sat on the Texas Supreme Court.[13]

That landmark event occurred in 1982 when Ruby Kless Sondock was appointed to the high court. She later recalled that she thought the letter from the governor's office was a joke and called the Capitol to verify that it was real.[14] Sondock had never dreamed of becoming a judge, but in 1973 she was the first female lawyer in Harris County appointed to a judicial position, initially in a family court and four years later in the 234th District Court. Although Sondock served on the Supreme Court of Texas for only six months, she opened the doors to the presence of women on the high court.[15] Barbara Culver, a Southern Methodist University law graduate, was appointed to a position on the supreme court in 1988 after serving as a state district judge for ten years. Her tenure was also brief—only ten months—but it confirmed that women were certainly competent to sit on the state's highest court.[16]

Not until 1992, however, was a woman elected to a six-year term on the Texas Supreme Court. Rose Spector, a St. Mary's graduate from

San Antonio, took her seat after serving as both a judge of a county court at law and of a state district court in Bexar County.[17] In 1995 Priscilla Owen joined Justice Spector on the high court. A graduate of Baylor's law school, Owen had practiced commercial litigation for seventeen years in the Houston firm of Andrews Kurth, where she was a partner. She was reelected to the supreme court in 2000, but left in 2005 when her appointment by President George W. Bush to the U.S. Fifth Circuit Court of Appeals was confirmed.[18] In 1997 Deborah Hankinson was appointed by Bush, then governor of Texas, to the high court. Hankinson's first career was as a teacher in the public schools, where she initiated curriculum and established resources to make special education more accessible to those students who needed it. Realizing that the law could impact education in a positive way, Hankinson entered SMU law school. After graduating she joined the firm of Thompson and Knight in Dallas. In 1995 Hankinson was appointed to the Texas Fifth Court of Appeals and two years later to the Texas Supreme Court, where she became the third woman justice.[19] Harriet O'Neill was elected to the court in 1998 and reelected to a second term in 2004. O'Neill's judicial career began when she was elected to a district court in Harris County. She then served on the Fourteenth Court of Appeals. A graduate of the University of South Carolina School of Law, O'Neill practiced law in Houston, concentrating primarily in complex business and commercial litigation before opening her own office to focus on mediating legal disputes. Justice O'Neill's term extends through 2010.[20] This remains an interesting question—will she be joined by other women justices while she is on the court? Only nine women have served on the Texas Supreme Court in its 171-year history. It appears that the same glass ceiling that a woman faces in becoming managing partner of a firm or dean of a law school exists on Texas' highest court as well.

On a more positive note, women fill many judicial positions in the state today although their access to the judiciary was slow in the beginning. The first woman to run for a judicial seat in Texas was Hortense Ward. In 1920 she presented herself as a candidate for a Harris County court position. Her campaign slogan was: "Don't vote for me because I am a woman but don't vote against me because I am a woman."[21] Ward, obviously, felt qualified for a judicial position, but she realized that gender was an issue in the race, which she lost. Even though women could cast ballots in this election, it was clear that most voters, including many women, did not yet feel that women belonged in the courtroom, especially in a seat of authority.[22]

Texas was not alone in moving very slowly in accepting women into the judiciary. A woman was named to a judicial position for the first time in the United States in 1870 when Esther McQuigg Morris became a justice of the peace in South Pass City, Wyoming.[23] By 1900 only five women in the country had served in any judicial or quasi-judicial capacity. Two decades later that number had risen by only ten. Even when women won the vote in 1920, the percentage of women on the bench did not substantially improve. In 1930 only twelve states had at least one woman judge. Not until 1979 did every state in the union have at least one woman serving in some judicial capacity.[24]

The assimilation of women into the judiciary proved to be a long, difficult climb in Texas, just as it was in the rest of the country. Judge Sarah Hughes remained the lone state district judge in Texas until 1957 when Beth Wright was appointed to preside over the Domestic Relations Court (later the 301st Family District Court) in Dallas County. Wright was admitted to the Texas Bar in 1941 after graduating from Southern Methodist University School of Law.[25] In the same year of Judge Wright's appointment, Pat Moore was elected judge of Lubbock County Court at Law No. 2. Judge Moore would go on to be elected the first woman judge of the Seventy-second District Court, which included Crosby and Lubbock counties, and would be reelected numerous times.[26]

As 1960 approached, there were only a handful of women occupying judicial positions in the entire state. That year an Amarillo lawyer, Mary Lou Robinson, became judge of the 108th District Court in Potter County, having previously served three years as a judge in the county courts.[27] Robinson, a 1950 graduate of the University of Texas law school, revealed that she decided in the seventh grade to become a lawyer because she had "a sense that life wasn't always fair, and while that couldn't be remedied altogether, there were things that the law and lawyers could do that make things better for people who didn't have the full advantages that society offered."[28] In 1973 Judge Robinson moved from the state district court to the Seventh Court of Appeals, where she became the first woman on an appellate bench in the state. In 1977 Justice Robinson scored another first when she advanced to chief justice of the Seventh Court of Appeals. She remained in that position until 1979 when President Jimmy Carter appointed her to the U.S. District Court for the Northern District of Texas, making her the second woman in Texas to become a federal judge.[29]

The first, and only the second in the country, was Judge Sarah Hughes, who became a household name when she swore in Vice President Lyndon Baines Johnson as president on that fateful day in Dallas.[30] Hughes' federal judiciary career, which began in 1961, was due to her own initiative. She later commented, "President Kennedy never would have appointed me if I hadn't let him know I was down here."[31] "I think you've got to ask for things. You can't wait to have things given to you."[32] Yet her appointment met with opposition from a powerful source, the American Bar Association, which claimed that Hughes was unqualified because of her age. (She was sixty-five at the time.) In spite of this opposition, Hughes' fellow Texans—Speaker of the House Sam Rayburn and Vice President Lyndon B. Johnson—were able to push the appointment through.[33] This political support, which was lacking for most women, was the key in Judge Sarah Hughes' successful ascent to the federal bench where she remained for fourteen years. She then took senior status and continued to hear cases until a stroke brought an end to her judicial career at the age of eighty-eight.[34]

In 1962 Eva Bloore Barnes was the first woman elected to the bench in Tarrant County. By the time this occurred, Barnes had been practicing law for thirty years. The newspaper article reporting on her swearing-in ceremony cited her qualifications for the office but seemed more interested in describing her outfit—a royal blue Chanel-style suit with matching pillbox hat. It seems that a woman's appearance still received more attention from the press than her professional qualifications.[35] Yet Judge Barnes was most serious about her judicial duties. Her domestic relations court was usually filled with cases in which children had been emotionally damaged by combative divorcing parents or absent parents. Judge Barnes worked tirelessly to improve the conditions in which children lived. As an assistant district attorney some years before, Barnes had spearheaded a move to reword portions of the Texas adoption laws. She frequently appeared on the bench without her robe, feeling that troubled families—especially the children—would be less fearful of the courtroom experience. Judge Barnes was reelected four times and retired in 1979.[36]

As late as the mid-1960s, women lawyers usually dismissed the idea of aspiring to the judiciary. Prejudice against women in the legal profession had kept judicial positions almost entirely in the male domain. Ruth Kern of El Paso commented after losing a race for judge in the early 1970s, "I was swamped in a local bar poll for candidates for judge, receiving only 22% of the vote, largely because of my sex. I believe the results would have been the same had my male opponent and I been running for Mother of the Year."[37] Women were not the "wheelers and dealers" in the political arena, so they did not have the support of the grassroots politicians. In partisan elections, the endorsement of a political party's leadership could be a plus for candidates, and women usually found that unavailable to them. Women also found it difficult to raise funds for election campaigns.

Nancy Westerfield faced all of these problems when she decided to run for a civil court bench in Harris County in 1972. She later recalled that as a result, she ran a "novice campaign." Westerfield had three male opponents in the race. Her slogan was "Harris County is ready for a WOMAN JUDGE. There are 60 judges in this county—all are men." Westerfield made the runoff and faced a longtime political figure. Her opponent campaigned against her by handing out emery boards with his name prominently displayed on both sides. As he gave them to voters, he commented, "I hope women do think of my opponent when they get a hangnail." Westerfield, who was in the first class to enroll at the University of Houston Law Center in 1948, lost a close race, receiving 49.7 percent of the vote. She inspired other women, however, to consider running for a judicial post.[38]

The year after Westerfield's trailblazing run for a judicial office, Mary Pearl Hall Williams was appointed to a county court at law bench in Travis County, making her the first female judge in that jurisdiction. Williams, a 1949 graduate of the University of Texas law school, began her career as an assistant attorney general. After working on the Civil Rights Compliance Staff in the Office of Emergency Preparedness in Washington, D.C., Williams returned to Austin where in 1980 she was elected to the 53rd District Court, a position she held until her retirement in 2000.[39]

In 1974 three women were on the ballot in Bexar County for judicial seats. Some felt that this was a coordinated effort to put together a women's ticket, but it seemed to be a coincidence. Carol Haberman, a St. Mary's law graduate, had served on the San Antonio City Council after practicing law for fifteen years. Rose Spector had been appointed a municipal judge in Olmos Park. Carolyn Spears had been admitted to the bar only five years earlier, acquiring a law license without graduating from law school. After time spent in the district attorney's office and in private practice, Spears ran in her first judicial race.[40] All three women won election. Suddenly, half the county court benches in San Antonio were held by women. Spector recalled, "Voters were very accepting of the idea of women judges. Lawyers were more skeptical."[41] By the end of the decade the three women had been elevated to district court benches. Judge Haberman was appointed to the 45th District Court in 1977, becoming Bexar County's first female district judge, while Judge Spears and Judge Spector were elected in 1980 to other civil district courts.[42]

In a rigidly segregated society like Texas, an African-American woman had little hope of becoming a judge. Yet in 1973 Charlye O. Farris was appointed to serve as a special judge in Wichita County in the absence of the regular judge. Farris, after serving her brief time on the bench, returned to her law practice in Wichita Falls.[43] Six years later Gabrielle Kirk McDonald became the first African-American, male or female, to be seated in the Southern District of Texas. After graduating at the top of her class at Howard University School of Law, McDonald worked for the Legal Defense Fund in the South where she did civil rights work in the area of employment law. Moving to Houston in 1969, she practiced law with her husband. Although her appointment to the federal bench was a landmark one, McDonald insisted that she had never aspired to be a judge. She remained in the position for nine years before stepping down. Judge McDonald then had the extraordinary experience of being elected by the U. N. General Assembly as one of eleven judges for a United Nations Tribunal Court scheduled to conduct the first war trial since Nuremberg. She was the only American and one of two women chosen for the court, receiving more votes then any other potential panel member. In all of these roles, Judge McDonald has shown a passion for justice and has used the rule of law to combat injustice. As she explained, "I believe in the rule of law not just intellectually. It's visceral for me. It's in my heart and soul . . . it's what protects people from anarchy."[44]

Joe Kegans, the first woman to sit as judge in a state district criminal court, had established a career as a tough, able lawyer but she never let people forget she was a woman. She hung a sign in her chambers that read, "Sure, God created man before woman. But then you always make a rough draft before the final masterpiece." For nineteen years Judge Kegans remained on the bench handling cases ranging from probation violations to ice-pick killers. At the same time, she was encouraging and protective to women lawyers who appeared in her court, becoming a mentor to many of them.[45]

The same year that President Carter appointed Mary Lou Robinson to a federal judgeship, he appointed another Texas woman, Carolyn Dineen King, to the United States Fifth Circuit Court of Appeals. King's journey to this lofty position exemplifies what many women of her time experienced. She graduated from Yale Law School in 1962 and after moving to Houston applied for a job in the U.S. Attorney's Office. Regardless of her exemplary credentials, she was rejected for the position, and the U.S. attorney admitted that he was not ready to hire a woman. Later that year King joined one of the city's largest law firms, but it took negotiating on her part to receive the same starting salary as the men. She spent ten years there as a corporate securities lawyer but moved to another firm when she was not offered a partnership, apparently due to her gender. When President Carter appointed her in 1979, King became the second woman named to the Fifth Circuit Court.[46] She made further history in 1999 when she became the first woman ever to become the court's chief justice.[47] Justice King held that position until 2006 when she was succeeded by another Texas woman, Edith Hollan Jones, who was appointed to the Fifth Circuit Court in 1985 at the young age of thirty-six. Jones, a University of Texas graduate, had already posted an impressive achievement when she became the first female partner in the Houston firm of Andrews, Kurth, Campbell, and Jones where she specialized in bankruptcy law.[48] In October 2007, Jennifer Walker Elrod was confirmed by the U.S. Senate to the Fifth Circuit Court. Elrod, a graduate of Harvard Law School, previously served as a state district court judge in Harris County.[49]

The fact that only six women have served on the Fifth Circuit

Court of Appeals since its inception in 1891 indicates that women are still a small minority on these higher courts. Jimmy Carter was the first president to make a conscious effort to appoint more women to the federal judiciary.[50] When he contacted Carolyn Dineen King, she reminded him that she was a Republican and therefore not a member of his party. Carter replied that party affiliation did not matter to him. He added that he was looking for a good lawyer and a woman and that she met both of those qualifications. In 2002 at the request of U.S. Supreme Court Chief Justice William Rehnquist, Justice King became the first woman to chair the Executive Committee of the Judicial Conference of the United States.[51]

If women in general were sparsely represented on the bench, minority women were totally absent until the 1965 Voting Rights Act was enacted. Some of these women, however, were trailblazers. When Harriet Murphy became a judge in Austin's municipal court, she was the first African-American woman appointed to a regular judgeship in the state. Judge Murphy would eventually serve as the presiding judge of the court.[52] Joan Tarpley was appointed to the state district bench in Dallas County, after serving as the first African-American woman on the county court at law.[53] Alice Bonner was the first to occupy a district judgeship in Harris County.[54] Perhaps the most unheralded occurrence took place in 1974 when Rosemary Saucillo Moreno was appointed to Houston's municipal court as its first Hispanic female. Moreno put herself through the University of Houston law school, graduating in 1965. After nine years on the bench, she returned to her law practice as a single mother after the death of her husband. When Judge Moreno died, Judge Berta Mejia, presiding judge of the Houston court, called her a mentor by explaining, "She opened the doors for me and other Latinas to pursue this career as a judge."[55]

The very first judicial post held by a woman in Texas was, actually, in a municipal court. Helen Viglini was named to the corporate court in Dallas in 1925. She did not remain on the bench long since she felt a strong pull toward the practice of criminal law.[56] There is no definitive record to indicate the names of women who served in municipalities' judiciaries over the next three decades. By the 1960s, however, women across the state were being appointed to these courts. Josephine Myrick Jameson was named to the municipal bench in Abilene.[57] Leona Malmstrom Franklin was the first woman justice in Victoria, and while on the bench served as the first woman president of the Texas Municipal Courts Association.[58] Both of these women had varied careers in law. After Jameson and her attorney husband moved to Abilene, she ceased working when her children were born. After her husband's untimely death, Jameson did graduate work in law at SMU and then joined an Abilene firm—Whitten, Harrell, and Erwin—that subsequently added her name to the firm. At that time she had two young sons. Jameson's journey in law is illustrative of how many women went about combining family and career—an issue that remained challenging for female attorneys. Franklin, who attended law school at UT while employed as a legal secretary for the Patterson law firm in Austin, was admitted to the bar in 1950 and joined the firm for which she had been working. Franklin became the first woman officer of the Texas State Junior Bar (later renamed Texas Young Lawyers Association). After her stint as a judge in Victoria, she was an attorney for Stewart Title Company and was an assistant Harris County attorney. When Kitty Schild was chosen as a municipal judge in El Paso, she was the first woman to occupy any judicial position in the county and paved the way for others to follow. After serving twelve years on the municipal court, she became judge of a county court at law. Schild also served as president of the Texas Municipal Courts Association.[59]

Yet it is apparent that judicial appointments of women were frequently handled differently from those of men. Janet Reusch's experience when she was appointed as a magistrate judge in the Western District of Texas in 1979 clearly illustrated the sexism present in the process. During her interview by an all-male committee prior to her confirmation, she was asked such questions as "Can you work without supervision?" and "Do you have difficulty making decisions?" This questioning was done in spite of the fact that Reusch's resume indicated that as an assistant U.S. attorney she had served as temporary head of the El Paso office and had been the government's trial attorney in thirty-seven criminal and civil trials. Before ending the interview, the same questioner asked about the color of the robe she planned to wear. Apparently, a joke had been circulated that Reusch should wear a pink robe with flowers around the collar. This interview might not seem remarkable, but as Reusch explained, a male with no prosecutorial experience was interviewed by the same committee a few months later. The tone of his interview was considerably different with no questions alluding to his lack of qualifications for the position or his preference for a robe color. Judge Reusch added that during her training at the Federal Judicial Center, the man in charge of the sessions made numerous sexist comments regarding the inability of women. The final insult was in constantly addressing the group as "gentlemen" in spite of the presence of two women.[60]

The number of women on the bench began to rise slowly in the 1980s as additional ones were either appointed or elected to positions. At the same time, the composition of the courts acquired more diversity. In 1983 Elma Salinas Ender of Laredo was appointed judge in the 341st Judicial District, making her the first Hispanic woman in Texas to serve in that capacity. Judge Salinas Ender, a graduate of St. Mary's University School of Law, explained that she tried to mentor younger women who wanted to become attorneys. She advised them to prepare "by studying hard, reading to expand their vocabulary, and getting involved in the community."[61] In 1989 Leticia Hinojosa, a Brownsville native, was appointed as the first judge of the newly created Hidalgo County Court at Law No. 4. She won election to the post the following year with 68 percent of the vote. Judge Hinojosa later recalled that her victory illustrated that "the public was ready for a Hispanic judge."[62] In

1987 Hannah Chow, a native of China, became the first Asian woman to preside over a state district court. A graduate of South Texas College of Law, Judge Chow admitted that she encountered more discrimination as a woman than as an ethnic minority, but she also believed that Texas was a place that women could easily succeed in practicing law.[63] In 1990 Guadalupe Rivera became the first Hispanic woman elected to a district court bench in the entire state of Texas.[64] Carmen Kelsey became Bexar County's first black district judge in 1993. Kelsey had worked for years in the juvenile section of the district attorney's office, eventually becoming its chief. When the bench of the 289th District Court was vacated, Kelsey with her vast experience in juvenile law was appointed and subsequently won election to the seat.[65]

When Carolyn Wright became the first African-American woman to win a countywide race for a district court bench in Dallas County, she was used to conquering new terrain. After graduating from Howard University School of Law, Wright had settled in Dallas where she opened a private practice. At that time, she was only the second African-American woman to practice full-time in the city. Wright described those beginnings as "breaking into a new frontier." That pioneering spirit would continue with her election to a state district court and then an appointment to the Fifth Court of Appeals.[66]

By the early 1990s there were 209 full-time female judges in Texas.[67] The growing presence of women on the bench did not mean, however, that gender bias had disappeared. As a result, the National Association of Women Judges and the National Organization of Women Legal Defense and Education Fund banded together to push the state and federal courts to review a perceived bias against women that they believed existed in the courts. A comprehensive overview of issues impacting women in the various state judiciaries was begun in 1988. The federal judiciary followed suit in 1992 by establishing a task force in each federal circuit. Their findings were similar and focused on three problems: (1) the lack of women seeking to become judges,

(2) inappropriate interactions that take place in the courtroom, and (3) the difficult act of balancing family life with the demands of a legal career.[68] The recommendations to remedy the problem of too few women justices were explained by U.S. Supreme Court Justice Ruth Bader Ginsburg: "Women hold up half the sky and they will do so in our courts. They need no favors. They need only equal respect for their talent and equal sharing by men of the job of bringing up the next generation."[69] A practical suggestion was focusing more on the positions from which women move into the judiciary, and after identifying them, work within the system to see that more women hold those positions. Many on the task force found unacceptable treatment, both explicit and implicit, of female lawyers by male judges. In addition to overt examples of gender bias—sexually derogatory statements, inappropriate sexual advances, calling women by "familiar" phrases—there were more subtle ones, as well. Male judges seemed to pay more attention to male attorneys and were more impatient with female ones. They also were viewed as making derogatory remarks toward women judges and even more so toward minority females on the bench.[70] In addressing the issue of managing both a family and a career, U.S. Supreme Court Justice Sandra Day O'Connor observed that women professionals still have primary responsibilities for the children and the housekeeping, spending roughly twice as much time on these areas as do their professional husbands.[71] The traditional responses to these problems has been to give the woman a choice of delaying or forgoing family life or to place women on a special track where they will not achieve as much but will have the opportunity to have families. Many feminist scholars and women judges reject this view as inherently unfair to women. Instead, they urge both men and employers, including the courts, to share in child-rearing.

A less serious incident of gender bias, but still one that upset women, occurred in 1999 when a Tarrant County judge ruled that women must wear skirts and blouses or dresses in his courtroom. As might be expected, women accustomed to wearing tailored pants suits objected vehemently to the new dress code. A subsequent article in the *Fort Worth Star-Telegram* suggested that male attorneys and witnesses be required to wear spats and cutaway coats. A week later the judge made a new ruling in which he stated, "[r]egarding women's dress code, I have concluded that it was probably the wrong thing to do and it is hereby rescinded." It appeared that female attire was still receiving attention, just as it had back in 1920.[72]

Although Justice Mary Lou Robinson had opened the doors of the state appellate courts to women in 1973, it took another two decades for them to become more than just a token on these courts. In 1981 when the Texas courts of civil appeals became courts of appeals with both civil and criminal jurisdiction, it was necessary to add justices in some of the districts. The Fourth Court of Appeals grew from three to seven justices. After a round of interviews with members of Governor Clements' staff, Shirley Butts was appointed to one of the new seats on the Fourth Court of Appeals. Governor Clements ultimately appointed twenty-five new appellate judges throughout the state—twenty-four men and Shirley Butts. Despite the novelty of her appointment, Justice Butts insisted that there was "no great furor." She added that her relationship with the male justices was one of collegiality and mutual respect.[73]

Three additional women were named to the appellate courts during the 1980s. Annette Stewart was appointed to the Fifth Court of Appeals in 1983,[74] Camille Hutson-Dunn was elected to the First Court of Appeals in 1984,[75] and Marilyn Aboussie joined the Third Court of Appeals in 1986. Being the first woman to hold her new appointment was not an unusual experience for Aboussie. She was the first female attorney in every law firm in which she practiced and the first woman judge of a court of record in Concho Valley. In 1998 Justice Aboussie became the first female chief justice of the Third Court, a position she held for five years until her retirement.[76] In 1992 Susan Larsen became the first woman on the Eighth Court of Appeals, where she authored 1,440 opinions during her twelve years on the bench.[77] The Second Court of Appeals welcomed Judge Maryellen Whitlock Hicks in 1993 as its first female justice. Hicks, the first African-American graduate of Texas Tech law school, had served as a municipal court judge and a state district judge before being named to the appellate bench.[78] Linda Reyna Yañez, who received her J.D. degree from Texas Southern University Law School and an LL.M. from the University of Virginia Law School, was not only the first woman named to the Thirteenth Court of Appeals in 1993 but also the first Hispanic woman to be seated on any Texas appellate court.[79] That same year Alma L. López was the first Hispanic woman on the Fourth Court of Appeals. Justice López also claims the distinction of being the first Hispanic woman to serve as the chief justice on an appellate court in the United States.[80] Patrice Barron, a Tulane University Law School graduate, was named to the Fourteenth Court of Appeals in 1994 as its first female justice[81] while Diane DeVasto was elected in 2003 to the bench of the Twelfth Court of Appeals. Judge DeVasto, a Baylor law graduate, had twenty-three years of experience on the bench—municipal, county, and state—when she became an appellate judge.[82]

A criticism that was frequently expressed in an effort to keep women off the bench was that they would rule differently than men. Those who opposed women in the judiciary insisted that women would let their emotions and their sensitivity overrule their logic and reasoning. Even though women have come to the judiciary by way of civil-rights work or advocacy for children and the poor, it does not appear that this background has affected their judicial prudence.[83] Nevertheless, the state's first all-female panel to hear oral arguments in an appellate court drew widespread attention in the early 1990s. The three justices were Margaret Mirabel, Michol O'Connor, and Alice Oliver-Parrott of the First Court of Appeals. The case itself did not generate much interest, but the fact that the court's ruling was solely in the hands of women aroused a great deal of discussion. There was still the perception in many circles that decisions rendered by women from the bench would be influenced by their gender. Obviously that did not happen.[84] The legal profession, as well as the public, was slowly recognizing that females in the judiciary—like Lady Justice— could administer fair and equal justice without prejudice or favor.

In 2005 the Fourth Court of Appeals made judicial history when it became the first all-female appellate court in the nation. It was composed of Justices Alma L. López, Catherine Stone, Karen Angelini, Sandee Bryan Marion, Phylis Speedlin, Sarah Duncan, and Rebecca Simmons.[85] The unique makeup of the court received much publicity and even raised some eyebrows. Chief Justice Alma López replied to those who thought it was unusual, "We women don't think so. We think it's time. The men had it for one hundred and something years."[86] Associate Justice Rebecca Simmons added, "These are all very hardworking women and capable jurists. That's what got them to the appeals court, not their gender."[87] It was a short-lived all-female panel, however; a male replaced one of the female justices the next year. And there is another side to the story. Four appellate courts in the state—the Sixth, Ninth, Tenth, and Eleventh—have yet to seat a female justice.[88]

In 2007 there are four women on the Criminal Court of Appeals, including Chief Justice Sharon Keller, who was the first woman on that court in 1994.[89] There is only one woman on the Texas Supreme Court, while the district appellate courts are currently represented by thirty-two women. When one realizes that twenty years ago women were almost nonexistent on these courts, it is apparent that progress is being made toward placing women on the bench.

Only five Texas women—Sarah Hughes, Mary Lou Robinson, Gabrielle McDonald, Carolyn Dineen King, and Edith Jones—had served on the federal bench, either district or appellate, until 1989 when Melinda Harmon, an Exxon litigator for thirteen years, was appointed to the U.S. District Court for the Southern District of Texas.[90]

Three years would pass before another woman, Lee Rosenthal, was appointed to a Southern District bench. Rosenthal, a graduate of the University of Chicago Law School, had clerked for the chief justice of the U.S. Fifth Circuit Court of Appeals before being hired by Baker Botts in Houston.[91] In 1994 Judges Harmon and Rosenthal were joined by Janis Graham Jack[92] and Vanessa Gilmore.[93] Jack graduated from South Texas College of Law and had a family law practice in Corpus Christi for twelve years before being named to the bench. Gilmore, the youngest sitting federal judge in the nation when she was appointed, graduated from the University of Houston Law Center and was a civil litigator with a Houston firm for twelve years. Nancy F. Atlas, appointed in 1995, was a graduate of New York University School of Law and had been an assistant U.S. attorney in New York before moving to Houston and practicing with Sheinfeld, Maley & Kay.[94] In 1998 Hilda G. Tagle, a University of Texas law graduate, became the first Hispanic woman to become a federal judge in Texas, having previously been a Nueces County Court at Law judge.[95] Like Gabrielle McDonald before her, Judge Tagle had broken the racial barriers that minority lawyers faced.

The advent of the twenty-first century placed an additional six women on the federal bench, including Barbara M. G. Lynn and Jane Boyle in the Northern District, Marcia Crone in the Eastern District, and Kathleen Cardone and Alia Ludlum in the Western District. Lynn, a graduate of Southern Methodist University School of Law, had practiced with Carrington Coleman Sloman & Blumenthal for twenty-three years before her appointment.[96] Boyle, also an SMU law graduate, had previously been an assistant district attorney in Dallas, an assistant U S. attorney, U.S. attorney, and U.S. magistrate judge.[97] Cardone, a graduate of St. Mary's, was formerly a state district judge and the presiding judge on the El Paso Municipal Court.[98] Crone, a University of Houston law graduate, engaged in private practice in Houston before being named U.S. magistrate judge for the Eastern

District.[99] Ludlum, a University of Texas law graduate, had been an assistant county attorney for Travis County, an assistant U.S. attorney, a part-time mediator in private practice, and U.S. magistrate judge for the Western District.[100]

In 1968 Congress expanded the federal judicial system by instituting the position of magistrate judge. Unlike the life-tenured judges of the U.S. district courts, these judges serve for a period of eight years and are assigned cases for jury or nonjury trials in an effort to manage increasing caseloads in the district courts. The women currently serving as magistrate judges in Texas are Nancy Koenig and Irma C. Ramirez in the Northern District; Nancy Stein Nowak and Pamela A. Mathy in the Western District; Caroline M. Craven and Judith Guthrie in the Eastern District; and Adriana Arce-Flores, Janice Ellington, Nancy K. Johnson, Mary Milloy, Dorina Ramos, Diana Saldaña, and Frances Stacy in the Southern District.[101] Judge Sarah T. Hughes, the lone federal district judge in Texas for almost two decades, did not live to see the advances made by women in the judiciary. She would not be surprised, however, because Judge Hughes had complete confidence in women's ability to rule from the bench.

The National Association of Women Judges (NAWJ) was organized in 1979 to alleviate what founder Joan Dempsey Klein called "the very lonely, very isolated lives of those women judges who may be the only one[s] on their bench in that locale or state. Often they are treated rather shabbily or are subject to subtle discriminatory practices in assignments and these judges find the NAWJ helps them to discuss mutual problems and feelings and to gain self-confidence."[102] At that time Texas had twenty-nine women judges in state courts—twenty-eight trial judges and one in an appellate court. When Justice Bea Ann Smith, a member of the Third Court of Appeals, attended her first NAWJ conference in 1997 she was the only Texas judge present. She returned home determined to recruit more Texas judges for the prestigious organization of 1,200 state and federal judges. In 2002, when

Smith was elected to the presidency of the NAWJ, Texas was represented by fifty-five judges.[103]

Seventy-five years after the first woman took a seat in the state judicial system, women represent 29 percent of all full-time judges in Texas. That figure translates today into 454 female judges as compared to 1,095 males on the bench. The real disparity appears within the ethnicity of the judges. Among women currently occupying the bench, 85 percent are Caucasian, 10 percent are Hispanic, 2 percent are African-American, less than 1 percent are Asian, and none are Native American.[104] While women in general are underrepresented in proportion to their population figures, ethnic minorities occupy too few positions in the judiciary. Barriers obviously still exist for these lawyers.

Judge Vanessa Gilmore is helping to erase some of those barriers. As Gilmore tells the story, she was giving a tour of the courthouse to a group of third- and fourth-graders when "[a] little girl raised her hand and asked me why the only portraits hanging on the wall were of old white men. I told her because in the past, those were the people who were chosen to be judges. But that was the past; things were changing. And one day I hoped she would see my portrait hanging there, along with a number of people who looked like her."[105] Gilmore may have planted the seeds of hope in a young girl who might grow up to be a judge.

Today a judgeship is considered a reasonable aspiration and a pursuable attainment for women. No longer are women considered unfit to sit on the bench just because of their gender. They have proved to be worthy of wearing the robes of justice.

Notes

1. Payne, *Sarah T. Hughes*, 78.
2. Ibid.

3. Ibid., 84.

4. James R. Evans Jr., "An Exceptional Legacy," *Heritage*, Spring 1998, 13–14.

5. Scholarship conducted in recent years has presented evidence that may indicate this was not the primary reason for choosing an all-woman court. Some of the findings suggest that Governor Neff may have been trying to place women in prominent roles to downplay the attention that Miriam "Ma" Ferguson was receiving. Ferguson, who would succeed Neff in just a few months, and her husband, Jim "Pa" Ferguson, were no allies of Neff.

6. Hollace Weiner, "A Case When Women Reigned Supreme," *Texas Bar Journal*. 59, 9:890–891.

7. Evans, 13.

8. *Dallas Morning News.*

9. Weiner, 891.

10. Ibid., As of 1998, the holdings set forth in *Johnson v. Darr* had been mentioned in cases and law review articles more then thirty-five times since the court's opinion was published, according to *Shepherd's Citations*. As precedent, the case has been used to support later arguments in appellate courts.

11. Evans, 15.

12. "Legislators Hear Mrs. Hortense Ward," *Houston Chronicle*, January 31, 1925. While in Austin Ward, true to her persevering personality, presented a bill to the legislature which would provide a court of domestic relations in Harris County. (*Houston Chronicle*, January 30, 1925).

13. A portrait of the 1925 court was hung in the Supreme Court Building in 1997. Judge Ruby Sondock, who participated with the dedication ceremony for the portrait, said, "If they could see us now!"

14. *Texas Bar Journal*, 55, 1:98.

15. *Texas Bar Journal*, 61, 1:87.

16. *Texas Bar Journal*, 37, 5:423.

17. Brandon, 86–87.

18. Justice Priscilla Owen, Texas Judiciary Online (accessed March 29, 2005).

19. Kelley Jones King, "A Judicial Profile: Texas State Supreme Court Justice Deborah Hankinson," http://www.texasbar.com (accessed March 28, 2005).

20. Justice Harriet O'Neill, Texas Judiciary Online (accessed March 29, 2005).

21. *Houston Press*, July 1, 1920, 2.

22. Although women could vote in this election—their first in which to participate after the passage of the Nineteenth Amendment—many of them did not do so. In fact, suffrage leaders were very disappointed in the small number of women across the country who exercised this hard-earned right. During the 1920s, many women continued to be apathetic toward voting rights.

23. Morello, 219. Although Morris had no legal training, she rendered seventy legal opinions in less than nine months. A milliner by trade, she had been instrumental in drafting and gaining passage of the 1869 Women's Suffrage Bill, which made Wyoming women the first in the world to win equal suffrage. See Morello, Chapter 9, Women on the Bench, for an interesting review of the first women in the judiciary.

24. Ibid.

25. Payne, *Dallas*, 278.

26. McArthur, *Handbook of Texas*, 4:823.

27. U.S. District Court, Northern District, http://www.txnd.uscourts.gov/judges/robinson.html (accessed March 10, 2005).

28. *Women and the Law Newsletter*, April 2005, 3.

29. U.S. District Court, Northern District.

30. Payne, *Sarah T. Hughes*, 242–56. Payne gives a riveting story of this event, as experienced by Judge Hughes.

31. *Texas Bar Journal*, 37, 4:326.

32. Jones and Winegarten, 99.

33. Payne, *Sarah T. Hughes*, 209, 224.

34. Ibid., 394.

35. Arnold, 50.

36. Arnold, 51. Years earlier, some women lawyers in Texas had suggested that

every legal professional in the courtroom should wear a robe. In that way, attire would not become an issue, and men and women would appear equal. That suggestion, however, was never even considered by the courts.

37. *Texas Bar Journal*, 37, 5:423.

38. *The Houston Lawyer*, July-August 1999, 48.

39. Woods, Craddock and Brown, 122.

40. Brandon, 85.

41. Ibid., 86.

42. Ibid.

43. Minority Attorneys File, Bill and Vara Daniel Center for Legal History, State Bar of Texas.

44. Gabrielle Kirk McDonald, "Raising the Bar: Pioneers in the Legal Profession," American Bar Association, http://www.abanet.org/publiced/bh_mcdonald.html (accessed November 8, 2004). In 1963 when Gabrielle McDonald entered law school, there were only 142 African-American attorneys in the entire country.

45. *Houston Chronicle*, January 7, 1997.

46. Carolyn Dineen King, Commission on Women in the Profession, American Bar Association, http://www.abanet.org/women/bios/king.html (accessed February 16, 2007).

47. "Local woman named first to head 5th U.S. Circuit," *Houston Chronicle*, n.d.

48. Fredrickson, *Andrews & Kurth*, 131–32.

49. Dale Lezon, "Elrod appointed U.S. appeals judge," *Houston Chronicle*, October 5, 2007, B2.

50. Morello, 239. President Carter appointed forty-one women to the federal bench—more than all previous administrations together. He insisted that merit standards be used as mandated by the 1978 Omnibus Judgeship Act and that political affiliations be deemphasized.

51. Carolyn Dineen King, see note 46 above.

52. Woods, Craddock and Brown, 122.

53. Payne, *Dallas*, 278.

54. Harris County Judicial Directory, 1978, Houston Metropolitan Research Center, Houston Public Library.

55. "Moreno, pioneering municipal court jurist," *Houston Chronicle*, undated.

56. "Women Attorneys Busy in Dallas Courts," *Daily Times Herald*, February 1, 1925.

57. *Texas Bar Journal*, 32, 10:813.

58. Judge Leona Malmstrom Franklin, interview by author, November 12, 2006.

59. *El Paso Bar Bulletin*, May 2005, 10.

60. Judge Janet Reusch, correspondence to author, March 30, 2007.

61. "Raising the Bar: Pioneers in the Legal Profession," American Bar Association, http://www.abanet.org/publiced/ender.html (accessed May 10, 2005).

62. Acosta and Weingarten, 264.

63. *Texas Bar Journal*, 53, 9:1051–52.

64. *El Paso Bar Bulletin*, May 2005, 10–11.

65. Brandon, 80.

66. Rob Haley, "Judicial Profiles," Dallas Bar Association, http://www.dallasbar.org/judiciary/profiles.asp?item=53 (accessed June 8, 2007).

67. Women Attorney Statistical Profile, Department of Research and Analysis (2003–04), State Bar of Texas, 2.

68. Texas Center for Legal Ethics and Professionalism, Guidelines for Gender Neutral Courtroom Procedures, http://www.txethics.org/reference_procedures.asp (accessed February 25, 2007).

69. "Women in the U.S. Judiciary," *Wikipedia,* http://en.wikipedia.org/wiki/Women_in_the_U.S._Judiciary (accessed February 26, 2007).

70. Texas Center for Legal Ethics and Professionalism.

71. "Women in the U.S. Judiciary," see note 69 above.

72. Arnold, 101.

73. Ellen Mitchell, "A Portrait of Senior Justice Shirley Butts," *San Antonio*

Lawyer, March-April 2006, 5–7.

74. Payne, *Dallas*, 278.

75. Judge Camille Dunn, video interview, Houston Bar Association Archives.

76. Marilyn Aboussie, http://www.stennis.gov/swips/marilynaboussie.htm (accessed March 15, 2007).

77. Jeanne C. "Cezy" Collins, "First Female Justice at the Eighth Court of Appeals Leaves Bench After 12 Years," *Forum for Texas Lawyers,* Fall 2004, 4–5.

78. *Texas Tech Alumni Magazine,* n.d., 5.

79. Judge Linda Reyna Yañez, Thirteenth Court of Appeals, http://www.13thcoa.courts.state.tx.us/court/justice_lyanez.asp (accessed March 20, 2007).

80. Fourth Court of Appeals, http://www.4thcoa.courts.state.tx.us/court/justice_alopez.asp (accessed March 13, 2008).

81. Confirmed by telephone with clerk of the Fourteenth Court of Appeals, May 25, 2007.

82. Confirmed by telephone with clerk of the Twelfth Court of Appeals, May 15, 2007.

83. Epstein, 145.

84. Judge Michol O'Connor, telephone interview by author, June 29, 2007.

85. "Women set to make U.S. judicial history," *Houston Chronicle*, April 2, 2005.

86. Ibid.

87. Ibid.

88. Telephone calls made by the author to each of these courts to confirm that none of them has had a woman justice, May 15, 2007.

89. *Newsletter of the Texas Supreme Court Historical Society*, Vol. 2 (November 1997), n.p.

90. Harmon succeeded Judge John V. Singleton, for whom she had clerked fifteen years earlier.

91. Judge Lee Rosenthal, Federal Judiciary Online (accessed February 22, 2007).

92. Judge Janis Jack, Federal Judiciary Online (accessed February 22, 2007).

93. Judge Vanessa Gilmore, Federal Judiciary Online (accessed February 26, 2007).

94. Judge Nancy Atlas, Federal Judiciary Online (accessed February 22, 2007).

95. Judge Hilda Tagle, Federal Judiciary Online (accessed February 27, 2007).

96. Judge Barbara Lynn, Federal Judiciary Online (accessed February 22, 2007).

97. Judge Jane Boyle, Federal Judiciary Online (accessed February 27, 2007).

98. Judge Kathleen Cardone, Federal Judiciary Online (accessed March 2, 2007).

99. Judge Marcia Crone, Federal Judiciary (accessed February 22, 2007).

100. Judge Alia Ludlum, Federal Judiciary Online (accessed March 2, 2007).

101. Federal Magistrates Judges Association, http://www.fedjudge.org/index.asp (accessed April 10, 2007).

102. Morello, 245.

103. *UT Law*, Spring 2003, 50.

104. All figures are taken from the reports of the Department of Research and Analysis, State Bar of Texas.

105. "Federal Judge Vanessa Gilmore: The Many-Splendored Faces of Today's Black Women," *Ebony*, March 1997.

Chapter Eight

Taking Charge

In 1938 an editorial written by Ben H. Powell, then president of the Texas Bar Association, appeared in the pages of the *Texas Bar Journal*. Powell was advocating a section within the organization just for women. He wrote, "It is undoubtedly true that the number of women lawyers will increase more and more rapidly as the years come and go. It seems to me that a committee composed of women lawyers only may be able to do much for the profession."[1] Much to President Powell's surprise, a body of women lawyers objected to being set aside in the "Special Committee on Activities of Women Lawyers." They wanted women to participate in any section of the bar that appealed to them. These women signed the response to the editorial: Chairman Mrs. C. S. Bradley, Vice Chairman Margaret Harris Gordon, Martha Lipscomb, Edwardine Couch, Adele Conger, Lanette Heilbron Glasscock, Betty Green, Joyce Burg, Mary Nan Bonham, Olga H. Lapin, Margaret Waters, Hattie Henenberg, Mae Ament, May Yelderman, and Marie M. Robinson.[2] The issue of whether women should become fully integrated into the mainstream bar organization or form their own female-driven organization would be debated for decades. There was little doubt, however, that women believed most official State Bar meetings did not include female lawyers, nor did they often address their presence in the profession.

The first recorded nationwide gathering of women lawyers took place in August 1893 in Chicago as part of the World's Columbian Exposition (also known as the Chicago World's Fair). Over thirty women from across the country heard speeches given by leading women lawyers and activists. Their primary focus was on the status of laws affecting women and the position of women in the legal profession. This conference was organized as a protest against the event's Board of Lady Managers, who decided the exhibits in the Women's Building would emphasize domestic, philanthropic, and artistic activities as being representative of women's role in the world. Obviously, these wealthy, politically moderate board members did not consider professional women suitable to include in the exhibits. Nevertheless, a group of professional women established their own clubhouse nearby, and during the six months of the fair they advocated for woman suffrage and highlighted the work of women lawyers, physicians, and educators. There were few women lawyers in the country at that time, but they recognized the value of coming together in their own venue to learn from one another and to encourage other women as they entered the profession.[3]

In the nineteenth century women lawyers frequently referred to themselves as "sisters in law."[4] They were aware that they were part of a distinct group of women. At a time when women received their identity from their place in the family, women lawyers defined themselves as sisters in the family of law. They were few in number and so geographically scattered that they keenly felt their isolation. From these feelings evolved the need to connect with one another in an all-female setting.[5]

In 1899 the Women Lawyers' Club was founded in response to

the American Bar Association's refusal to admit women. In 1911 the organization changed its name to the National Association of Women Lawyers (NAWL) and began publishing the *Women Lawyers Journal*, which addressed general legal issues, advocated for women's rights, and highlighted the advancements being made by women in the profession.[6] By the time the ABA ended its exclusion of women in 1918, NAWL was established firmly enough to continue its independent existence. The issues important to NAWL were those affecting women in general and women lawyers in particular—the legal status of women, laws of marriage and divorce, property rights of married women, and proposed legislation affecting women, as well as the disabilities or opportunities encountered by women lawyers.[7] Not only was it important to have a group assertively working toward finding solutions in these areas, but the emotional support, practical advice, and professional mentoring received among its members were affirming to those women who were such a minority in the legal profession. It seems that some Texas women were active in NAWL in the early years, because the names of Joyce Burg, Hazel Lyons Franz, Lanette Heilbron Glasscock, Mary Santee Hanson, and Marguerite Rawalt appear in reports as holding offices or serving on regional committees.[8] Rawalt, who was president of NAWL in 1942, had attended the University of Texas as an undergraduate and then served as an assistant to Governor Pat Neff from 1921 to 1924. After a divorce, she moved to Washington, D.C., where she enrolled in George Washington University School of Law, graduating in 1933. Although Rawalt had a long career with the Bureau of Internal Revenue in Washington and served as president of the Federal Bar, she became a member of the Texas Bar in 1938.[9]

The State Bar of Texas never prohibited women from joining. But since membership was not mandatory in the early years of the twentieth century, however, few women apparently chose to belong.[10] Florence Rabe Ramer and Irene Brown are reported to be the first female members. Elected to membership in 1915, they attended the convention that year, and both were asked to address the meeting. They delivered their brief message of thanks, after which they were warmly welcomed. Whether the two women attended any more meetings is not known.[11]

While few women participated in the activities of the State Bar, they were usually invited to join local bar associations. The Dallas Bar Association seemed quite receptive to female members as early as 1920 when they elected Helen Viglini to membership. On the day she was elected, a toast titled "Women and the Law" was offered at the meeting.[12] Other Dallas women—Sarah Menezes, Grace Fitzgerald, Hollie B. Martin, Isabelle Abright, Sarah Hughes, Edith Wilmans and Hattie Henenberg—were elected as members over the next few years. Fitzgerald was listed in 1926 as the only female member of the organization to have a committee assignment, to the Membership Extension Committee. That same year the Dallas association placed Sarah Menezes in charge of a luncheon program at the Adolphus Palm Garden Room during which Menezes presented the male speaker, a bankruptcy referee.[13] In spite of these women's active status in the organization, their numbers did not increase. In 1934 there were just eleven women among the 470 members of the Dallas Bar Association. All of these women were in private practice—primarily solo—except for one who was the legal aid attorney with the city of Dallas and another who worked as an assistant court reporter.[14] Sarah Hughes joined the Dallas Bar Association because she felt membership was essential to her career. The presence of these new members in the organization attracted so much attention that they were invited to speak before local organizations, especially women's groups. Sarah Hughes, for one, eagerly accepted these invitations.[15]

Women lawyers in Houston did not have the same experience as their Dallas sisters, for they did not feel welcomed by the male-led bar association. Billye N. Russell, a graduate of Houston Law School,[16] passed the bar in 1932 and opened a solo practice.[17] She initially refused to join the Houston Bar Association because every announcement of forthcoming meetings contained the word "stag," implying that only men were welcome. Moreover, the association often held its gatherings in private clubs that did not admit women.[18] The Houston Bar Association's composite photograph in 1931 pictures only four females among 498 male attorneys. Twelve women appear in the photographs from 1936.[19] This lack of inclusiveness was, no doubt, the impetus for women forming their own organization. In 1934 a group led by Joyce Burg founded the Harris County Women Attorneys Association. Burg later recalled, "There were just a few [women], not many of them practicing. We put on a Gridiron Skit. The judges were our guests, and it really went over."[20] Nevertheless, the organization soon disbanded. There were probably too few women lawyers to maintain an organization. Or, perhaps, they were just too busy trying to make a living.

San Antonio's women lawyers were more successful in their efforts. They formed the San Antonio Council of Women Lawyers in 1935 "to promote the welfare and interest of women lawyers, to maintain the honor and integrity of the profession of law."[21] Yet, at the same time, they explained that their intention was to supplement the San Antonio Bar Association rather than separate from it. By 1939 the San Antonio women's organization had twenty-five members and was studying the juvenile courts, divorce laws, and equal rights for women.[22]

Another group, the Fort Worth Women Lawyers, was organized in 1941. Its officers were Vera Fogg, Juliet Sedberry, Mrs. Maurice B. Phipps, Louise Buckles, Jewell Lemons, and Eva Bloore Barnes.[23] It is not known if all of the women were lawyers or whether some held supportive positions in the legal profession. There is no record of how long this group remained active. Yet its very formation is an indication that women believed that an all-female organization would be beneficial to them in their careers.

Even when women were members of local bar associations, they played only a limited role in these groups. The combination of discrimination, women's areas of practice, and their family obligations made women almost invisible members of these networking organizations. They frequently felt like uninvited guests when they ventured to attend social events. Janet Reusch recalled her experience in El Paso in the mid-1970s. The El Paso Bar Association held annual banquets which were attended only by men. Reusch, one of a handful of women lawyers in El Paso, decided to attend one of these gatherings. When the word got out, the message came back that she would be "bodily evicted" if she appeared. But three male attorneys said they would accompany her as protection. As Reusch tells the story, "The expected brawl did not occur. No one tried to throw me out even though my brave protectors never appeared . . . In fact, all attorneys who spoke to me were friendly. And older attorneys, in true gentlemanly style, said they were glad I was there."[24] Just a few years later, Janet Reusch was elected the first female president of the El Paso Bar Association.[25]

Women periodically returned to the debate of whether to form their own bar associations to collectively address the legal and cultural restrictions they faced or whether to become integrated into the established bar organization. Sometimes an all-female group began as an informal gathering with no intention of becoming a formal organization. In 1968 a group of women attorneys in Dallas began meeting once a month at the Adolphus Hotel to prepare programs and activities for the annual meeting of the American Bar Association, which was to be held in Dallas the following year. After their success with the ABA event, they continued to meet informally to exchange information on job opportunities, to discuss legislative changes, to encourage more female candidates to run for both the judiciary and public office, and to discuss those legal issues pertinent to women's advancement in the field. By 1972 they had created their own letterhead, which read "Committee for Women in Government." Their primary activity was supporting the appointment of women to new courts in Dallas County. The group finally incorporated on May 16, 1984, as the Dallas Women

Lawyers Association. They outlined their purpose as "united for their mutual benefit with a goal of elevating the standards of women in the profession."[26]

In the meantime, the Travis County Women Lawyers' Association was organized and by 1977 had thirty-three members. Its founding members included Bea Ann Smith, Margaret Cooper, Sue Sheppard, Mary Pearl Williams, and Harriet Murphy. The group stated their mission as strengthening the image of women lawyers in the community. By 1988 the Travis County association had over 200 members. One way it has accomplished its mission is by giving three scholarships annually to women law students. These scholarships are named for Marian O. Boner, Charlye Farris and Edna Cisneros, and Mary Pearl Williams. The Boner scholarship is awarded to a female University of Texas (UT) law student who has a history of community service, while the Williams award is given to a UT student who shows exceptional leadership ability. The Farris-Cisneros scholarship, created in reaction to the *Hopwood* court decision in 1994,[27] is awarded to a minority woman who is entering law school as a first-year student. In addition to its focus on education, the organization continues to work toward the elimination of bias gender. A more recent initiative, Lawyers for Women Fighting Breast Cancer, will link members of Travis County Women Lawyers' Association with breast cancer patients and their families who need pro bono legal services. Law students at UT will assist with the pro bono work.[28]

Forty years following the first attempt at forming a women's association in Houston, two women attorneys began discussing the need for a separate organization. Mary McKerall, the lone female in the county attorney's office, and Michol O'Connor, an assistant district attorney, decided to hold a meeting to discern interest for an organization. They approached Judge Ruby Sondock, who they knew was supportive of a women's bar association. Judge Sondock offered her courtroom as an after-hours meeting place. An article appeared in the local newspaper announcing the meeting. In it McKerall explained, "We would not be in competition with the Houston bar." O'Connor added, "We don't have an organization to speak for women lawyers. Yet often the bar will ask what women think on some issues."[29] The news article drew a large number to the meeting on August 25, 1976. McKerall later remembered, "I walked over . . . not knowing whether any but a few would be there. I should have worn protective gear. Instead of being alone, I needed to get out of the way of the many women who filled the courtroom that day."[30] The gathering resulted in the formation of the Association of Women Attorneys (AWA), which chose Burta Raborn as its first president. Their annual judiciary reception grew out of a dinner meeting in the 1980s where judges, who thought they treated women attorneys "just fine," and AWA members, who had a completely different perception of the situation, came together to clear the air. Monthly meetings include State Bar CLE–accredited presentations on subjects of common interest. Scholarships are given each year through the AWA Foundation to female students in each of Houston's three law schools. At times the organization has questioned whether there was still a need for a women's organization. They have always answered that question in the affirmative. As former president Cameron Vann explained, "AWA is all about relationships . . . we provide a networking opportunity for solo practitioners as well as attorneys from law firms, corporations, and government entities . . . It is nice to know that we're able to help a few of those up and coming women who take on the challenge of law."[31]

The Bexar County Women's Bar Association was conceived in 1983 to provide a local forum for dialogue and the exchange of ideas about women in the legal profession. An additional goal was to place more women in leadership positions in the San Antonio Bar Association. As one of the early members recalled, "[W]e felt our needs were not being adequately met by the San Antonio Bar Association, especially for those of us who are solo practitioners or who are actively involved in trial practice . . . We also needed other women to network with, and [we] wanted to start a mentor program."[32] The initial membership roster listed seventy-four women and three men. As the Bexar County Women's Bar Association approaches its twenty-fifth anniversary, its 300 members include attorneys, judges, legal assistants, friends, honorary members, and students. While the organization has continued to be a source of support and encouragement for women attorneys, it has also provided services to the community, among them establishing a waiting room for children in the district attorney's office, designing a child-support formula which was accepted by Bexar County judges, sponsoring an Elder Law Handbook, having a Law Day luncheon for high school students, and raising money for Bexar county charities through its annual "Bench Bunch."[33]

Lubbock women lawyers began having lunch together on a regular basis in the early 1980s, but they did not officially organize into a bar association. This may have been in deference to the male lawyers who did not see the need for a separate organization for women. Then an incident occurred that spurred the women into action. A male judge greeted a young female prosecutor at a social gathering, but instead of shaking the woman's outstretched hand, he kissed the woman on the mouth.[34] Women lawyers who witnessed the incident began meeting together to give support to the prosecutor and other women lawyers in the area. This was the beginning of the Lubbock County Women Lawyers Association. One of their first debates was whether to allow male members. They decided in the affirmative. After all, they were not antimale; it was the treatment women sometimes received from men that disturbed them. The organization's first president was Maria Luisa Mercado, who was followed by Carolyn Jordan, Barbara Benson, and Carolyn Moore. The Lubbock County Women Lawyers Association has continued to address issues confronting women in the legal profession.[35]

Women lawyers retained their memberships in local bar associations, but these groups were slow to place them in positions of leadership. Emma Stullken Webb was an early president of the Bastrop County Bar Association.[36] In 1953, another incredibly early date for the election of a woman, Pat Moore was elected president of the Lubbock County Bar Association.[37] By the 1980s more groups were choosing women as officers. The Dallas Bar Association elected Harriet Miers as its president in 1984.[38] Exactly twenty years later the Dallas Bar elected Rhonda Hunter as its first African-American president. Hunter, a graduate of Southern Methodist University law school and a specialist in family law, had served the Dallas Bar Association in board-level positions for fourteen years before being chosen to lead the organization.[39]

Others who were the first women to serve as president of their local associations were Beverly Tarpley in Abilene,[40] Lynne Liberato in Houston,[41] Nancy Sample Garms in Amarillo,[42] Beryl Crowley in Washington County,[43] Janet Reusch in El Paso,[44] Ann Gardner in Tarrant County,[45] Karen Johnson in Travis County,[46] Debra Drayovitch in Denton,[47] Shirley Selz in Corpus Christi,[48] Paula Dunham in Jefferson County,[49] and Sue Hall in San Antonio.[50] When Hall was elected president in 1991, she had previously served as treasurer, secretary, and vice president and was the first woman to hold each of these offices. When asked about these overdue breakthroughs, Hall said, "I don't think anyone is mean spirited . . . It's just that very few people think of changing the way things have always been done."[51] Women elected as presidents of their bar associations expressed hope that the attention given them because of their gender would not overshadow their goals and accomplishments.

While she was serving as the first female president of the Houston Bar Association, in 1994, Lynne Liberato commented that she was sometimes impatient with the "first woman" label, but she realized that women brought a new perspective to these roles. She explained, "I know that for now, I view this job through the lens of my gender . . .

The experienced woman training a new male employee who earns more than she; the woman who has been asked routinely in job interviews what type of birth control she uses; the woman who has been excluded from the celebration of an office success because, she was told, the men would have less fun if women were there. These experiences and others like them shape the perception and expectations of women." Liberato added that the diversity created by women in leadership roles would benefit the legal profession by changing the dialogue and, ultimately, producing a stronger organization and a stronger community.[52]

State Bar membership became mandatory for all licensed attorneys in 1939.[53] Yet women continued to play a limited role even as their numbers increased. The first woman to hold an elected office in the State Bar of Texas was Louise Raggio. In 1964 she was named chair of the Family Law Section where her leadership helped to change the face of family law in Texas. When Raggio ran for a position on the Board of Directors in 1978, she was defeated. Undaunted, she ran again the following year and met with success. It was customary to present the new board members a gift. Raggio received a gift that was identical to that of the male officers—a pair of gold cuff links engraved with the seal of the State Bar. Apparently no thought had been given to an appropriate gift for a woman since there had never been a female director. Raggio came up with a solution by putting her cuff links on a chain and wearing them around her neck. She was later given a gold pendant with the State Bar insignia, but she kept the cufflinks as her "badge of acceptance."[54]

Women gradually moved into the top positions in the State Bar hierarchy. Harriet Miers, who was already considered a trailblazer in the legal arena, attained the ultimate position when she was elected bar president for 1992–93. Subsequent to Miers' tenure, four women have been elected to the top post.[55] For 1996-97 members chose Colleen McHugh, a St. Mary's law graduate who is currently a member of the

University of Texas Board of Regents. As president she led the successful legislative efforts to increase legal services funding for disadvantaged Texans. McHugh was also the first woman to chair the State Bar of Texas Board of Directors.[56] Betsy Whitaker, a Southern Methodist University law graduate, led the bar in 2003–04. When she was elected, one of her goals was to reconnect all the members of the State Bar and to provide them with a wide array of technological advances as tools in practicing law.[57] Lynne Liberato, an alumna of South Texas College of Law and a partner at Haynes and Boone in Houston, was president of the bar in 2000–01. During her tenure, MYTexasBar—the first comprehensive Web portal for lawyers in the country—made its debut.[58] The fifth woman and the 126th lawyer to hold the highest office in the State Bar was Martha Dickie, who served in 2006–07. Dickie, a partner in Akin & Almanza in Austin, is a graduate of the University of Texas School of Law and practices general civil litigation. Dickie compared her tenure as president to "a safari—not a trip from point A to point B, but an adventure filled with surprise, lack of routine, new people, new landscapes, and new experiences."[59]

The debate on whether women wanted to have their own section of the bar that began in the 1930s was finally resolved in 1980 when the Women and the Law Section was formed. Beryl Crowley, a member in the beginning, remembers that it was originally a special committee called "Effective Involvement of Women in the Bar."[60] By 1982 there were 218 members.[61] The mission of the Women and the Law Section is "to encourage and facilitate active and effective participation of women in the legal profession and to address women's current needs and the issues affecting them." The section's projects include helping pass legislation that is gender-related, sponsoring CLE seminars for further education, and providing outreach from a woman's perspective to schools and civic clubs. The Women and the Law Section also presents annually the Sarah T. Hughes Women Lawyers of Achievement Award and the Ma'at Justice Award.[62]

A new committee of the State Bar of Texas was formed in 1989 to study the role of women in the profession. It was intended to be a special committee for only one year. Yet a survey that was distributed at the time to both women and men indicated that gender bias was still an important issue to many bar members. Thus the "temporary" committee was made a standing committee of the State Bar known as Women in the Profession. Since that time the committee continues to assess the status of women in the legal profession, identifies barriers that prevent women lawyers from full participation in the profession, and develops programs and materials to address discrimination against women lawyers. The committee makes recommendations to the State Bar Board of Directors when problems need to be studied for possible action. The primary purpose of the Women in the Profession Committee is to be an advocate for all women lawyers in the State Bar.[63]

In spite of the various women's bar associations across the state, there was not a statewide women's organization until 1994. The seeds for such an organization were planted during a meeting of the State Bar Board of Directors. A cartoon making light of family violence produced chuckles as it was passed around among the men. The women at the meeting, however, did not consider domestic violence a laughing matter. That incident spurred the formation of Texas Women Lawyers (TWL).[64] Although membership in the State Bar had always been open to women and in recent years women had been elected to positions of leadership, many female lawyers felt that the state organization did not always address issues important to women in the legal profession. Women were particularly concerned about bills proposed by the bar's Women and the Law Section which had not been included in the bar's legislative package. These bills would have prohibited discrimination in certain private clubs, set forth civil commitment procedures for sexually violent predators that were being released from prison, and allowed a judge to order alimony in a divorce case. Another high priority of this newly formed group was the implementation of the recommendations from the Texas Supreme Court's Gender Bias Task Force, which was appointed by the high court to address discrimination in the court system. As Susan Morrison, a former president of TWL, explained, "[We] were fed up with the slow progress . . . some would say 'indifference' . . . by the State Bar on women's issues." The founders of Texas Women Lawyers, concerned that the implementation committee was not addressing gender bias in a timely manner, decided an organization was needed to keep women's issues in the forefront.[65] TWL continues to act as an umbrella organization to bring together women's bar associations across the state to develop networking resources, to promote women in the legal profession, and to become effective advocates in achieving equity for women, not just in the legal field, but in society as a whole. Texas Women Lawyers' initial mission statement was "to own the universe." Today it is "WOMEN MEAN BUSINESS" (and the capital letters are theirs).[66]

In recent years women lawyers from Texas have become more involved with national legal organizations. The American Bar Association remained a male domain for decades. Consequently, few women participated in any of its activities even if they joined. One exception to this was Louise Raggio, who in 1966 traveled to the ABA convention in Montreal to make a speech on the passage of the Marital Property Act of Texas. Raggio, a trailblazer with the ABA just as she was with the State Bar of Texas, chaired the Family Law Section of the ABA in 1975–76.[67] Thirty years later, Kim Askew, a partner in the Dallas offices of Hughes & Luce, was chosen in 2006 to chair the American Bar Association's Section of Litigation, the largest section in the ABA. She is the first lawyer of color to serve in this position. The litigation section is a legal publisher, a provider of CLE programming, a source of news and analysis, and a strong national voice in discussions concerning the profession. Askew, a Georgetown University law graduate, was introduced to bar work through the Dallas Bar Association and then expanded her efforts to the State Bar of Texas, where she chaired the State Bar Board of Directors. "National leaders all had to have opportunities at other levels," explained Askew. "I didn't get involved in these organizations to be a leader. I learned about issues that I cared about and identified places where I thought I could contribute." The reality that a woman from Texas would head the litigation section of the American Bar Association after so many women were discouraged—indeed, barred—from becoming litigators in the past is a strong indicator of true progress in the legal profession in our state.[68]

A Texas woman has served as the top officer in another legal organization. Algenita Scott Davis was elected president of the National Bar Association in 1990 as the third female to hold the position. The National Bar Association (NBA) had been organized in 1925 when there were fewer than 1,000 African-American lawyers in the nation. Over the past eighty years, the NBA has grown in size and influence.[69] Until Davis attended Howard University for her undergraduate degree in business, she thought she wanted to be a mathematician. A friend there convinced her to study law. After graduating from law school she returned to her hometown of Houston. At the time of her election to the NBA presidency, Davis was a corporate attorney with the largest bank holding company in Texas. Since she was also a wife and the mother of two young children, balancing family and career made for a busy life. Davis said, however, that she lived by the credo: "Do all that you can do." Then she added, "The law is a profession for hardworking and energetic individuals. That means the law is a profession for women . . . it's a natural."[70]

A century after Edith Locke received her license to practice law, women lawyers in Texas have proven that they can learn the law, establish professional careers, and provide leadership in bar associations. Those pioneering women lawyers kept trying to convey this message to their families, their communities, and, most importantly, to the legal profession. It may have taken one hundred years, but women have shown that law is a natural pursuit for women and that they have been extraordinarily successful in the quest. It has been a long, difficult journey, but today there are almost twenty-five thousand women lawyers in the state of Texas. Lady Justice would be proud!

Notes

1. *Texas Bar Journal*, 1, 12:356.

2. *Texas Bar Journal*, 2, 7:234.

3. Cott, 353–57. The World's Columbian Exposition in 1893 introduced the public to the many talents and abilities of women. By having their own building at the fair, women were able to display their creations, as well as promote women's involvement with community life. Obviously, it was not a real women's rights convention, but it was a starting point for women to develop their own public voices. See also Jeanne Madeline Weimann, *The Fair Women: The Story of the Woman's Building, World's Columbian Exposition* (Chicago: Academy Chicago, 1981).

4. Drachman, 1–4.

5. Ibid., 61–65. The country's first generation of women lawyers so felt the need for contact with one another that they formed the Equity Club. Although it was centered at the University of Michigan, one of the first law schools to admit women, the members intended that women in other areas could join. In order to do this, they would exchange letters on a regular basis. Although the club only existed for four years, Drachman states that "it became one of the most inspirational voices of the women lawyers movement." For more, see Virginia G. Drachmen, *Women Lawyers and the Origins of Professional Identity in America: The Letters of the Equity Club*, 1887–1890 (Ann Arbor: University of Michigan Press, 1993). See also Anne Firor Scott, *Natural Allies: Women's Associations in American History* (Chicago: Academy Chicago, 1981). Scott, an eminent women's historian, argues that women's associations have shaped community and national life for over a century. Although she writes primarily about voluntary groups working to enhance a community's cultural life, she reveals how all-female organizations are a natural for women, who connect and collaborate with one another in a unique way as they work toward a common goal.

6. Dusky, 143.

7. Epstein, 259.

8. *Who's Who*, 12, 31, 39, 41; *Derry*, 285.

9. *Derry*, 285.

10. Membership in the state organization was voluntary until 1939, when it became mandatory.

11. Proceedings of the Texas Bar Association (1915), 12–13.

12. Payne, *Dallas*, 129.

13. Ibid., 128, 131.

14. Ibid., 166.

15. Payne, *Sarah T. Hughes*, 29–30.

16. Houston Law School was an early proprietary law school in Texas. It opened in 1912.

17. Houston Law School Papers, RG-2, Box 1, Houston Metropolitan Research Center, Houston Public Library.

18. Fredrickson, *Houston Bar Association*, 79.

19. Photographs hanging in offices of Houston Bar Association.

20. *Houston Lawyer*, January-February, 1986, 41. Women in the Houston Bar Association formed their own section in 1947, thinking it would give them a way to become more involved. Although they were successful in electing Wilminor Carl to the board of directors in 1951, the section soon floundered and was dissolved.

21. *Texas Bar Journal*, 2, 2:39.

22. Ibid., 39–40.

23. *Texas Bar Journal*, 4, 4:199.

24. Janet Reusch, correspondence to author, December 29, 2006.

25. Reusch correspondence, see note 24 above.

26. Payne, *Dallas*, 276; Payne, *Sarah T. Hughes*, 304–305; Elizabeth Vrato, *Counselors* (Philadelphia: Running Press, 2002), 41–42.

27. In *Hopwood v. Texas*, 78 F.3d 932 (5th Cir. 1996), four white plaintiffs who had been rejected from The University of Texas School of Law challenged the institution's admissions policy on equal protection grounds and prevailed. After seven

years as a precedent in the Fifth Circuit, the *Hopwood* decision was abrogated by the U.S. Supreme Court in 2003.

28. Travis County Women Lawyers' Association, http://www.utexas.edu/law/news/2006/111506-justice.html (accessed June 26, 2007).

29. "Women lawyers to organize," *Houston Chronicle*, August 23, 1976, section 2, 3.

30. Mary McKerall, interview by author, May 23, 2007. McKerall explained that the legal sorority alumni group that so many of them had belonged to was no longer meeting their needs. They wanted a group that could take a position on issues and promote action, if necessary.

31. Association of Women Attorneys, http://www.awahouston.com (accessed February 25, 2007).

32. *Texas Bar Journal*, 53, 9:1053.

33. Carol E. Jendrzey, correspondence to author, May 10, 2007.

34. Carolyn Moore, correspondence to author, June 11, 2007.

35. Ibid.

36. *Texas Bar Journal*, 45, 1:129.

37. McArthur, *Handbook of Texas*, 4:823.

38. Raggio, 194–95.

39. Selwyn Crawford, "Dallas Bar trailblazer props open a door," *Dallas Morning News*, Sept. 7, 2006.

40. *Texas Bar Journal*, 68, 9:852.

41. "Women change the face of local legal scene," *Houston Chronicle*, July 13, 1992, 13A.

42. *Texas Bar Journal*, 58, 2:188.

43. *Texas Bar Journal*, 55, 1:98.

44. *El Paso Bar Bulletin*, Spring 2005, 10.

45. Second Court of Appeals, http://www.2ndcoa.courts.state.tx.us/court/justice-agardner.htm

46. Woods, Craddock and Brown, 126. Johnson also served as the executive director of the State Bar of Texas from 1990 to 1994.

47. Michelle Houston, correspondence to author, July 9, 2007.

48. Dick King, correspondence to author, July 9, 2007.

49. Jefferson County Bar Association, correspondence to author, July 9, 2007.

50. Brandon, 87.

51. Ibid.

52. Lynne Liberato, "Through lens of gender, a 'first woman' speaks," *Houston Chronicle*, February 15, 1994, 17A.

53. Angela A. Dorau, "State Bar of Texas," *Handbook of Texas*, 6:72.

54. Raggio, 201.

55. *Texas Bar Journal*, 55, 1:13.

56. *Texas Bar Journal*, 59, 6:514.

57. *Texas Bar Journal*, 66, 6:494–98.

58. *Texas Bar Journal*, 64, 6:550.

59. *Texas Bar Journal*, 69, 7:642–645.

60. *Texas Bar Journal*, 55, 1:98.

61. *Centennial Bar History*, 21.

62. Women and the Law Section, http://www.txwomenlawsection.org (accessed July 15, 2007). The 2005-2006 State Bar Annual Report on Status of Women indicates that 97% of the Women and the Law Section are female.

63. Women in the Profession, http//www.texasbar.com/Template.cfm?Section=Minority_and_Women _Lawyers&CONTENTID=6318&TEMPLATE=/ContentManagement/Content Display.cfm (accessed July 7, 2007).

64. Susan Morrison, interview by author, March 23, 2007.

65. Janet Elliott, "Women Split with Bar," *Texas Lawyer*, January 30, 1995, 26–27. Women involved in initial discussions about forming a statewide group included Kathryn Tullos, Nancye Betherum, Ann Graham, and Irene Jackson. Betherum served as TWL's first president.

66. Suzanne Squyres, "Texas Women Lawyers keeps women's issues on forefront," *Women's Enterprise USA*, March 2004, 20.

67. Raggio, 188, 197–98.

68. *Texas Bar Journal*, 69, 9:874.

69. *Texas Bar Journal*, 55, 1:13; Dusky, 143. The American Bar Association excluded black lawyers from membership until 1940. See Appendix C for Texas women who have received the Gertrude Rush Award, named for one of the National Bar Association's founders.

70. *Texas Bar Journal*, 55, 1:13.

Epilogue

What is there to conclude about the incredible journey of so many women over the past one hundred years except that they were incredible women? Their stories, however, reveal much about them that goes beyond that description.

They were intuitive, listening to an inner voice rather than being guided by the sentiments of others. When told they were taking men's places in law school, they did not retreat. Rather, they insisted that the practice of law could accommodate both men and women. They firmly believed that women brought unique qualities to the profession that would only enhance it.

They were bold, daring to enter a profession that for all practical purposes was closed to them and continued to be an unwelcoming environment. They became outspoken on issues that were not necessarily popular, but ones they considered necessary to move the legal profession forward and to benefit society at the same time. When they saw unacceptable practices becoming commonplace, they were willing to take the necessary steps to end them, even if their actions jeopardized their careers.

They were persistent, finding ways to jump hurdles placed before them. This may have slowed them in their journey, but they did not give up. When told that the courtroom was no place for women, some nevertheless became successful litigators and proved the naysayers wrong. When they were discouraged from running for elective office, they persisted and became effective public servants.

They were tough, refusing to crumble when confronted with criticism, discrimination, and harassment. It was discomforting to be told that they could not be good mothers and good lawyers at the same time. It was not easy to be rejected for a job because of their gender or color. Nor was it pleasant to be harassed because they were female and considered the weaker sex.

Above all, they were dedicated. Believing that our country was founded on just and equitable laws, women felt compelled to see that every citizen was treated with justice and equality. They saw themselves as an instrument through which our legal system flowed. Whether in a firm or solo practice, courtroom or government agency, elected position or faculty chair, they represented the law that treats everyone as an equal.

Who are "they," you ask? They are Texas women, past and present, who have chosen to focus their careers and much of their lives on the practice of law. We, the rest of society, are indebted to them for their boldness, persistence, toughness, and dedication in changing the landscape of law forever.

And, of course, women still exhibit these traits today. It is essential that they continue to be intuitive, bold, persistent, tough, and dedicated because there may still be hurdles to jump, rocky roads to travel, and complex turns in the pathway to navigate. One of the biggest problems facing female lawyers in the twenty-first century is combining their two worlds, family and career, if they choose to take that path. Solving this problem will require the collaborative efforts of the entire legal field. It appears that women are leaving the profession in greater numbers than ever before. That is not a healthy trend for either women lawyers or the profession as a whole. This issue must be resolved for the next generation of lawyers.

Women today comprise 31 percent of the State Bar of Texas and 48 percent of the law students in the state. They have a rich heritage provided by those who have gone before. They face a promising future as Texas faces the continuing need for dedicated lawyers. And so the journey continues.

Appendix A

State Bar of Texas Women Fifty-Year Lawyers (as of Spring 2007)

Name	*Year Admitted*	*Law School Attended*
Mrs. George M. Alford	1942	Southern Methodist University
Dr. Doris E. Anderson	1950	University of Texas
Judge Ann P. Baker	1957	University of Texas
Sybil Balasco	1956	University of Houston
Judge Theo L. Bedard	1954	University of Texas
Sara M. Benchoff	1954	University of Texas
Sarah W. Biedenharn	1955	Yale University
Dorothy L. Boucher	1950	Baylor University
Jane A. Brasch	1955	Southern Methodist University
Dorothy C. Busch	1956	University of Texas
Judge Shirley W. Butts	1954	University of Texas; University of Virginia
Wilminor M. Carl	1929	University of Texas
Ada Cronfel	1955	University of Texas
Betty Ross Crook	1955	Georgetown University
Barbara Culver Clack	1951	University of Texas
Eleanor B. Darnall	1956	Southern Methodist University
Beverly G. Derting	1951	Baylor University
Mary M. Domask	1946	unknown
Virginia E. Duff	1947	Southern Methodist University
Helen G. Elliott	1953	University of Houston
Frances T. Farenthold	1949	University of Texas

Name	*Year Admitted*	*Law School Attended*
Charlye O. Farris	1953	Howard University
Rae Ann Fichtner	1952	George Washington University
Barbara Finney	1942	University of Texas
Leona M. Franklin	1950	University of Texas
Lanette H. Glasscock	1931	San Antonio School of Law
Frances H. Goodwin	1956	George Washington University
Leah S. Guerry	1954	Southern Methodist University
Judge Carol R. Haberman	1957	St. Mary's University
Frances A. Hancock	1940	Samford University
Judge Naomi R. Harney	1957	University of Houston
Beatrice B. Hightower	1940	University of Texas
Nancy Lee Howard	1956	University of Texas
Kathleen B. Inglish	1936	self-study
Rachel F. Johnson	1957	South Texas College of Law
Bettye J. Lambert	1954	University of Houston
Kathleen J. Lindsey	1938	University of Texas
Barbara B. Mansell	1950	St. Mary's University
Patricia H. Marschall	1955	University of Texas
Ruth W. McCracken	1947	University of Alabama
Argentina C. Meurer	1955	University of Texas
Katherine B. Nelson	1956	University of Texas
Juliette M. Nichols	1944	University of Texas
Judge Gladys M. Oakley	1957	University of Houston
Rosa J. Pace	1956	University of Texas
Louise B. Raggio	1952	Southern Methodist University
Dorothy G. Rea	1949	University of Texas
Judge Mary Lou Robinson	1949	University of Texas
Marian S. Rosen	1954	University of Houston
Barbara W. Ruud	1949	College of William and Mary
Jeannette Sadler	1945	Southern Methodist University

Name	*Year Admitted*	*Law School Attended*
Hulda K. Sellingsloh	1940	University of Houston
Susan W. Sessions	1948	Southern Methodist University
Jean M. Sheppard	1956	Southern Methodist University
Elsie Brown Silverman	1955	George Washington University
Adele B. Simpson	1948	unknown
Nita K. Smith	1945	Southern Methodist University
Nancy E. Sutton	1942	University of Texas
Beverly J. Tarpley	1951	University of Texas
June Wilson Teer	1951	Baylor University
Ann Van W. Thomas	1942	University of Texas
Helen W. Watkins	1944	George Washington University
Lois Watson	1956	University of Texas
Nancy V. Westerfield	1955	University of Houston
Jean L. White	1946	Southern Methodist University
Judge Mary Pearl Williams	1949	University of Texas

APPENDIX B

Ma'at Justice Award

Ma'at, the Egyptian goddess of justice, symbolizes truth, order, righteousness, and the emergence of order out of chaos. The State Bar of Texas Women and the Law Section established the Ma'at Justice Award in 1995 to recognize and celebrate individual attorneys or an association of attorneys who have contributed to the furtherance of justice in our society. Every year the Women and the Law Section awards the Ma'at Justice Award to an individual who is actively addressing the needs and issues affecting women both in the legal profession and in the community. Past winners are:

1995	Jonita Borchardt of Denton
1996	Nancye Bethurem of Dallas
1997	Ralph H. Brock of Lubbock
1998	Ana Mejia-Dietche of Austin
1999	Collin A. Petty of Houston
2000	Iris Hefter Robinson of Houston
2001	Paula W. Hinton of Houston
2002	Justice Deborah Hankinson
2003	Carolyn F. Moore of Lubbock
2004	Beverly Tarpley of Abilene
2005	Ronnie E. G. Harrison of Houston
2006	Shelia Enid Cheaney of Austin
2007	ileta Sumner of San Antonio

Appendix C

Gertrude E. Rush Award

The Gertrude E. Rush Award, given in honor of the only woman cofounder of the National Bar Association, stands as an award of merit expressive of the spirit and commitment of Gertrude E. Rush. The Rush Award standards demand that the recipient should manifest the pioneering spirit epitomized by Gertrude E. Rush, demonstrate leadership in the community and in his or her profession, demonstrate concern for human and civil rights, and be a model for excellence in legal education and perseverance in the law, public policy, and social activism.

Women members of the State Bar of Texas who have been past recipients are:

1995	Algenita Scott Davis
1997	The Honorable Barbara C. Jordan (posthumously)
2003	Charlye O. Farris, The Honorable Harriet M. Murphy

APPENDIX D

Margaret Brent Award

The Margaret Brent Women Lawyers of Achievement Award, established by the ABA Commission on Women in the Profession in 1991, recognizes and celebrates the accomplishments of women lawyers who have excelled in their field and have paved the way to success for other women lawyers.

Members of the State Bar of Texas who have been past recipients are:

1994	Professor Barbara Jordan
1995	Louise B. Raggio
1998	Irma L. Rangel
1999	Carol E. Dinkins
2001	The Honorable Gabrielle Kirk McDonald
2003	Charlye O. Farris
2004	Catherine A. Lamboley
2005	Carolyn Dineen King

Appendix E

Sandra Day O'Connor Award for Professional Excellence

The Texas Center for Legal Ethics and Professionalism presents the Sandra Day O'Connor Award for Professional Excellence to women lawyers in Texas who have achieved professional excellence within their area of specialty and who personify excellence on a local or statewide level. Justice O'Connor has graciously endorsed this award.

Past recipients of the award are:

2004	Louise Raggio, The Honorable Rose Spector
2005	Harriet Miers, The Honorable Mary Lou Robinson
2006	Adelfa B. Callejo, Myra A. McDaniel
2007	The Honorable Ruby Kless Sondock

APPENDIX F

Sarah T. Hughes Women Lawyers of Achievement Award

In 1992, the State Bar of Texas Women and the Law Section established the Sarah T. Hughes Women Lawyers of Achievement Award. The award honors the accomplishments of women who have achieved outstanding recognition in the professional area and who, by doing so, have paved the way for success for other women attorneys. The award recognizes women attorneys who have achieved excellence in their respective fields and have influenced other women to pursue legal careers, opened doors for women lawyers in a variety of job settings that historically were closed to women, advanced opportunities for women within a practice area or segment of the profession, or otherwise served their profession or community in a manner that has benefited the legal profession.

Past recipients of the award are:

1993	Louise B. Raggio, Harriet Miers
1994	Dean Barbara Aldave
1995	Barbara Jordan
1996	Frances “Sissy” Farenthold
1997	Justice Shirley W. Butts
1998	Gaynelle Griffin Jones
1999	Evelyn H. Biery
2000	Justice Ann McClure
2001	Justice Barbara Rosenberg
2002	Susan Horton
2003	Justice Alma L. Lopez
2004	Charlye O. Farris
2005	Pauline Higgins
2006	Judge Barbara Lynn
2007	Judge Judith K. Guthrie

APPENDIX G

Women Attorneys: Attorney Statistical Profile (2006–07)

Published January 30, 2007

STATE BAR OF TEXAS
Department of Research and Analysis

Women Attorneys: Attorney Statistical Profile (2006-07)

This report profiles active women attorney members of the State Bar of Texas as of December 31, 2006, roughly the midpoint of the Bar's fiscal year. Numbers and percents are given by key demographic variables including gender, race/ethnicity, years licensed in any jurisdiction, age, graduating law school, primary occupation, law firm size, TYLA membership, section membership, and board certification. Inclusion of Bar fiscal year 1996-97 data allows for comparison.

	Women Attorneys				All State Bar Attorneys			
	1996-97 N = 15,691		2006-07 N = 24,469		1996-97 N = 61,638		2006-07 N = 79,409	
Gender								
Male	0	0%	0	0%	45,946	75%	54,546	69%
Female	15,691	100%	24,469	100%	15,691	25%	24,469	31%
Race/Ethnicity								
Caucasian/Anglo	13,010	86%	18.751	80%	52,181	90%	63,942	85%
African-American/Black	876	6%	1,696	7%	1,894	3%	3,153	4%
Hispanic/Latino	885	6%	1.922	8%	2,948	5%	5,334	7%
Asian/Pacific Islander	198	1%	732	3%	449	1%	1,433	2%
Native American Indian	40	<1%	75	<1%	135	<1%	225	<1%
Other Race	122	1%	354	2%	401	1%	915	1%
Years Licensed *								
2 or less years	2,833	18%	3,643	15%	7,063	11%	7,656	10%
3 to 6 years	3,820	24%	4.136	17%	9,617	16%	9,394	12%
7 to 10 years	3,078	20%	3,573	15%	8,233	13%	9,195	12%
11 to 15 years	3,205	20%	4,270	17%	9,915	16%	11,336	14%
16 to 20 years	1,948	12%	3,540	14%	9,317	15%	9,928	13%
21 to 25 years	493	3%	2,913	12%	6,725	11%	9,369	12%
Over 25 years	314	2%	2,393	10%	10,768	17%	22,526	28%
Median Years Licensed	8 yrs.		12 yrs.		13 yrs.		16 yrs.	
Age								
21 to 25 years	211	1%	351	1%	444	1%	537	1%
26 to 30 years	2,761	18%	3,545	14%	6,751	11%	7,257	9%
31 to 35 years	3,139	20%	3,957	16%	8,818	14%	9,583	12%
36 to 40 years	3,463	22%	3,949	16%	10,544	17%	10.544	13%
41 to 45 years	2,906	19%	3.428	14%	10,799	18%	9,895	12%
46 to 50 years	1,869	12%	3,519	14%	9,235	15%	10.832	14%
51 to 55 years	788	5%	2,922	12%	5,956	10%	10,671	13%
56 to 60 years	291	2%	1,744	7%	3,187	5%	8,683	11%
61 to 65 years	110	1%	664	3%	2,072	3%	5,088	6%
More than 65 years	146	1%	388	2%	3,814	6%	6,310	8%
Median Age	38 yrs.		41 yrs.		42 yrs.		46 yrs.	
Member Class--TYLA/Senior **								
TYLA Member	7,490	48%	10,367	42%	19,717	32%	23,424	29%
Senior Member	8,201	52%	14,102	58%	41,921	68%	55,985	71%

State Bar of Texas Department of Research and Analysis

Women Attorneys: Attorney Statistical Profile (2006-07)

	Women Attorneys				All State Bar Attorneys			
	1996-97		2006-07		1996-97		2006-07	
	N = 15,691		N = 24,469		N = 61,638		N = 79,409	
Law School Attended								
Baylor University	845	5%	1,251	5%	4,246	7%	5,120	7%
St. Mary's	1,227	8%	1,887	8%	4,467	7%	5,792	7%
South Texas	1,791	12%	2,813	12%	6,497	11%	8,704	11%
Southern Methodist	1,422	9%	2,091	9%	5,498	9%	6,712	9%
Texas Southern	432	3%	852	4%	1,446	2%	2,313	3%
Texas Tech	905	6%	1,545	6%	3,569	6%	5,031	6%
Texas Wesleyan	110	1%	761	3%	397	1%	1,689	2%
University of Houston	2,321	15%	3,112	13%	6,949	11%	8,648	11%
University of Texas	3,010	19%	4,156	17%	14,004	23%	15,596	20%
Out-of-State/Other Law School	3,468	22%	5,552	23%	13,707	23%	18,456	24%
Primary Occupation								
Private Law Practice	7,616	59%	12,636	59%	37,183	69%	48,911	68%
Government Attorney	2,384	18%	3,599	17%	5,815	11%	7,871	11%
Full-Time Judge	334	3%	454	2%	1,378	3%	1,549	2%
Law Faculty	102	1%	214	1%	324	1%	507	1%
Corporate/In-House Counsel	1,366	11%	2,329	11%	4,876	9%	6,845	9%
Other Law Related	462	4%	964	4%	1,261	2%	2,079	3%
Other Non-Law Related	300	2%	616	3%	1,410	3%	2,059	3%
Retired-Not Working	418	3%	272	1%	1,504	3%	1,599	2%
Unemployed-Looking	---	---	211	1%	---	---	378	1%
Unemployed-Not Looking	---	---	291	1%	---	---	407	1%
Firm Size (private practitioners only)								
Solo Practitioners	2,393	33%	3,902	33%	12,444	35%	16,508	35%
2 to 5 attorneys	1,658	23%	2,683	23%	8,869	25%	10,889	23%
6 to 10 attorneys	562	8%	845	7%	2,992	8%	3,462	7%
11 to 24 attorneys	595	8%	996	8%	3,052	9%	3,900	8%
25 to 40 attorneys	377	5%	560	5%	1,683	5%	2,018	4%
41 to 60 attorneys	203	3%	298	3%	996	3%	1,120	2%
Over 60 / 61 to 100 attorneys ***	1,442	20%	1,320	11%	5,544	16%	4,662	10%
101 to 200 attorneys ***	---	---	199	2%	---	---	734	2%
Over 200 attorneys ***	---	---	1,115	9%	---	---	3,523	8%
Median Firm Size	4 attys.		5 attys.		4 attys.		4 attys.	
Members of State Bar Sections								
Section Members	6,203	40%	9,259	38%	25,176	41%	31,693	40%
Non Section Members	9,488	60%	15,210	62%	36,462	59%	47,716	60%
Members of One Section	2,927	19%	5,077	21%	11,002	18%	15,855	20%
Members of Two Sections	2,031	13%	2,611	11%	8,145	13%	9,247	12%
Members of Three Sections	812	5%	980	4%	3,481	6%	3,837	5%
Members of Four or More Sections	433	3%	591	2%	2,548	4%	2,754	3%

State Bar of Texas Department of Research and Analysis

2

Women Attorneys: Attorney Statistical Profile (2006-07)

Attorneys can belong to multiple sections, therefore the percents do not sum to 100%	Women Attorneys				All State Bar Attorneys			
	1996-97		2006-07		1996-97		2006-07	
	N = 15,691		N = 24,469		N = 61,638		N = 79,409	
Section Membership								
Administrative and Public Law	335	2%	369	2%	1,111	2%	1,081	1%
African-American Lawyers	113	1%	184	1%	242	<1%	336	<1%
Alternative Dispute Resolution	302	2%	323	1%	1,203	2%	1,139	1%
American Indian Law	41	<1%	26	<1%	123	<1%	105	<1%
Animal Law	24	<1%	151	1%	50	<1%	253	<1%
Antitrust and Business Litigation	152	1%	160	1%	1,084	2%	1,119	1%
Appellate	389	2%	571	2%	1,324	2%	1,713	2%
Asian-Pacific Interest	36	<1%	82	<1%	101	<1%	186	<1%
Aviation Law	20	<1%	30	<1%	190	<1%	244	<1%
Bankruptcy Law	---	---	345	1%	---	---	1,238	2%
Business Law	657	4%	752	3%	3,936	6%	3,879	5%
Computer and Technology	122	1%	147	1%	912	1%	786	1%
Construction Law	155	1%	301	1%	1,026	2%	1,802	2%
Consumer and Commercial Law	249	2%	219	1%	1,724	3%	1,306	2%
Corporate Counsel	579	4%	812	3%	2,448	4%	2,878	4%
Criminal Justice	317	2%	571	2%	1,442	2%	2,214	3%
Entertainment and Sports Law	97	1%	136	1%	503	1%	523	1%
Environmental and Natural Resources	350	2%	353	1%	1,537	2%	1,269	2%
Family Law	1,227	8%	1,909	8%	3,575	6%	4,462	6%
General Practice, Solo, and Small Firm	236	2%	381	2%	1,562	3%	1,785	2%
Government Lawyers	209	1%	294	1%	539	1%	725	1%
Health Law	405	3%	467	2%	1,236	2%	1,215	2%
Hispanic Issues	77	<1%	142	1%	257	<1%	402	1%
Individual Rights and Responsibilities	50	<1%	57	<1%	176	<1%	182	<1%
Insurance Law	---	---	357	1%	---	---	1,520	2%
Intellectual Property Law	206	1%	361	1%	1,284	2%	1,850	2%
International Law	206	1%	194	1%	1,049	2%	811	1%
James C. Watson Inn	2	<1%	23	<1%	72	<1%	154	<1%
Judicial	1	<1%	26	<1%	3	<1%	56	<1%
Justice of the Peace	17	<1%	16	<1%	56	<1%	51	<1%
Juvenile Law	255	2%	362	1%	588	1%	813	1%
Labor and Employment Law	959	6%	1,045	4%	2,811	5%	2,799	4%
Litigation	1,398	9%	1,603	7%	7,239	12%	7,416	9%
Military Law	12	<1%	32	<1%	172	<1%	230	<1%
Municipal Judges	43	<1%	87	<1%	195	<1%	245	<1%
Oil, Gas and Energy Resources Law	247	2%	346	1%	2,103	3%	2,357	3%
Poverty Law	---	---	196	1%	---	---	340	<1%
Public Utility Law	106	1%	108	<1%	425	1%	403	1%
Real Estate, Probate & Trust Law	1,063	7%	1,655	7%	5,723	9%	7,020	9%
School Law	182	1%	238	1%	578	1%	574	1%
Sexual Orientation & Gender Identification Issues	---	---	59	<1%	---	---	170	<1%
Taxation	220	1%	314	1%	1,504	2%	1,674	2%
Women and the Law	482	3%	407	2%	500	1%	424	1%

State Bar of Texas Department of Research and Analysis

3

Women Attorneys: Attorney Statistical Profile (2006-07)

Attorneys can have multiple board certifications, therefore the percents do not sum to 100%	Women Attorneys 1996-97 N = 15,691		Women Attorneys 2006-07 N = 24,469		All State Bar Attorneys 1996-97 N = 61,638		All State Bar Attorneys 2006-07 N = 79,409	
Board Certifications								
Board Certified Attorneys	801	5%	1,282	5%	5,780	9%	7,060	9%
Attorneys Not Board Certified	14,890	95%	23,187	95%	55,858	91%	72,349	91%
Attorneys Board Certified in One Area	724	5%	1,191	5%	4,591	7%	5,907	7%
Attorneys Board Certified in Two Areas	68	<1%	82	<1%	1,050	2%	1,029	1%
Attorneys Board Certified in Three or More Areas	9	<1%	9	<1%	139	<1%	124	<1%
Attorneys Board Certified In:								
Administrative Law	59	<1%	52	<1%	177	<1%	162	<1%
Bankruptcy Law: Business	29	<1%	20	<1%	185	<1%	160	<1%
Bankruptcy Law: Consumer	24	<1%	29	<1%	152	<1%	159	<1%
Civil Appellate Law	87	1%	113	<1%	346	1%	408	1%
Civil Trial Law	55	<1%	68	<1%	1,250	2%	1,173	1%
Consumer and Commercial Law	3	<1%	6	<1%	40	<1%	68	<1%
Criminal Law	69	<1%	128	1%	650	1%	836	1%
Estate Planning and Probate Law	96	1%	146	1%	498	1%	654	1%
Family Law	187	1%	261	1%	600	1%	705	1%
Health Law	---	---	18	<1%	---	---	47	<1%
Immigration and Nationality Law	17	<1%	41	<1%	67	<1%	102	<1%
Juvenile Law	---	---	33	<1%	---	---	58	<1%
Labor and Employment Law	54	<1%	177	1%	254	<1%	544	1%
Oil, Gas, and Mineral Law	20	<1%	15	<1%	268	<1%	262	<1%
Personal Injury Trial Law	72	<1%	126	1%	1,494	2%	1,768	2%
Real Estate Law: Commercial	51	<1%	48	<1%	481	1%	490	1%
Real Estate Law: Farm and Ranch	10	<1%	7	<1%	118	<1%	99	<1%
Real Estate Law: Residential	37	<1%	38	<1%	326	1%	329	<1%
Tax Law	17	<1%	22	<1%	217	<1%	231	<1%
Workers' Compensation Law	---	---	34	<1%	---	---	92	<1%

For more information, contact:
State Bar of Texas
Department of Research and Analysis
P.O. Box 12487
Austin, TX 78711-2487
(800)204-2222 ext. 1724
research@texasbar.com
www.texasbar.com/research

Footnotes

* Based on year first licensed in any jurisdiction.

** Texas Young Lawyers Association membership is automatic for attorneys less than 37 years of age and for attorneys of any age who have been licensed for less than four years.

*** The firm size categories '61 to 100 attorneys', '101 to 200 attorneys', and 'Over 200 attorneys' were introduced in 2004.

--- Indicates that the given category or group was not in existence.

General Notes

All data represent active attorney bar members in good standing. Some figures are estimates as not all demographic data is known for all attorneys; individual data items will not sum to the column headers in these instances. Percentages may not sum to one hundred due to rounding. Bar geography, such as county membership and various district memberships, is based on members' official address. Bar members' official address was determined by work address; if work address was unavailable, home address was used.

State Bar of Texas Department of Research and Analysis

4

BIBLIOGRAPHY

Archival Sources

Bill and Vara Daniel Center for Legal History, State Bar of Texas.

Minority Attorneys File.

Women Attorneys File.

Houston Bar Association Archives.

Interview of Joyce Burg by Eric L. Fredrickson, October 1, 1990. Video.

Interview of Barbara Finney by Eric L. Fredrickson, October 1, 1990. Transcript.

Interview of Judge Camille Dunn, December 18, 1996. Video.

Photographic Composites of Houston Bar Association Members.

Houston Metropolitan Research Center, Houston Public Library.

Houston Law School Collection.

Women's Biographical Scrapbooks.

City Directories of Amarillo, Austin, Beaumont, Corpus Christi, Dallas, El Paso, Fort Worth, Galveston, Houston, Lubbock, San Antonio, Wichita Falls.

South Texas College of Law, Fred Parks Law Library, Special Collections.

1928 Catalog.

Files, Women Students.

Files, Women Faculty Members.

South Texas College of Law News Publications.

University of Texas, Tarlton Law Library, Audio-visual Center.

Martindale American Law Directories 1902, 1905, 1908, 1910, 1912, 1915, 1920, 1922, 1925, 1930. New York: G. B. Martindale, Publisher.

Martindale-Hubbell Directories 1935, 1940. New York: Martindale-Hubbell Publishing Company.

University of Texas, Tarlton Law Library, Special Collections.

Baade Collection.

Cactus, 1918 Yearbook.

Dorothy Most Scrapbook.

Helen Hargrave Papers.

Kappa Beta Pi Legal Sorority Records.

Published Sources

Acosta, Teresa Palomo, and Ruthe Winegarten. *Las Tejanas: 300 Years of History.* Austin: University of Texas Press, 2003.

Aldave, Barbara Bader. "Women in the Law in Texas: The Stories of Three Pioneers." *St. Mary's Law Journal* 25:289–301.

Amandes, Richard. "The History of the School of Law of Texas Tech University." *Texas Tech Law Review* 1 (1969): 31–58.

Anglin, Chris. "First female alumna lived full life in law." *Annotations*. South Texas College of Law 25 (April 1997): np.

Arnold, Ann. *History of Fort Worth Legal Community*. Austin: Eakin Press, 2000.

Baade, Hans W. "Law at Texas: The Roberts Gould Era (1881–1893)." *Southwestern Historical Quarterly* 86 (October 1982): 161–196.

Barnes, Janette. "Women and Entrance to the Legal Profession." *Journal of Legal Education* 23:276–308.

Barrera, Lisa Lizette. "Minorities and the University of Texas School of Law (1950–1980)." *Hispanic Texas Journal of Law and Policy* 4:99–104.

Bench and Bar of Texas. Austin: H. Evans, 1937.

Biskupic, Joan. *Sandra Day O'Connor: How the First Woman on the Supreme Court Became Its Most Influential Judge*. New York: HarperCollins Publishers, 2005.

Brandon, Jay. *Law and Liberty: A History of the Legal Profession in San Antonio.* Dallas: Taylor Publishing Company with San Antonio Bar Association, 1996.

Butler, Marguerite C. "The History of Texas Southern University, Thurgood Marshall School of Law: The House that Sweatt Built." *Thurgood Marshall Law Review* 23

(1997): 45–53.

Campbell, Amy Leigh. *Raising the Bar: Ruth Bader Ginsburg and the ACLU Women's Rights Project.* Xlibris, 2003.

Carroll, Susan J. *Women as Candidates in American Politics.* Bloomington: Indiana University Press, 1994.

Castleberry, Vivian Anderson. *Daughters of Dallas.* Dallas: Odenwald Press, nd.

Chafe, William H. *The Paradox of Change: American Women in the Twentieth Century.* Oxford: Oxford University Press, 1991.

Committee on History and Traditions of the State Bar. *Centennial History of the Texas Bar 1882–1982.* Burnet: Eakin Press, 1981.

Cook, Fiona Hale, ed. *Who's Who Among Women Lawyers 1939.* Boston: Fiona Hale Cook, 1939.

Cott, Nancy F., ed. *No Small Courage: A History of Women in the United States.* New York: Oxford University Press, 2000.

Crawford, Ann Fears, and Crystal Sasse Ragsdale. *Texas Women: Frontier to Future.* Austin: State House Press, 1998.

Crawford, Vicki L., Jacqueline Anne Rouse and Barbara Woods, eds. *Women in the Civil Rights Movement: Trailblazers & Torchbearers 1941–1965.* Bloomington: Indiana University Press, 1990.

Crooker, John H. Jr., and Gibson Gayle Jr. *Fulbright & Jaworski: 75 Years (1919–1994).* Houston: Fulbright & Jaworski, 1994.

Cupp, Ruth Willis. *Portia Steps Up to the Bar: The First Women Lawyers of South Carolina.* Raleigh: Ivy House Publishing Group, 2003.

Derry, Laura Miller, ed. *Digest of Women Lawyers and Judges: Biographical Sketches and Data of Women Lawyers of U.S. and its Possessions.* Louisville: Dunne Press, 1949.

Drachman, Virginia G. *Sisters in Law: Women Lawyers in Modern American History.* Cambridge: Harvard University Press, 1998.

———. "Women Lawyers and the Quest for Professional Identity in Late Nineteenth Century America." *Michigan Law Review* 88:2440.

Duskey, Lorraine. *Still Unequal: The Shameful Truth about Women and Justice in*

America. New York: Crown Publishers, Inc., 1996.

Elliott, Janet. "Women Split with Bar." *Texas Lawyer,* January 30, 1995.

Enstam, Elizabeth York. *Women and the Creation of Urban Life, Dallas Texas, 1843–1920.* College Station: Texas A&M University Press, 1998.

Epstein, Cynthia Fuchs. *Women in Law*. Urbana: University of Illinois Press, 1993.

Epstein, Phyllis Horn. *Women at Law: Lessons Learned Along the Pathways to Success.* Chicago: American Bar Association, 2004.

Evans, James R. Jr. "An Exceptional Legacy." *Heritage*, Spring 1998, 13–14.

Farrer, Nancy L. "Of Ivory Columns and Glass Ceilings: The Impact of the Supreme Court of the United States on the Practice of Women Attorneys in Law Firms." *St. Mary's Law Journal* 28:529–573.

Fernea, Elizabeth W., and Marilyn P. Douglas. *Texas Women in Politics*. Austin: Foundation for Women's Resources, 1977.

Flexner, Eleanor. *Century of Struggle: The Woman's Rights Movement in the United States*. Cambridge: The Belknap Press of Harvard University Press, 1975.

Ford, Carole Bell. *The Women of CourtWatch: Reforming a Corrupt Family Court System.* Austin: University of Texas Press, 2005.

Frankel, Noralee, and Nancy S. Dye, eds. *Gender, Class, Race & Reform in the Progressive Era*. Lexington: University Press of Kentucky, 1981.

Fredrickson, Eric L. *Andrews & Kurth L.L.P.: The First 100 Years of Excellence.* Houston: Andrews & Kurth L.L.P., 2002.

———. *A Commitment to Public Service: The History of the Houston Bar Association*. Houston: Gulf Publishing Company, 1992.

Freeman, J. H. *The People of Baker Botts*. Houston: Baker & Botts, 1992.

Garza, Hedda. *Barred from the Bar: A History of Women and the Legal Profession*. New York: Franklin Watts, 1990.

Gordon, Lynn D. *Gender and Higher Education in the Progressive Era*. New Haven: Yale University Press, 1990.

Gray, Kathlyn. *The New Power of Women in Politics*. Hillsdale, N. J.: Enslow Publishers, Inc., 1994.

Hard, William. "Will Texas Do Better by Its Married Women?" *The Delineator* 80 (November 1912): 317.

Harrington, Monica. *Women Lawyers: Rewriting the Rules.* New York: Penguin Books, 1993.

Harris, Barbara J. *Beyond Her Sphere: Women and the Professions in American History.* Westport: Greenwood Press, 1978.

Harvey, Brett. *The Fifties: A Woman's Oral History.* New York: HarperCollins Publishers, 1993.

Higgins, Kim. "Joan Tarpley: The Embodiment of Empowerment." *Eclipse*, January-February 2006, 48–49.

Hoff, Joan. *Law, Gender & Injustice: A Legal History of U. S. Women.* New York: New York University Press, 1991.

Huber, Stephen K., and James E. Myers. "Admission to the Practice of Law in Texas: An Analytical History." *Houston Law Review* 15 (March 1978): 485–535.

Hyman, Harold M. *Craftsmanship and Character: A History of the Vinson & Elkins Law Firm in Houston 1917–1997.* Athens: The University of Georgia Press, 1998.

Jones, Nancy Baker, and Ruthe Winegarten. *Capitol Women: Female Legislators 1923–1999.* Austin: University of Texas Press, 2000.

Kissinger, Ashley. "Civil Rights and Professional Wrongs: A Female Lawyer's Dilemma." *Texas Law Review* 73:1420–1459.

Lasher, Patricia, and Beverly Bentley. *Texas Women: Interviews and Images.* Austin: Shoal Creek Publishers, 1980.

Lipartito, Kenneth J., and Joseph A. Pratt. *Baker & Botts in the Development of Modern Houston.* Austin: University of Texas Press, 1991.

Litoff, Judy Barnett, and David C. Smith. *American Women in a World at War: Contemporary Accounts from World War II.* Wilmington, Delaware: Scholarly Resources Inc., 1997.

Lopez, Vianei. "Women in the Law: Moving from the Past to the Future." *Houston Lawyer* 31 (November-December 1993): 164–196.

Matthews, Glenna. *The Rise of Public Woman: Woman's Power and Woman's Place in the United States 1630–1970*. New York: Oxford University Press, 1992.

Meyer, Annie Nathan. *Women's Work in America.* New York: Henry Holt and Company, 1891.

Meyerowitz, Joanne, ed. *Not June Cleaver: Women and Gender in Postwar America 1945–1960.* Philadelphia: Temple University Press, 1994.

Mitchell, Ellen. "A Portrait of Senior Justice Shirley Butts." *San Antonio Lawyer,* March-April 2006, 5–7.

Morello, Karen Berger. *The Invisible Bar: The Woman Lawyer in America, 1638 to the Present*. New York: Random House, 1986.

Mossman, Mary Jane. *The First Women Lawyers: A Comparative Study of Gender, Law and the Legal Professions.* Portland, Oregon: Hart Printing, 2006.

Newton, Nancy Jo, and W. Frank Newton. "Legal Education in Texas." In *Centennial History of the Texas Bar 1882–1982*, 159–176. Burnet: Eakin Press, 1981.

O'Connor, Sandra Day. *The Majesty of the Law: Reflections of a Supreme Court Justice.* New York: Random House, 2004.

"Our Place in History: A Celebration of Women in the Law at the University of Texas School of Law." *Texas Journal of Women and the Law* 25:289–301.

Payne, Darwin. *As Old as Dallas Itself: A History of the Lawyers of Dallas, the Dallas Bar Association, and the City They Helped Build.* Dallas: Three Forks Press, 1999.

———. *Indomitable Sarah: The Life of Judge Sarah T. Hughes.* Dallas: Southern Methodist University Press, 2004.

Raggio, Louise Ballerstedt, with Vivian Anderson Castleberry. *Texas Tornado*. New York: Citadel Press, 2003.

Rhodes, Deborah L., ed. *The Difference "Difference" Makes: Women and Leadership.* Stanford: Stanford University Press, 2004.

Rikleen, Lauren Stiller. *Ending the Gauntlet: Removing Barriers to Women's Success in the Law.* Thomson/Legalworks, 2006.

Robbins, Mary Alice. "More Women Move into Firm Management." *Texas Lawyer,* September 11, 2002 (reprint).

Roberts, Sherilyn. "Charlye Ola Farris Ahead of Her Time." *Eclipse*, January-February 2007, 40–41.

Robinson, Leila J. "Women Lawyers in the United States." *The Green Bag*, 1890, 24.

Rogers, Brian. "Karen Tandy, Class of '77 Appointed Head of DEA." *Texas Tech Lawyer*, Spring 2004, 7–8.

Rogers, Mary Beth. *Barbara Jordan: American Hero*. New York: Bantam Books, 1998.

Scott, Anne Firor. *Natural Allies: Women's Associations in American History*. Urbana: University of Illinois Press, 1991.

Shapley, Haley. "Demetris Sampson: A Servant to All." *Eclipse*, January-February 2006, 46–47.

Sheffield, Ric. "On Film: A Social History of Women Lawyers in Popular Culture 1930 to 1990." *Loyola of Los Angeles Entertainment Law Journal* 14:73–114.

Silverthorne, Elizabeth, and Geneva Fulgham. *Women Pioneers in Texas Medicine*. College Station: Texas A&M University Press, 1997.

Smith, J. Clay Jr., ed. *Rebels in Law: Voices in History of Black Women Lawyers*. Ann Arbor: University of Michigan Press, 2000.

Solomon, Barbara Miller. *In the Company of Educated Women: A History of Women and Higher Education in America*. New Haven: Yale University Press, 1985.

Squyeres, Suzanne. "Texas Women Lawyers keeps women's issues on forefront." *Women's Enterprise Texas*, March 2004, 20.

Stevens, Robert. *Law School: Legal Education in America from the 1850s to the 1980s*. Chapel Hill: University of North Carolina Press, 1983.

Stuntz, Jean A. *Hers, His, & Theirs: Community Property Law in Spain and Early Texas*. Lubbock: Texas Tech University Press, 2005.

Swaim, Betty Ann McCartney, ed. *The Bench and Bar of Waco and McLennan County 1849–76*. Waco: Texian Press, 1976.

Texas Bar Journal 1938– . Austin: State Bar of Texas, 1938– .

Texas State Historical Association. *The New Handbook of Texas, v. 1–6*. Austin: Texas State Historical Association, 1996.

Vrato, Elizabeth. *The Counselors*. Philadelphia: Running Press, 2002.

Weiman, Jeanne Madeline. *The Fair Women*. Athens, Ohio: Ohio University Press, 1976.

Weisberg, D. Kelley. "Barred from the Bar: Women and Legal Education in the United States 1870–1890." *Journal of Legal Education* 28:485–507.

Welch, June Rayfield. *The Colleges of Texas: A Survey of the Lone Star State's Institution of Higher Learning Past and Present*. Waco: Texian Press, 1981.

Welter, Barbara. *Dimity Convictions: The American Woman in the Nineteenth Century*. Athens, Ohio: Ohio University Press, 1976.

Winegarten, Ruthe. *Black Texas Women: 150 Years of Trial and Triumph*. Austin: University of Texas Press, 1995.

———. *Black Texas Women: A Sourcebook*. Consulting editors, Janet Humphrey and Frieda Werder. Austin: University of Texas Press, 1996.

Winegarten, Ruthe, and Cathy Schecter. *Deep in the Heart: The Lives & Legends of Texas Jews*. Austin: Eakin Press, 1990.

Winegarten, Ruthe, and Judith N. McArthur. *Citizens at Last: The Woman Suffrage Movement in Texas*. Austin: Ellen Temple Publisher, 1987.

Woloch, Nancy. *Women and the American Experience*. New York: Alfred A. Knofp, 1984.

Wood, Allen. *The Early Bench, Bar and Practice of Law in Corpus Christi*. Corpus Christi: Corpus Christi Bar Association, 1996.

Woods, Julia A., Ashley Craddock and Regan Marie Brown. *Austin Lawyers: A Legacy of Leadership and Service*. Birmingham, Alabama: Association Publishing Company, 2005.

Wortman, Marlene Stein, ed. *Women in American Law, Volume 1*. New York: Holmes and Mier Publishers, Inc., 1985.

Yarborough, Ralph. "A History of Law Licensing in Texas." In *Centennial History of the Texas Bar 1882–1982*, 181–193. Burnet: Eakin Press, 1981.

Young, Allegra Jordan. "Celebrating 100 Years of Women at UT Law." *UT Law: The Magazine of The University of Texas School of Law* (Spring 2006): 19–23.

Unpublished Sources

Almaraz, Roxanne. "Irma Rangel: Lawyer, Educator, Legislator." Unpublished paper. Women in the Legal Profession, Stanford University Law School, Spring 2004.

Czelusta, Keycie. "Grace Under Pressure: Judge Sarah T. Hughes and the Cases that Shook Texas." Unpublished paper. Women in the Legal Profession, Stanford University Law School, April 5, 2002.

MacKenzie, Charles Alfred. "A History of the Baylor University School of Law from the Lectures of Abner S. Lipscomb through the Deanship of Abner V. McCall." Master's thesis, Baylor University, August 1988.

Olsson, Nils Greger, and Dustin Kim. "Annual Report on the Status of Women and Racial/Ethnic Minorities in the State Bar of Texas (2005–2006)." State Bar of Texas Department of Research and Analysis.

Skinner, Michelle. "Hortense Sparks Ward." Unpublished paper. Women's Legal History, Stanford University Law School, Spring 2005.

Tabares, Norma. "Adelpha Callejo." Unpublished paper. Women's Legal History, Stanford University Law School, Fall 1999.

Texas Supreme Court. Licensing Dates for Texas Attorneys.

Government Documents

Statistics of the Population of the United States at the Tenth Census 1880. Washington, D.C.: Government Printing Office, 1883.

Twelfth Census of the United States Taken in the Year 1900, Volume II, Occupations Report. Washington, D.C.: U.S. Census Office, 1902.

Thirteenth Census of the United States Taken in the Year 1910, Volume IV, Occupation Statistics. Washington D.C.: Government Printing Office, 1914.

Fourteenth Census of the United States Taken in the Year 1920, Vol. IV, Occupation Statistics. Washington, D.C.: Government Printing Office, 1923.

Fifteenth Census of the United States Taken in the Year 1930, Volume IV, Occupations by States. Washington, D.C.: Government Printing Office, 1933.

Sixteenth Census of the United States Taken in the Year 1940, Volume III, The Labor Force, Part 5. Washington, D.C.: Government Printing Office, 1943.

Newspapers

Abilene Reporter-News

Austin American-Statesman

Chicago Legal News

The Dallas Morning News

Dallas Times Herald

El Paso Times Herald Post

Houston Business Journal

Houston Chronicle

Houston Post

The New York Times

The Washington Post

Personal Contacts

Adams, Marvin. Correspondence received September 28, 2006.

Albritton, Gayle. Correspondence received October 4, 2006.

Aleman, Azalea. Correspondence received December 1, 2006.

Atterbury, Julia. Telephone interview June 29, 2007.

Cade, Patricia. Telephone interview May 11, 2007.

Cloyd, Robyn. Telephone interview July 6, 2007.

Condon, Professor Matthew. Correspondence received February 21, 2005.

Darst, Lisa. Correspondence received April 25, 2005.

Day, Kathy. Correspondence received November 25, 2006; November 27, 2006.

El Paso Public Library. Correspondence received May 27, 2005.

Finney, Barbara. Correspondence received October 17, 2006; March 29, 2007.

Franklin, Judge Leona. Interview November 12, 2007.

Grimes, Kay. Correspondence received September 11, 2006.

Houston, Michelle. Correspondence received July 9, 2007.

Huffman, Dean Walt. Correspondence received March 31, 2007.

Hurwitz, Karen. Correspondence received November 9, 2006; November 11, 2006.

Jackson, Sarah. Correspondence received May 23, 2005.

Jefferson County Bar Association. Correspondence received April 2, 2007.

Jendrzey, Carol E. Correspondence received May 10, 2007.

Johnson, Professor Vincent. Correspondence received April 2, 2007.

Kidwell, Shelia. Correspondence received June 7, 2007.

King, Dick. Correspondence received July 9, 2007.

Lambert, Mark. Correspondence received January 31, 2005; February 14, 2005; April 1, 2005; May 18, 2005; May 19, 2005; May 20, 2005; May 24, 2005.

Lanehart, Chuck. Correspondence received April 1, 2005.

Lang, Victor. Correspondence received April 19, 2005.

Lord, Evelyn. Correspondence received January 28, 2006.

MacNaughton, Ann. Interview June 15, 2007.

McClure, Justice Ann Crawford. Correspondence received April 11, 2005.

McKerall, Mary. Interview May 20, 2007. Correspondence received May 25, 2007.

Milner, Camille. Correspondence received March 27, 2005.

Monroe, Monte. Correspondence received April 15, 2005.

Moore, Carolyn. Correspondence received June 29, 2007.

Morrison, Susan. Interview March 28, 2007.

O'Connor, Judge Michol. Telephone interview June 30, 2007.

Plain, Marian. Correspondence received March 30, 2005.

Quackenbush, Barbara. Interview March 29, 2007.

Raggio, Louise. Correspondence received October 11, 2006.

Reusch, Judge Janet. Correspondence received December 29, 2006; March 27, 2007.

Robbins, Suzanne Geiss. Correspondence received November 9, 2006; November 11, 2006.

Rosenthal, Judith. Correspondence received June 28, 2006; July 5, 2006; July 21, 2006.

Spearman, Patricia. Correspondence received September 30, 2006.

Widener, Michael. Correspondence received February 18, 2005.

Wilson, William. Correspondence received April 2, 2007.

Online Sources

American Bar Association

Baylor School of Law

Business and Professional Women

Dedman School of Law

Federal Judiciary

Handbook of Texas Online

National Association of Women Judges

National Association of Women Lawyers

National Bar Association

Southern Methodist University

South Texas College of Law

State Bar of Texas

St. Mary's University School of Law

Tejano Voices

Texas Center for Legal Ethics and Professionalism

Texas Courts

Texas House of Representatives

Texas Judiciary

Texas Tech University School of Law

Texas Wesleyan University School of Law

Texas Woman's University

Texas Women Lawyers

Thurgood Marshall School of Law, Texas Southern University

University of Houston Law Center

University of Texas School of Law

Women's Legal History, Stanford University Law School

INDEX

Index

Index

O

Q

R

T